Selfies

Searching for the Image of God in a Digital Age

Craig Detweiler

Brazos Press
a division of Baker Publishing Group
Grand Rapids, Michigan

Published by Brazos Press
a division of Baker Publishing Group
PO Box 6287, Grand Rapids, MI 49516-6287
www.brazospress.com

Printed in the United States of America

Library of Congress Cataloging-in-Publication Data
Names: Detweiler, Craig, 1964– author.
Title: Selfies : searching for the image of God in a digital age / Craig Detweiler.
Description: Grand Rapids : Baker Publishing Group, 2018. | Includes bibliographical references and index.
Identifiers: LCCN 2017052602 | ISBN 9781587433986 (pbk. : alk. paper)
Subjects: LCSH: Self—Religious aspects—Christianity. | Social media—Religious aspects—Christianity. | Self-portraits.
Classification: LCC BT713 .D48 2018 | DDC 302.23/1—dc23
LC record available at https://lccn.loc.gov/2017052602

18 19 20 21 22 23 24   7 6 5 4 3 2 1

green
press
INITIATIVE

For Stephen Dickter
1975–2012
Cinematographer, Scholar, Friend

Gone too soon.
We should have written this together.

133286

Contents

Acknowledgments

To my editor, Bob Hosack, who has the patience of Job and the persistence of Nehemiah. Without your encouragement, I never would have started this project (or completed it). To Brian Bolger, Brandy Scritchfield, Jeremy Wells, Shelly MacNaughton, and the Brazos Press team, who get the job done with minimal drama. Such service is increasingly rare and refreshingly independent in a corporatized world.

To the many cities, schools, churches, and conferences that hosted my extended *iGods* tour. Your earnest and urgent questions regarding how to navigate the accelerated moment we find ourselves in have challenged me to dig deeper and write faster (two things that do not necessarily go together).

To my colleagues at Pepperdine University, Michael Feltner and Kendra Kilpatrick, who granted the sabbatical to finish this book, and Sarah Stone-Watt, John Mooney, Michael Smith, and John Sitter, who protected and preserved my time zealously.

To my students, who are the canaries in our cultural coal mine. We armed you with a constant companion that did not include an owner's manual. My apologies that as digital natives, you've had to do most of the work (while we've watched with a disapproving eye). You make me remarkably hopeful.

To my essential readers, Kathryn Linehan and Gus Peterson. Where do you turn when you're lost among words on the page? To faithful friends willing to offer both affirmations and hard truths.

To the photographers, artists, and friends who allowed me to publish their images in this book. Thank you for exercising such faith and courage in putting yourselves out there to model how much healthy selfies can communicate. May your faces continue to shine.

To my family, who have borne the brunt of my late nights and sheltered weekends. Thank you to Zoe and Theo for answering my questions with boundless enthusiasm. You have been vital teachers and inspirational media leaders. Keep up the creative work.

All honor to Caroline for being my ever faithful, ongoing conversation partner. Forgive me for disrupting your sleep. I have so much gratitude for all of your unattributed suggestions, ideas, and corrections. I offer my ongoing appreciation for your keen eyes, sharp ear, and winsome smile.

1

Introduction

How Do You Solve a Problem Like the Selfie?

I have always wanted to be <u>me</u> without making it difficult for you to be <u>you</u>.

—Howard Thurman[1]

D ID YOU SEE the "Smiling Selfie in Auschwitz"? An American teen-ager touring Auschwitz stirred up a firestorm of criticism when she posted a picture of herself smiling amid a concentration camp (and even included a blushing smiley face emoticon). Her Twitter handle, "Princess Breanna@PrincessBMM," played into so many stereotypes of the millennial generation as entitled, spoiled, and insensitive. The iPhone earbud dangling in her photo only enhanced the notion that she was drifting cluelessly through a Nazi death camp to a private soundtrack, trampling the memory of those snuffed out in such a horrific genocide. To many, her selfie communicated ahistorical insensitivity, her smile seemingly mocking the six million lives lost under the Nazis' horrific genocide. Breanna was lambasted across social media (and traditional media outlets). As her

1

infamy grew, the Alabama teen tweeted, "I'm famous, ya'll."[2] The outrage was swift and unsparing.

My family was in Europe when this online debate exploded. We were teaching at a summer program in London. Thanks to my book *iGods*, I was invited by CNN to comment on the controversy for their *Belief Blog*. It was obvious that the student's reaction (and even her efforts to explain her reasons for smiling) were not easily defended. She talked about connecting with her deceased father through the experience. They had studied the Holocaust together just before he passed away. While most wondered, "What kind of monster could walk through gas chambers and come away smiling?" I saw a teen, perhaps still in personal grief, connecting with her father across time. Rather than attack, I chose to offer a defense of this teenager who was being grilled across the Twitterverse.[3]

We'd taken our children to the Anne Frank House in Amsterdam and to the Memorial to the Murdered Jews of Europe in Berlin just days earlier. Our kids were eager to tour the Anne Frank House. Though they had been introduced to Anne's poignant *Diary of a Young Girl* in school, they had become even more interested in her home thanks to its appearance in John Green's young adult novel *The Fault in Our Stars* (2012). The book portrays two teens, Hazel and Gus, who fall in love while battling cancer. They travel to Amsterdam in search of a famous author who inspired Gus. The house where Anne Frank hid from the Nazis serves as the backdrop for a romantic first kiss between Hazel and Gus in the novel (and the 2014 movie). While Anne's fascination with movie stars is documented in the glamour shots still pinned to the walls, some appropriately questioned whether kissing in the Anne Frank House was insensitive.[4] Hazel herself struggles with whether kissing in such a historic place is insensitive to Anne's memory as a Holocaust victim. She ultimately rationalizes that Anne enjoyed teen romance within that house and surely might be pleased that others would dare to pursue love in the same place.

In Berlin, while my family pondered the enormity of the Holocaust at the Memorial to the Murdered Jews of Europe, others played hide-and-seek amid the tomblike stelae. We took photos, but we didn't run around with childlike abandon. The gravity of the place weighed heavily on our hearts. At the Jewish Museum in Berlin, we were haunted by the Holocaust

Tower. When the door closed behind us with a thunderous boom, the huge, oppressive walls and darkness bore down upon us. Yet we also watched countless school groups cruise in, take a quick pic, and hop out. To them, the memorials were a backdrop for yet another selfie.

Should we be encouraged that so many young people were touring these memorials? Or outraged that they didn't know how to act properly in a place steeped in so much suffering and pain? They grabbed the requisite tourist snapshot but may not have grasped where they were, what they were surrounded by, or what opportunities for reflection were present. They fell into a trap described eloquently by poet T. S. Eliot: "We had the experience but missed the meaning."[5] How many times have I been guilty of cruising through an ancient ruin or a famous museum in search of the requisite shot, the approved tourist photo? It is far too easy to treat the world as a stage dressed for our best selfie. We can sleepwalk through places and experiences designed to move us and come away with selfies that distracted us from our setting, blinded us to the transcendent or eternal.

But who needs to wake up whom?

I feel like the responsibility for explaining the gravity of Auschwitz falls upon those who've gone before Breanna. In the Bible, God repeatedly urges his people, "Remember the days of old; consider the generations long past" (Deut. 32:7). In his autobiographical *Night*, survivor Elie Wiesel reminds us why we must continue to teach and speak and visit horrific places like Auschwitz: "For in the end, it is all about memory, its sources and its magnitude, and, of course, its consequences."[6] Miroslav Volf writes that "if no one remembers a misdeed or names it publicly, it remains invisible."[7] How can we convey solemnity to a generation that never experienced the Holocaust? There are many forms of teaching.

Israeli artist Shahak Shapira crafted a creative and confrontational response to inappropriate selfies posted at the Memorial to the Murdered Jews of Europe.[8] He photoshopped the most insensitive photos taken at the Berlin memorial onto historical images from the concentration camps. The YOLO (you only live once) spirit of the contemporary selfies was juxtaposed with the haunting reality of piles of Jewish bodies discovered at the conclusion of World War II. Shapira posted his examples of public shaming online at Yolocaust.de. He included an email address where these worst offenders could ask Shapira to remove their embarrassing image. Within one week, 2.5 million people had visited the Yolocaust.

Shapira noted, "The crazy thing is that the project actually reached all 12 people whose selfies were presented. Almost all of them understood the message, apologized and decided to remove their selfies from their personal Facebook and Instagram profiles." A gentleman who captioned his photo with "Jumping on dead Jews @ Holocaust Memorial" asked for forgiveness: "I have seen what kind of impact those words have and it's crazy and it's not what I wanted. . . . And I am sorry. I truly am."[9] Shapira honored such surprising changes of heart by removing the Yo-locaust site altogether. Pain caused by offensive selfies was transformed via repentance.

Questions of what spaces or occasions are sacred aren't limited to instances of genocide. A quick internet search for "inappropriate selfies" reveals all kinds of lapses in judgment, including smiling selfies with the deceased at funeral parlors. Perhaps these young people haven't been taught that when a Jewish family gathers to sit *shiva* following the burial of the deceased, mirrors in the house are covered. It is a time of introspection. Prayers and focus are to be directed toward God, not ourselves. Crowds that turn their backs to masterpieces in order to snap a selfie with a Van Gogh have vexed art museums and curators. In front of the *Mona Lisa* at the Louvre or *Starry Night* at the Museum of Modern Art, plenty of visitors are looking *away* from the painting, more interested in themselves on their screens.[10] Contemporary artist Kara Walker anticipated how people would interact with her massive installation *A Subtlety, or the Marvelous Sugar Baby* (2014) at a former Domino Sugar Factory in Brooklyn.[11] A seventy-five-foot sculpture of an African American mammy with the naked body of an Egyptian sphinx is anything but subtle. This African figure is composed of refined white sugar, a bracing commentary on economic and sexual exploitation of black women in America. Signs encouraged visitors to post pictures of their experience with the hashtag #karawalkerdomino. Walker knew that a ten-foot-tall vagina would prompt insensitive reactions from visitors because "human behavior is so mucky and violent and messed-up and inappropriate."[12] How should we respond to our complicated feelings about identity, race, power, gender, sexuality, and the sacred?

After thousands of people clicked and commented on my CNN article about Auschwitz, I realized that we desperately need places to process our conflicted thoughts about selfies. Our intense relationships with our phones seem to have only exacerbated our frustrations with each other. We haven't sorted out a code for digital decorum. What is sacred amid so many selfies? The digital era has disrupted so many established industries and traditions. Institutions are scared. Civic and religious leaders feel threatened. Social media is creating epistemological problems and raising foundational questions: What is truth? What sources can be trusted? As our culture boils, most of us have retreated to our phones. We are so busy broadcasting ourselves that we have no time to worry about our neighbors. We tell our children to be patient and loving and kind, but we haven't figured out what that means in our online activities. With devices in hand, we all too easily treat others as a position or a problem rather than as a person. We may acknowledge this is a problem, but few of us have the time, energy, or resources to propose a solution, to mine our spiritual and ethical resources in search of rehumanizing precedents. We will not rise above our political divide until we recognize the glory and dignity of each other on (and off) line. Digital discipleship is a new concept, still being sorted out.

One point of agreement seems to be that selfie takers are selfish. We blame our devices, but mostly we blame each other. "Kids today . . ." "In my time . . ." "We never . . ." A survey of college students joined the chorus, calling selfies "arrogant, self-absorbed, disgusting, degrading, ridiculous, vapid, useless, selfish, shameless, vain and hedonistic."[13] We chastise ourselves for self-interest, even while we're posting. A cycle of self-loathing follows. Some Facebook friends of mine suggested they'd never be interested in a book about such a superficial subject. The word "selfie" is perceived so negatively, even as passé. The Chainsmokers satirical dance single, #Selfie, gave us ample reasons to hate those who exclaim, "But first, let me take a selfie."[14] And yet I pressed on, energized by what I've studied and encouraged by what I've discovered.

Because they are a recent phenomenon, selfies have only begun to be studied by researchers. The iPhone 4 debuted in 2010. By including a front-facing camera, Apple enabled users to see (and photograph) themselves more easily than ever before. A quick "click" and iPhone owners could share their image far and wide. By 2013 the word "selfie" had become so ubiquitous that the Oxford English Dictionary proclaimed it "the word of the year." Art critic Jerry Saltz defined it this way: "A fast self-portrait, made with a smartphone's camera and immediately distributed and inscribed into a network, [a selfie] is an instant visual communication of where we are, what we're doing, who we think we are, and who we think is watching."[15] Parents and teachers have been flummoxed by how quickly the smartphone has captured adolescents' attention. Teens have been handed a potent tool without an operating manual. Never have so many been able to reach so many so quickly. Smartphones have remarkable democratizing power. They also have the ability to surveil the public like never before. More diverse voices are being heard and more colorful faces seen. And yet algorithms may be splintering us into smaller and smaller groups of like-minded people. A new tribalism may emerge that threatens democratic ideals. We are still trying to figure out how to respond to this powerful and prolific form of communication. Could a deeper appreciation of selfies renew our affirmation of everyone's God-given dignity and worth?

I wade into the maelstrom as parent and professor. Smartphones and selfies are ever present in my home and classroom. I'm not sure what to think about them. They can be a distraction and also a delight. To sort out my own ambivalence, I will merge research from classicists, art historians, psychologists, and communication professors with my training as a theologian and visual storyteller. I may end up with a book that frustrates experts in their field, but my aspirations are to offer an alternative route into a conversation regarding social and technological shifts that impact us all. Consider this an exercise in theological aesthetics—how to see more clearly, reflect more deeply, and respond more perceptively.

Are Selfies Dangerous?

Taking a selfie may be an act of genuine joy. We may want to preserve a private moment of victory or pleasure to relish and recall. It may be just a reminder for us. We may want to lock in our minds a time of deep satisfaction. Photographs have always been a way to commemorate a major rite of passage: weddings, births, graduations. To these major life transitions we may now add a concert, a game, a vacation, a retreat. These peak experiences are distinguished from the more mundane days that tend to blend together. Some of us are actively trying to find beauty amid the mundane. We pause to capture a perfect cappuccino or an especially exquisite pizza. I am all for private moments of profound gratitude. Surely these are central

Atop Mount Thielsen

to the gift of life. As the wise writer of Ecclesiastes encourages us, "Go, eat your food with gladness, and drink your wine with a joyful heart, for God has already approved what you do" (9:7).

Selfies have been proven to be far more than a threat to civility and sacred spaces. They can undermine our health and well-being. Selfies can be dangerous. A Spanish man was gored to death when he tried to take a selfie amid the running of the bulls in Pamplona. A fifteen-year-old in India photographing himself holding his father's gun died when he accidentally pulled the trigger instead of pushing the photo button. Two Polish parents taking a selfie stepped off ocean cliffs in Portugal and tumbled to their deaths in front of their children. We can get cut off from our surroundings, lose focus, and suspend judgment in pursuit of the perfect picture. It was widely reported that in 2015 more people died from taking selfies than from shark attacks.[16] How much risk will you assume to get the ultimate selfie on a mountaintop, in front of a train, or with a wild animal? The blind pursuit of the perfect image, ignoring our surroundings and context, can have grave consequences.

Have you seen the extreme selfies of Russian daredevils Kirill Oreshkin and Alexander Rusinov taken atop skyscrapers?[17] They constantly aspire to new heights, taking on new risks, in search of even more death-defying selfies. How do their pictures make you feel? Dizzy and disoriented? Exhilarated and alive? Do we admire their bravery or shake our heads at such risky behavior? I appreciate the audacity of those in search of an extreme selfie. *National Geographic* celebrated how "the selfie generation gets outside."[18] The pursuit of peak experiences may involve getting back to nature, from scaling a mountain to fording a rushing river with a GoPro strapped to our heads. Images on Instagram may inspire us to get off road, to dive off cliffs, to explore glorious national parks. The Russians' frightening feats provoke mixed feelings and high anxiety. We may understand why they took the #bestselfieever but wish they would stop. We hope they realize the enduring truth that "pride goes before destruction, a haughty spirit before a fall" (Prov. 6:18) before it is too late.

Our conflicted thoughts reflect the mixed feelings we have about selfies. Sometimes we admire the ingenuity; on other occasions we condemn such grandstanding. We may loathe the duck faces gathered on Instagram or love the spontaneity that accompanies Snapchat. We may be happy for our friends' peak experiences but envy them at the same time. How many of us have wanted to break a tourist's selfie stick in two? Selfies are loved and hated with equal intensity. As we've seen with Princess Breanna, a pose struck out of personal satisfaction may be received as an offensive boast. Did you follow the shaming of sorority girls that were caught on camera taking selfies during an Arizona Diamondbacks baseball game?[19] The male television announcers bemoaned "every girl locked into their phone." "Oh, Lord." "Welcome to parenting 2015; they're all just completely transfixed by the technology." They mock their "selfie with a hot dog, selfie with a churro, selfie just of a selfie." The announcers conclude, "Help us, please, somebody, help us! Can we do an intervention?" Online condemnation was also swift: "They have the combined IQ of a burnt tater tot." Afterward, it was discovered that the D-backs' stadium announcer had just asked the crowd to take selfies as part of a contest/promotion. There is always so much more to the story.

I wonder if the disdain we unleash upon sorority girls taking selfies actually reveals disdain for young women in general. Our comments regarding selfies may unmask our misogyny. Are we too quick to judge the selfie generation, a generation that has never been taught to think critically about what the act of taking a self-portrait and posting it on the internet entails? The online outrage we unleash upon adolescents belies the patience promoted by the apostle Paul. In Romans 10:14 he resists the temptation to condemn others: "But how can they call on him to save them unless they believe in him? And how can they believe in him if they have never heard about him? And how can they hear about him unless someone tells them?" (NLT). We have been quick to condemn and slow to listen (or see).

Adolescents have been offered a license to post without any accompanying ethical framework. Is it fair to blame teens for misusing tools that didn't exist in our childhood? If I had been given a phone with an ability to take and post pictures when I was thirteen, I would not have photographed many things to be proud of. What kinds of public mistakes would I have made if emboldened by this new possibility? We are now all engaged in what sociologist Erving Goffman calls "the arts of impression management."[20] Thanks to social media, adolescents are often forced to grow up in public at earlier ages and stages. They are embarking upon an ancient challenge, to know thyself, while broadcasting each awkward step along the way. Is it fair to criticize the young for not acting more maturely?

Today's pings are just a more sophisticated version of *Pong*. As one of the original video games, *Pong* was slow, methodical, even predictable. And yet we loved it. *Pong* didn't require much sophistication. The speed could be shifted, but the rules remained the same. Hit it back. The game could be locked in place, stuck in an endless loop. One could walk away for a while and nothing would change. Take an eye off the screen, a hand off the controller, and one may not even lose a point. Today's teens are playing ping, not *Pong*. Pings are those beeps and blurps that tell us we have a new message, a new update, a new headline to consider. Pings are the notifications that float across our screen all day long. They are rooted in instant messaging and constant connection.

Nowadays, we *all* assume that we are *all* available at *all* times, and we *all* expect (maybe even demand) an immediate response. Parents may panic if their teens fail to respond to a text message asking for an update. Relationships may end if we fail to respond to our friends' online drama in a timely manner. To opt out is often to drop out of that social circle. We may be permanently removed from the group chat. Nobody wants to break a Snapchat streak. *Pong* involved one ball on one screen. Ping

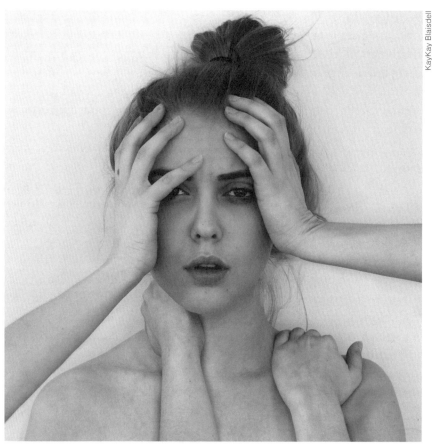

KayKay Blaisdell

Focus

involves multiple balls and can be played across multiple screens. To keep up with Snapchat, Instagram, Facebook, and Twitter takes an enormous amount of attention. Responding to so many simultaneous pings can be stressful—perhaps far more stressful than we realized when we handed a thirteen-year-old their first smartphone.

We made sure our children had our number in case of emergency. But after that, it was simply learn by doing. The pings come in the form of red dots or flashing lights. They're numbered. The job of young people is to respond to the pings in a timely and satisfying manner—*for the rest of their lives*. That can be an overwhelming inbox for a tween to handle. It might even leave them feeling a bit stressed out. The game we've placed teens within—your worth can and will be measured in hard numbers of friends, followers, and likes—never ends. It is always on, even when they're taking the risky move of not paying attention. Conversations and rankings are occurring even while we sleep. We can plunge off the social cliff if we don't keep our eye on the bouncing ball of pings and pongs. Some parents expect an immediate response to their texts and yet complain when their children's faces are buried in their phone. Talk about a double bind.

The greatest danger selfies pose may be not to our bodies but rather to our souls, our psyches, our selves. When we make our private moments public, something volatile may occur, as Princess Breanna discovered. Thanks to social media, our selfies become an occasion for a public referendum. Our friends and followers can now vote on our appearance, adding commentary, even forwarding it on to others. Our private moments veer quickly toward public property, fair game for memes and repurposing in a myriad of ways. While it can be gratifying to feel the affirmation of the crowd, it can also be devastating when our posts fail to generate the kinds of attention we seek. When we post a selfie, we put ourselves out there, into the social stream, to sink or swim. We may subject ourselves to far more judgment and cruelty than is healthy or sustainable. We may adapt our identities to conform to the social standards already established on Instagram, Snapchat, or Twitter. While it is great to develop a strong sense of aesthetics (for Instagram) or humor (for Snapchat) or newsworthiness (for Twitter), each of these platforms may limit or box in our developing personas. Where do we find a core identity that is poised to endure the ups and downs of being "hearted" or "unhearted" online?

We may we turn to social media to bolster our self-image. Selfies are a convenient way to ask, Who am I? Yet we need a more reliable source for our confidence and courage than each other. How do we process darker moments of doubt or sorrow or confusion? Where do we post those feelings? Is there an app for that? This book will challenge readers to go deep, to lean into the feelings that may lurk behind or beneath our selfies. We may question whether we are smart, pretty, or desirable. We may battle feelings of inadequacy. Who hasn't struggled with loneliness or belonging? We will investigate why researchers have found that Instagram is the worst app for young people's mental health.[21] We will turn to psychology and sociology, art and literature, theology and Scripture to anchor our understanding of ourselves. My hope is that we will turn to God as the source of our self.

This book will also ask collective questions about where we are heading. Studying selfies is one way to ask, Who are we? Almost forty years ago, Christopher Lasch derided "the culture of narcissism" creeping into American life.[22] Almost twenty years ago, Robert Putnam lamented the decline of civic activity and the ways in which we are now "bowling alone."[23] Those who insist we are even more self-centered today might point to how the titles and focus of our popular magazines have shifted, as photographer Fred Ritchin notes: "I always use a quote by Paul Stookey (of the singing group Peter, Paul and Mary) about popular magazines. They used to be called *Life* (about life), then it was *People* (not about life, but just about people), then it was *Us* (not even about all people, but just about us), then it was *Self* (not even about us). It's a question of how we extend ourselves into the world."[24] As we have focused further on our own image and needs, we may have lost fundamental notions of what "we the people" means. My anecdotal experience of teens suggests that they may not inherently want an education, a church, and a media that is "all about them." Yet those who've come before us have increasingly asked, What's your status? At the end of our efforts to self-actualize has arisen an identity crisis. Our ability to update our profile pictures ad nauseam hasn't resulted in more security. Instead, it has riddled us with questions: How do I look? Do people like me? Does anybody care?

So much of the anxiety swirling around social media arises from a crisis of identity. We are uncertain who we are and whose we are. We are unclear on an individual and a collective level. Philosopher Charles Taylor chronicled how "the sources of the self" have shifted across human history.[25] We have made an inward turn, seeking to define ourselves within a natural world that may reveal a moral order. We recognize that humans have rights without necessarily knowing where those rights spring from. As work has become more mechanized, we have turned toward ecstatic experiences to transcend the mundane. The technological era has ushered in instantaneous communication, generating unparalleled wealth *for some*. The iGods of Silicon Valley have prospered, but those who cannot keep pace with the changes feel left behind. The apocalyptic visions springing from the mouths of politicians around the globe have capitalized on this sense of uncertainty. I am almost old enough to recall the last time

Americans struggled through massive social upheaval. Not since the civil rights movement, women's liberation, and *Easy Rider* have we seen such a clash between generations and ideologies. Thanks to the ubiquity of smartphones and our ability to broadcast our thoughts and images, tensions are rising again. Interestingly, they may be arising for similar reasons. We are seeing and hearing more from the same groups who sparked tumult in the sixties—youth, women, minorities. Media ownership may still be concentrated among a few white males, but the ability to be seen and heard is now available to (almost) all. Is our current culture war rooted in a hatred of selfies or in a disdain for particular faces now showing up and speaking out?

One way to define identity is by the via negativa: "who we aren't." In theology, the via negativa is an opportunity to clear our minds of misconceptions. It begins as an act of humility, acknowledging how much we don't know about God. Lately we have mostly applied the via negativa to others as a form of comparison: "Thank God I am not like them." We may judge others solely upon appearances. Selfies can devolve into occasions for envy or spite. We know we should be happy for our friends' promotions, marriages, cars, vacations, and kids, but sometimes it is tough to love their wonderful lives. The apostle Paul insists, "We do not dare to classify or compare ourselves with some who commend themselves. When they measure themselves by themselves and compare themselves with themselves, they are not wise" (2 Cor. 10:12). When we need perspective, let us look toward God rather than our smartphones. In theology, the *via negativa* wisely speaks of God as ineffable, immutable, and wholly other. St. Thomas Aquinas declares, "This is the ultimate in human knowledge of God: to know that we do not know Him."[26] This realization allows us to respect the impenetrable mystery of God and softens us in relation to our neighbors. Imagine the transformation that may occur if we approach social media with humility rather than hostility. As G. K. Chesterton wrote, "How much larger your life would be if your self could become smaller in it."[27]

Identity can also be found by whom or what we embrace—a *via positiva*. When we focus upon what we know of God—the glory of God's creation, the sacrificial love of Jesus, the indwelling of the Spirit—we may respond with praise and thanksgiving. Joy and gratitude may reign. Our identity can spring from a place so robust that we can operate out of faith rather than fear. "For God gave us a spirit not of fear but of power and love and self-control" (2 Tim. 1:7 ESV). We must resist the temptation to define ourselves tribally, to divide the world into mine versus yours. Selfies can be used to establish borderlines, to keep some out and let others in. But strength does not arise from only huddling with people who look like us, dress like us, agree with us. I hope we will summon a strength above and beyond ourselves that allows us to venture out with confidence and compassion rather than fear. We can love and appreciate others because we know that we are loved and affirmed by God.

The Search

This is a study of our self-portraits. It is an exploration of why we paint, sculpt, write, analyze, and photograph ourselves. From an absurdly early age, we start to portray ourselves on paper. Kids render themselves as a hamburger on stilts. We love when children place themselves in the world, with a sun in one corner, maybe some grass, a dog, some form of shelter, and hopefully a parent or two close by. We may put these early self-portraits on

Zoe Detweiler

Self-portrait by Zoe, age 3

the refrigerator or even frame them. On the back, parents make a note, "Zoe, self-portrait, age 3." So why do we affirm this carefree activity as natural but condemn such self-imaging as narcissistic when it involves a camera on a smartphone? Aren't they aids for navigating important developmental stages?

Why do we portray ourselves? We want to be remembered, to have our presence noted. We post so many selfies for similar reasons, mostly having to do with this side of paradise. We want to be recognized, to be noticed, to feel loved and adored. So much of our online activity is about being seen, singled out, affirmed. We fuss and fret over our self-image because we know that it is how we will be introduced to large swaths of the world. In a globalized economy, before people meet us (in person), they are likely to see us (online). And if we connect in real life (IRL), we will probably follow up that meeting with some form of mediated communication (from texting to Facebook to LinkedIn). We are our online profile—with all the accompanying pressure, possibilities, and limitations associated with it.

We take selfies for many reasons, from documenting our lives, to promoting our products (which may include our self and our services) to keeping up with our families. When we post a selfie we connect with the world beyond ourselves. Selfies are a form of visual query. We hope to elicit a reaction. Psychologist Sherry Turkle writes poignantly about how for kids raised by parents attached to their phones, "Longed for here is the pleasure of full attention, coveted and rare."[28] We so rarely give (or receive) undivided attention. Who cares enough to turn off their notifications or even power down in order to be fully present in your life? We all want to be noticed. Selfies are a way to see and be seen. Even when we scroll through others' posts, we are noting who is liked and what is loved. Mother Teresa noted, "If we have no peace, it is because we have forgotten that we belong to each other—that man, that woman, that child is my brother or my sister. If everyone could see the image of God in his neighbor, do you think we should still need tanks and generals?"[29]

We are in the midst of an identity crisis both as individuals and as a larger community. We are uncertain who we are. Are we kind, sensitive, and caring? Gorgeous, beautiful, and alluring? Powerful, chiseled, and victorious? Fun, carefree, and adventurous? Our selfies suggest that we'd like to check "all of the above." When it comes to race, gender, and sexuality, the categories get even more complicated and the debates much more heated. When a young African American–Thai woman falls in love with

a nonbinary Latinx, a retired, red-blooded, American cisgender male may
have difficulty sorting out what the proliferation of identifiers for these
shifting identities means. The confusion and frustration of older generations has manifested in highly combustible ways. When we're unfamiliar
with what we're seeing, we will likely have difficulty understanding. Yet
rather than taking our dissonance as an opportunity for reflection, we
may turn it into an occasion to rant or lash out across the gulf. We take
to social media in search of our selves, our community, our sanity. Some
see our selfies as a convenient and communicative art; others find them
utterly appalling. But we must remember that seeing and hearing clearly
are prerequisites for followers of Jesus. I am trying to perceive and receive
selfies as the face of God.

Our identity crises usually begin with the question, Who am I? The Bible
begins with the question, Who is God? The Spirit of God hovers over the
waters in the beginning of creation (Gen. 1:2). We catch a glimpse of this
creative Spirit when God says, "Let us make mankind in our image, in our
likeness" (v. 26). Further clarity arrives when the Bible reiterates "created"
three times, "So God created mankind in his own image, in the image of
God he created them; male and female he created them" (v. 27). A plural
God creates a plural people. We are made to be in relationship, in community. This call to community challenges our hyper-individualistic ways
and also challenges masculinized notions of God. The rigorous work of
Elizabeth A. Johnson expanded my understanding of the wonder of God.
She writes, "If women are created in the image of God, then God can be
spoken of in female metaphors in as full or limited a way as God is imaged
in male ones."[30] We (not just we who are "he") are God's best answer to
the question, Who is God? Yet the trinitarian nature of God, Jesus, and
the Spirit also challenges us to seek more than just earthly relationships.
Cambridge professor Sarah Coakley considers how "twoness, one might
say, is divinely ambushed by threeness."[31] While it is wonderful to be in
relationship with each other, our desires still draw us toward something
More, found in the mystery of the Trinity.

Rather than seeing selfies as the problem, I approach selfies as the start
of a solution. In *Paradise Lost*, John Milton sought to "justifie the wayes of
God to men."[32] I am endeavoring to point the ways of men and women to
God. When we're taking selfies, we are searching for identity and seeking
a response from each other. We focus upon ourselves and then send our

selfies into the larger community. We may seek affirmation, recognition, and even eternity. Selfies are a search for God via God's image: us. When we search for beauty or identity, we are longing for God. When we seek love and affirmation, we are longing for God. And when we post pictures of ourselves being silly or smart or even sexy, we are longing for God. This book reaches back to our genesis, to the radical notion that we are created in the image and likeness of God, the *imago Dei*. As we rediscover that God (and not we ourselves) made us, we may shift how we see ourselves, how we treat our neighbors, and how we care for creation. We are relational people made in the image of a relational, Triune God.[33] Instead of "taking selfies" in a possessive way, perhaps we can "receive" selfies as a sacred gift from the original Giver. Making images is a deeply soulful, generative activity. The beauty of God's creation (us) and the joyous gift of life inspire our best selfies.

Behind all the social, psychological, educational, and economic reasons why we may be taking selfies, we are seeking relationships with God, with each other, and with our selves. The mania we bring to self-imaging via social media may be directly proportional to our hunger for the divine. French philosopher Blaise Pascal identified this craving, this helplessness, as rooted in what was once true happiness but now remains only an empty print or trace. He described the frantic nature of one who "tries in vain to fill [this emptiness] with everything around him, seeking in things that are not there the help he cannot find in those that are, though none can help, since this infinite abyss can be filled only with an infinite and immutable object; in other words by God himself."[34] Is social media a frustrating search for help that only has one solution? When we overdo the self-serving, self-promoting possibilities of Instagram or Twitter, it can get ugly. Really ugly. But English mystic Julian of Norwich said, "Sin is behovely." She considered sin useful, even necessary, "because it brings us to self-knowledge—knowledge of our own fallibility—which in turn moves us to seek God."[35] Psychologist Dan Allender notes how "every person enjoys dignity and suffers from depravity. The structure of personality is a result of the interaction of these two dynamics."[36] Coakley considers desire as central to our humanity: "the precious clue woven into the crooked human heart that ever reminds its relatedness and its source."[37] In other words, our search for love and connection points to the nature of our origins in relationship to God. We will study the history of self-portraits in an effort to promote reflection upon our own selfies. As we develop self-knowledge and self-awareness, I hope we will begin to recognize the ways in which we are the image of God despite our frailty, fearfulness, anxiety, and sin. Our self-images may have been fractured by bad experiences at home, at school, on the job, online, or even in our churches. Thankfully, self-images can be restored. Our selfies can be redeemed. May we cast aside our old, manic, false selfies in order to put on a new selfie, in Christ and for the community.

Methodology: Eyes to See

My methodology begins with watching and listening. What are people saying and singing and doing? A selfie may be a cry for help from the depths. A post may spring from a desire to be noticed, a longing to be affirmed. The "Smiling Selfie in Auschwitz" arose from personal pain: the death of a father. To make it to Germany was a life goal for Breanna, an opportunity to reconnect with one she loved and lost and longs to see again. The selfie may shout "Look at me!" but who is the intended audience? She posts for her father, who is in heaven, hopefully smiling down on her, seeing her acknowledgment of his ongoing influence and presence in her life. It also may be an address to God in heaven for carrying her this far through a heavy season of grief. Selfies may be insensitive and inappropriate attention-grabbing devices. But whenever a child shouts, "Mom! Dad! Look at me!" what is the appropriate response?

Much of Jesus's ministry focused on developing eyes to see and ears to hear. He wants followers dialed in to their surroundings, aware of what's happening in their community. How do we recognize the opportunities in front of us and make the right choices about who or what to pay attention to? Jesus was embedded within a religious culture that had clear codes regarding what was appropriate and what was forbidden. There was a hierarchy of laws designed to keep God's people clean and above reproach. Jesus wondered, What about the people getting crushed by that system? Don't we need to see them too? Breanna got vilified on the internet with lightning speed. Her post clearly violated the sensibilities of the masses. But how do we bring her into a new ethical understanding? Through condemnation? We see the patience of Jesus in how he handles those who interrupt his journey, cut into his plans, derail his destination. While his disciples worry about staying on schedule, Jesus seems eager to pause, to focus on the person begging to be noticed.

Why is Princess Breanna smiling in her selfie? She spoke of it as correspondence with her deceased father, but still—her father's dead, she's touring Auschwitz, and she's smiling? Does her smile mask a deeper truth? After surveying an incredibly diverse cross section of college students across America, Donna Freitas found "the most pressing social media issues students face: the importance of *appearing* happy"—and not just happy, students told her, but "blissful, enraptured, even inspiring." Almost 75 percent of students surveyed agreed that "I try always to appear positive/happy with anything attached to my real name."[38] Freitas calls this vexing dilemma "the happiness effect." Breanna has lost her father, tours a death camp, and yet, due to social expectations, has almost no option other than to smile (and include a happy face emoji). In grief, teens put on a brave face. In disappointment, adolescents act inspired. In crisis, the next generation appears blissful. Freitas summarizes the dangers of such dissonance: "In our attempts to appear happy, to distract ourselves from our deeper, sometimes darker thoughts, we experience the opposite effect. In trying to always appear happy, we rob ourselves of joy."[39]

We are quick to condemn, slow to understand. And yet we expect (and maybe even demand) understanding and empathy from others in relation to our own selfies. Like Breanna, we may be unprepared to deal with the unintended consequences of our posts. Things we post in an effort to define who we are and where we are (in life) can become occasions for ridicule, defamation, and debate, which can launch us into deeper self-crises.

Listen to the music of the Grammy Award–winning band Twenty One Pilots. In their 2016 music video for "Stressed Out," the band rides through suburban Columbus, Ohio, on Big Wheels tricycles.[40] The toy tricycles have been blown up to adult size, making the men seem smaller, younger, more childlike. Singer and songwriter Tyler Joseph is dealing with the gap between what he was told and what he has experienced. Having been promised that when he got older, his fears would shrink, he's now even more insecure and aware of how he cares what other people think. This present reality creates a strong sense of nostalgia in Joseph, a desire to return to simpler days. These homeschooled kids stop at the boyhood home of drummer Josh Dun. They retreat to his old bedroom. Joseph snaps back to days of make believe, when he dreamed of building a rocket ship to travel to outer space. But his dream is shattered by a harsh reality—namely, the need to "wake up" and "make money." The chorus boils down his dilemma to a tight couplet:

> Wish we could turn back time, to the good ol' days,
> When our momma sang us to sleep but now we're stressed out.[41]

Adults may be tempted to dismiss such longing for childhood as arrested development. Everyone would like to dodge the painful realities of rent or college loans. But this attitude pays short shrift to the psychic pain that adolescents are identifying with in the song. How can they get to adulthood when their current crises refuse to abate? Why are our adolescents so stressed out? Haven't we taken care of them, provided a roof over their head and shoes on their feet? We also handed them video games, iPads, and smartphones. What else could they possibly need? A user's manual explaining how to handle all those electronic prompts and pressures might have been helpful.

We have attached adolescents to devices with constant connection—an electronic leash—and then wondered why they feel like they are being tugged in too many directions. Social media insists we are born to perform, to command attention, to be celebrated by any means necessary. Such expectations can be exhausting and overwhelming. Profile management can feel like an endless and draining task. Our apps are always keeping score, tracking our progress. Social media can have echoes of *The Hunger Games*, watching our competitors flame out in real time. We may feel trapped and hemmed in.

Stressed-out teens may be comforted by the knowledge that the psalmist knows how they feel. The psalmist also experienced a sense of being hemmed in and surrounded on all sides.

> The cords of death entangled me;
>   the torrents of destruction overwhelmed me.
> The cords of the grave coiled around me;
>   the snares of death confronted me.

> In my distress I called to the LORD;
>   I cried to my God for help. (Ps. 18:4–6)

This book seeks to honor that cry and attempts to look and listen carefully. What do our selfies communicate? Selfies can be silly or serious, casual or curated. They reflect our moods, our memories, our state of mind. They may be moments that we want to hold on to or replies that we expect will be thrown away. Snapchat makes our self-imaging disposable fun. Yet, throughout history, our most enduring self-portraits have arisen from thoughtful reflection and soul searching. They express our creativity and depth. Unlike our disappearing Snapchat self-images, the portraits of ourselves that endure are more comparable to the carefully curated images we post on Instagram. They express art and soul via our bodies. I hope this book will inspire us to create our best selfies yet.

In Luke 7, Jesus embarks on an itinerant healing ministry. He performs miracles in Capernaum and Nain, even raising a widow's son from the dead. As his fame spreads, Simon, a local religious leader, invites Jesus to dinner. Jesus responds to the gracious invitation by reclining in the Pharisee's home at his table (v. 36). As news of Simon's special guest spreads, an infamous woman crashes the dinner party. Her reputation may have resulted in a label like "slut." She stands away from the table, behind Jesus, weeping on his feet. To cry at someone's feet is quite a form of contrition. How much shame, pain, and confusion might have prompted her tears? Was she trying to summon words but couldn't figure out where to start? Perhaps she was trying to interrupt a party she hadn't been invited to. Maybe she even had some history with Simon, having already felt prejudged, condemned as beyond forgiveness. She wipes off her tears with her hair, kisses Jesus's feet, and then pours perfume from an alabaster jar upon them.

Simon takes what he knows of the woman as an occasion to also judge Jesus, saying, "If this man were a prophet, he would know who is touching him and what kind of woman she is—that she is a sinner" (Luke 7:39). Simon has already labeled the woman as condemned. Her reputation disqualifies her from a seat at the table, from any form of recognition. But Jesus turns her interruption into a teachable moment. He talks about loans and the divergent debts that two people accrued. There is so much discussion in the Bible about money. God is not a fan of usury or the rich getting richer on the backs of the poor. Jesus describes how one person owes the loan officer ten times more than the other. There is a big gap between $250,000 of student debt and $25,000 in college loans. Jesus then asks who would be more grateful, more relieved, by the forgiveness of that debt. Simon rightly answers, "I suppose the one who had the bigger debt forgiven" (v. 43). Jesus concurs and then turns Simon's question back upon him, "Do you see this woman?" (v. 44).

Simon thought that Jesus had failed to see the woman's moral failings. But Simon had failed to see the love and contrition communicated by the woman's tears. Jesus points out how inhospitable Simon had been compared to the woman. Simon did not offer water to clean Jesus's feet. Simon did not kiss or welcome him. Simon fell short as a host but still dared to stand in judgment of those excluded from his table. Yet the sinner acted with humility, grace, and considerable financial sacrifice in pouring out her perfume. Jesus says, "I tell you, her many sins have been forgiven" (Luke 7:47). How fascinating that he acknowledges the *numerous* mistakes she's made. Jesus answers the question in Simon's heart saying, in essence, "I am a prophet. I know who is touching me and what kind of woman she is, that she is a sinner." But Jesus is also the kind of prophet who does something far more scandalous—he dines with and even forgives the ashamed.

This is the kind of patience and insight I want to practice with texting teens and harried parents. How can I judge them when I am so guilty of treating others impersonally, preferring to text instead of talk? How can I condemn others for self-centeredness while attempting to update my own status on Facebook? Let he who has never tweeted cast the first disparaging tweet! We all need to be forgiven for our lack of digital decorum. Condemnation is quick and easy; compassion takes time and patience. We need eyes to see and ears to hear.

Selfies is an extension of my initial foray into theology and technology, *iGods*.[42] While that book covered the largest companies and formats driving social media, *Selfies* aspires to get further into digital discipleship and stewardship. How do we love God and serve our neighbors through social media? Does the lure of the selfie shift our focus too narrowly upon ourselves? How can we deflect or at least accurately reflect the glory of God in each of us without glorifying ourselves? A key question resides in the ambitious construction of the Tower of Babel (Gen. 11:1–9)—who or what is being elevated?

Shamir Fauntleroy

No gang signs, just degrees

Some churches have already reduced the implications of the gospel to individualistic salvation. In their 2005 book *Soul Searching*, sociologists Christian Smith and Melinda Lindquist Denton introduced the term "moralistic therapeutic deism" to describe the core theological beliefs of the American adolescents they surveyed in their national study of youth and religion. Yet they did not place the blame on the teenagers for thinking faith was all about rewards granted by God for good behavior. They challenged parents, teachers, and church leaders to present a far more robust gospel that moved adolescents beyond themselves toward service and community.[43]

Adults may have ample reasons to worry about the long-term effects of selfies. But rather than merely castigate youth, I will take a long look at both the history of art and the history of faith. *Selfies* will offer a reasoned, biblically informed response. It follows the theological method of Swiss Catholic theologian Hans Urs von Balthasar (1905–88).[44] His biblical reflections begin with the beautiful creation in Genesis, "the glory of the Lord." Balthasar's theology centers on God's most beautiful action, the ultimate form of the good: the incarnation of Jesus Christ. Because of Jesus, Balthasar posits, "we have a real and inescapable obligation to probe the possibilities of there being a genuine relationship between theological beauty and the beauty of the world and in spite of all the dangers inherent in such an undertaking—to probe the feasibility of a genuine encounter between divine revelation and antiquity."[45] We will look back in order to forge a way forward. Beautiful things (like God's creation—us) inspire beautiful actions (like photo-taking, art-making, and justice-seeking), which reflect beautiful thoughts about God and each other.

This book is about learning to see ourselves (and others) as God sees us. My methodology is rooted in reflection but is designed to inspire more active selfie making. Each chapter concludes with discussion questions that encourage us to take stock of our habits and challenges intended to expand our artistic range. Some may need to put down their phones and enjoy a much-needed rest. Others may end up snapping even more photos of themselves and their neighbors. We are living in an era of expansive possibilities for self-expression. I'm thrilled to highlight students and friends who are plunging ahead as thoughtful image makers.

A Survey of Selfies

This book will study the history of self-portraits in order to enliven our contemporary practices. We begin in antiquity and proceed into the twenty-first century of Snapchat filters and augmented reality. An appreciation and understanding of beauty will spark our consideration of ethics in a digital age. Each chapter follows a similar path. We will look at images, question our actions, and turn to the Holy Trinity and the Bible for wisdom moving forward. As with life, we begin with general revelation, our senses, our reason, and our experience, and we judge them against our norming norm, the special revelation of Scripture. We will, I hope, develop (or recover) a more robust visual theology over the course of our study. I proceed in the inclusive spirit summarized by Dwight Hopkins: "Theological anthropology, drawing on one being created in God's image and heeding the call from Jesus, means a kind of democratic participation, promoting everyone's equal value and equal access to all the best created by human culture, fostering the ownership by working people of the wealth they created, men's and women's mutual sharing in the domestic and public spheres, and harmonious interweaving of ecological and human systems."[46] I am advocating for a biblical understanding of *shalom*, a peaceable kingdom that makes room for everyone to prosper. Eboni Marshall Turman notes how "it is in the uncomfortable dialogues that include all the voices, and in the transformative practices that employ all the bodies that the identity of Christ and the identity of Christ's body converges."[47] The giving and receiving of our selfies is a transformative practice involving our bodies that can become an occasion to celebrate the diversity of the body of Christ.

In *Selfies* we will explore core questions of identity—who we are as individuals, created in the image of God, and who we are as a people, challenged to love one another. Any discussion of selfies must consider the charge that a culture of narcissism has now birthed a new wave of narcissists. Today's teens didn't invent self-interest, but they have been saddled with the burden of profile management. In chapter 2 we travel back to the ancient world, to the source of the term, rereading the myth of Narcissus and considering how the Greeks' understanding of beauty might reflect how we view ourselves today. In chapter 3 we look at changes in technology that allowed Renaissance painters to rise in social status—the use of mirrors, for example, to master self-portraits and increase their fame (and fortune). In chapter 4 we examine how our finest writers have mined memory to forge an alternate future.

In chapter 5 we will discuss how to read a photograph and, more importantly, how to read a person. It is tough to place so much responsibility on a single image. How do we train ourselves to see through the images we're projecting via social media? Chapter 6 plunges into psychology. We will endeavor to get behind the images we're projecting. What we want is to understand what our selfies say and what we're seeking. Chapter 7 is about where we are today. Why do we take selfies and where are our selfies headed? In chapter 8 we discuss the augmented reality we experience via Snapchat filters and apps like Meitu. Could our interest in playing with our appearance via Bitmojis and Animojis reflect a longing for the glory promised in the biblical book of Revelation? Could the transfiguration of Jesus provide a powerful preview of our future? We are created as selfies of God, but we are tempted to erect selfies as God. This is the tension we live within. Some may focus on how to make selfies for God; this book will focus on how to be selfies with God. We proceed with caution, in humility, and full of anticipation.

Questions to Consider/Discuss

Each chapter will conclude with questions to consider as discussion starters. This book could serve as the basis for a class or a small-group study.

1. What do you think about selfies? Do you find them distracting? Delightful? When have you seen a selfie violate a sacred space or moment?
2. What's the most dangerous selfie you've ever taken? Has something you've posted blown up bigger than you expected and ended up hurting more than you imagined? What was that like?
3. How do you view yourself? Do selfies bolster or undercut those feelings? What does God say and feel about you?

Selfie Challenge

Each chapter will also conclude with a selfie challenge—an opportunity to put these concepts into practice using the cameras on our phones. Sometimes we will strive to #knowthyselfie. At other times, we will endeavor to #lovethyneighborasthyselfie. This first selfie challenge is an opportunity to take a #selfiewithGod.

We send selfies to each other as a way to communicate our place and mood. You may be content, angry, enthused, or confused. Get started by taking a selfie to give God a status update on you. Try to communicate your feelings without a smile.

Portrait of a Thin-Faced, Bearded Man

2

Reflected Beauty

The Ancient Self

WE WERE IN SEARCH OF MUMMIES. Aren't most twelve-year-old boys fascinated with creepy things? My son was dragging me through the British Museum in search of Egyptian artifacts, especially the mummies. Indiana Jones movies and the Revenge of the Mummy ride at Universal Studios fueled his imagination. My aspiring anthropologist cruised past ancient Assyria, skipped the Parthenon, and headed toward the third-floor gallery labeled "Egyptian Life and Death." The coffins were tucked into the back of an upper floor. Visitors had to dig in order to find the Egyptian relics. At last, we made it to a room full of mummies seemingly waiting to rise and haunt my son for life. While he focused on the cloth still wrapped around their bodies, I searched for a gold-plated funerary mask of King Tut or other pharaohs. A few items sparkled, but my eye gravitated toward the portraits covering the coffins. These modest paintings were not gold. The subjects didn't resemble ravens or cats or any kind of sphinx. They weren't even flat. These funerary portraits seemed shockingly contemporary. They looked like people I know, students I've taught. They wore tunics and had shiny wreaths in their hair, but they looked like my colleagues. These were not gods or kings, just people. A two-thousand-year gap in human history collapsed.

Historians date *Portrait of a Thin-Faced, Bearded Man* to 160–80.[2] The bearded man stares directly at us. The shadows on his cheeks and nose are clearly defined. His curly hair and robust beard are rendered with exquisite detail. A light shines in the man's dark brown eyes.[3] I want to know more about this person. What was his name? Why did he die? What worried him? What did he relish about life? Centuries may separate us from ancient Egypt, Greece, Nubia, Judea, China, or Rome—we have longer life spans, far more mobility, an array of devices at our disposal—yet when I stare at this portrait, I feel a shocking sense of solidarity across time.

This chapter will consider ancient notions of humanity, of beauty, of the self. Only the wealthy and powerful could afford to have their effigy sculpted in the ancient world. How should we receive and perceive these images? What wisdom can be gleaned from ancient myths and empires?

Goddesses and Olympians: Beauty in the Ancient World

Some days are better than others. We may love the sunlight on our face, the way an outfit complements our body, the fresh cut of our hair. When we like our appearance, it is often time to take out our phone. The right selfie can earn a flurry of likes, loves, and comments from "stunning" to "gorg" or even "adorbs." How great it is when social media summons words of encouragement.

But what if we don't conform to preestablished standards of beauty or perfection? We are often hiding behind so many layers of artifice that it is rare to let our true selves emerge. While we are tempted to perform for our Instagram followers, perhaps the selfie is one of the noblest ways to fight back against the forces that seek to impose external standards of beauty upon us. These beauty standards have ancient roots. The Egyptians celebrated the beauty of their queens, like Nefertiti and Cleopatra. Few in the ancient world were more obsessed with beauty than the Greeks. The balance and proportions assigned to goddesses like Aphrodite became a

Metropolitan Museum of Art, Purchase, 1952

Marble statue of Aphrodite

standard for centuries to follow. Yet the Greeks never had a notion of bro-
kenness as beautiful. What about a boy born with mitochondrial disease
or a woman with cerebral palsy? Do standards instituted in the ancient
world continue to serve as our measuring rod?

So many of our struggles with body image spring from these ideals
regarding kings and queens, gods and goddesses. We have been measuring ourselves against Greco-Roman standards for centuries. They still
dominate our museums, our magazines, and our media. A study led by
Brigham Young University found that 96 percent of girls and 87 percent of
boys had interacted with Disney princesses by age four.[4] Girls who engaged

the most with princess culture (via movies, shows, dolls, costumes, etc.) had the lowest body esteem. For boys, engagement with princesses actually enhanced their body image. Lead researcher Sarah Coyne concludes, "Disney Princesses represent some of the first examples of exposure to the thin ideal. . . . As women, we get it our whole lives and it really does start at the Disney Princess level, at age three and four."[5] A quick glance at magazine covers demonstrates how much "thin" remains "in." The inclusion of even one "plus-sized" model in the *Sports Illustrated* swimsuit edition makes headline news. Cover girl Ashley Graham remarked on her pioneering achievement, "Girls who are insecure about their bodies, girls who feel fat, girls who have cellulite, girls who have stretch marks on their body—those are all the things that I had as a kid and I never had a woman like me growing up to look at."[6] Perhaps the preponderance of selfies on social media has pressured companies to alter their advertising images. The present pushes back against the past.

Casting decisions in Hollywood still have a major impact on audiences' self-perceptions. Lithe (mostly) Caucasian bodies still dominate the prime-time television schedule. Breakthrough roles for Kerry Washington in *Scandal* and Taraji P. Henson in *Empire* and Rami Malek in *Mr. Robot* are slowly altering the "overwhelming whiteness" of network TV, but what images have been predominant?

Issues of weight satisfaction, size-perception accuracy, appearance evaluation, and body concerns continue to dominate reality TV's makeover shows. The success of *Extreme Makeover* begat *The Biggest Loser*, *Bridalplasty*, and *Revenge Body with Khloe Kardashian*. Consider the message inherent in an E! network show titled *Botched by Nature*, for which the executive producers are all men, including the two plastic surgeons who host the show. Dr. Anne Becker found that within three years of Western television arriving in rural communities in Fiji, adolescent women were developing shape preoccupation and engaging in purging behavior to control their weight. Becker concludes, "Understanding vulnerability to images and values imported with media will be critical to preventing disordered eating and, potentially, other youth risk behaviors."[7] America is exporting anxiety to women around the globe via our televised images of perceived success and desirability. Ouch.

Men have also struggled to reflect the athletic ideals portrayed in Greco-Roman sculpture. Sarah Grogan considers how these idealized

Metropolitan Museum of Art, Fletcher Fund, 1925

Fragments of a marble statue of Diadoumenos
(copy of Polykleitos)

images contribute to contemporary insecurities. Grogan notes the arrival
by the seventh century BC of "a broad-shouldered, narrow-hipped ideal
that has become known as the 'Daedalic' style, after the mythical Daedalus
who according to legend was the first Greek sculptor. At this stage, the male
body was idealized and presented in a strictly stylized way, with emphasis
on clearly defined muscles that were carved into the surface pattern on the
marble."[8] When Italians rediscovered the Greco-Roman ideals, it sparked
an artistic renaissance. Michelangelo carved an equally naked and iconic
David, ready to slay Goliath.

Photographer Robert Mapplethorpe brought chiseled nude males back into
vogue in the 1980s and '90s. His polished black-and-white style influenced

advertising campaigns for Calvin Klein underwear featuring the sculpted torso of Mark Wahlberg. Today, most movie stars are expected to resemble superheroes like the mighty Norse god Thor. There are plenty of special effects in those Marvel movies, but those weren't digitized muscles on Chris Hemsworth. Men may have fewer reasons to complain, though, since social pressure on males is far less intense than it is on females. Susan Bordo contrasted the "unbearable weight" placed upon women's physical appearance, while men tend to be judged in terms of achievements rather than looks.[9] Nevertheless, for both men and women, the social pressures to conform to an externalized ideal are rising. How can we experience what poet Gerard Manley Hopkins describes as "God's better beauty, grace"?[10] We can start by recognizing the stories we tell ourselves, unmasking the ideals that drive us to distraction. To develop a healthier selfie, we may need to consider how the ancient world counterbalanced the pursuit of a beautiful body.

Gazing at Ourselves

How many articles have been written about the next generation being lazy, entitled, and narcissistic? Cultural historian Christopher Lasch derided "the culture of narcissism" emerging in the 1970s.[11] Tom Wolfe famously labeled his fellow baby boomers as "the me generation."[12] Decades later, *Time* declared the boomers' children, the millennials, as the "Me Me Me Generation."[13] *Psychology Today* warned of a "narcissism epidemic."[14] Studies indicate that even if adolescents agree with the assessment, it still bothers them: "millennials experience more anger, frustration and sadness over the label than other generations."[15] Nobody likes to be stereotyped. And yet this summation has become so pervasive so quickly. Has our acceptance of these conclusions become so widespread that it is forming a lazy new mythology about the self-absorption of today's teens and twentysomethings?[16]

While scientists debate survey data, I've noticed almost no discussion of the roots of the phenomenon—Narcissus himself. We're applying psychological diagnoses and tossing out labels that spring from a story that we may understand in only superficial ways. Perhaps we should reread the myth of Narcissus. As Ovid describes the scene, Echo was stripped of the gift of speech (or at least self-expression). She cannot determine her own fate but can only respond with fragments of what she's heard. This curse cripples her ability to communicate, especially with a beautiful young man like Narcissus. Echo takes the risk of stepping out. As he approaches, she reveals herself with arms open wide. What a vulnerable, unguarded position. Those who've been hurt rarely open themselves up for rejection. Alas, Narcissus spurns her. "Hands off! Embrace me not! May I die before I give you power over me."[17] Is he afraid to be touched? Some people recoil at the notion of a hug or a kiss. They get tense when affection is involved. In our digital era we may be more comfortable texting than talking. We go to great lengths to avoid awkward moments. Ovid suggests that Narcissus sees connecting with Echo as a surrendering of power. To some degree, he's right. Allowing another person to enter our life, to be in relationship, forces us to set aside our sole agenda. To relate to others, we have to think about the needs of someone beyond ourselves. That is a form of shared power, of suggesting that we are not the center of the universe.

Echo risks the pain of rejection. Narcissus does not honor her humility or sacrifice. He stops communicating, with no announcement or explanation. Today's teens call this "ghosting"—when one completely disappears (online).[18] In our electronic age there is so much electronic miscommunication. When we can't read each other's faces we eliminate important nonverbal clues. So much drama could be avoided through face-to-face (but potentially awkward) conversation. Reading faces is essential in a relationship. With her love rejected, Echo retreats to a cave in the woods, living in isolation until she becomes gaunt, wrinkled, and dried up. Her bones fade and she becomes only a voice, a faint echo (or ghost) of her former self. Being overlooked and ignored, heard but unseen, is a devastating curse.

How did a beautiful youth become fixated on his own reflection? This story reveals some of our collective blind spots that have led us to so readily assign this posture to adolescents. According to ancient wisdom, an obsession with the beauty of our own image can be deadly. Roman mythology warned of the perils Narcissus faced in gazing into a glassy pond. Self-love and blindness have always been dangerous, but perhaps a new generation is discovering the cost of becoming distracted by its own image, wrapped up in appearances. Many overlook what Narcissus missed when he became enraptured with himself. He missed Echo's call to love and relationship. Narcissism can be costly.

Gazing at ourselves was a temptation well before mirrors were perfected. While the selfie may bear remarkable similarities to the gaze of Narcissus,

Erica Bogosian

Narcissus and Echo

it can also offer an opportunity to take stock, to assess oneself. There is a vast difference between self-absorption and self-reflection. We must learn how to appreciate beauty without drowning in a pool of self-obsession. The transformations of Echo and Narcissus are equally tragic because their story begins with the possibility of finding love and connection. It ends in isolation and death—a timeless cautionary tale.

Narcissus reaches into the water, seeking to hug his own neck. What did that gesture look like? It may be comparable to when we extend our arms to snap a selfie. Our hand rises for an odd, unnatural moment. Ovid inserts editorial commentary: "O fondly foolish boy, why vainly seek to clasp a fleeting image? What you seek is nowhere; but turn yourself away, and the object of your love will be no more. That which you behold is but the shadow of a reflected form and has no substance of its own."[19] What a poignant description: "the shadow of a reflected form." What a haunting curse it is to love only an image, devoid of substance. Reflections are so pale, so thin, compared to a real person in the flesh.

This ancient myth reflects our ongoing, fundamental fears. Nobody wants to be alone. Nobody wants to disappear. Nobody wants to be heard but not seen. We want to be loved, to experience connection, to stare into the eyes of someone who adores us. Our obsession with social media is rooted in those fears and longings. We want to be noticed. We want others to acknowledge us. We post a photo in the hope that others will notice, will comment, will like us. We try to capture our best side on a good hair day, when the light seems favorable to our cheekbones, our profile, our figure. We want to be acknowledged as beautiful. Like Narcissus and Echo, we send out friend requests hoping someone will respond positively. It is risky. We might get hurt. When we experience rejection, it may be comforting to stare at the screen. We may turn inward, following Echo, toward an (electronic) cave. We may follow the path of Narcissus, focusing upon our self-image. We may alter our appearance in order to see ourselves as we like to be seen. We may project an aspirational image in the hope of living into our best selves. Yet we may discover that maintaining this ide-alized or false self can be exhausting. It can be quite costly when people discover what we're really like, how alone we feel, how trapped we are by the images of our own (re)making.

What did ancient audiences glean from these myths, and how might they shed light on our contemporary blindness? Louise Vinge notes how Ovid places a story about too much talking (or Echo's failure to hear) beside a tale of Narcissus's inability to see.[20] They are each stuck in a world of mere reflections. Narcissus fails to properly discern Echo's words or his image; he is both deaf and blind. He also fails to recognize that the body he's drawn to is only a reflection. He keeps reaching into the water, longing for a connection. Ovid writes, "He himself is eager to be embraced,"[21] but the spring is called *fallax*, deceptive. We need healthy and reliable reflections in our lives—supportive friends, loving families, an unchanging God.

How many of us reach out on social media, hoping for a connection? Despite all the likes or loves we may amass, we may come away strangely dissatisfied. We have failed to recognize that a computer program will be hard-pressed to offer the human, physical connection we seek. There is no such thing as a virtual hug. It is an illusion. Vinge notes that what Narcissus sees in the water and mistakes for another person is called both *imago* and *umbra*; the words for "shadow" and "reflection" are interchangeable.[22] Neither are embodied. Ovid describes this boy as *imprudens*—inexperienced and ignorant. He isn't actually in love with himself, but only with a shadow or reflection of his true self. Psychologist Julie Kristeva suggests that "Narcissus kills himself because he realizes that he loves a fake. The moral condemnation that concludes the Ovidian myth thus reveals the concomitance of *narcissism* and the *fake*."[23] Even today we search for authenticity: real love, genuine connection.

Escaping Our Echo Chambers

Narcissus gets so absorbed in his appearance that he falls for his reflection, and Echo ends up alone. This is the danger of self-absorption. We may miss out on the love and opportunities that surround us. How could Narcissus and Echo have escaped their isolation? I've heard students talk more and more about loneliness in recent years. We may be more connected in virtual ways (through social media), but we are increasingly alone in our rooms, wondering why everyone else is out having fun (according to their social media posts and projections). When I ask undergrads struggling with loneliness if they ever venture out into the hallway of their dorm, most indicate that they just stay in their room, or at least within their suite of rooms. We reach out via texts and tweets but rarely knock on someone's door, not wanting to risk appearing awkward. Yet the isolation of hiding behind the screens in our own rooms can be a self-defeating box.

Social media feeds our self-absorption by increasingly trapping us in a filter bubble connected to our known likes. As search engines and their algorithms get to know who we like, what we seek, and how we click, they begin to offer information that conforms to our preferences. In a world with an overabundance of options, it can be helpful to have filters to tailor our news or relationships for us—yet a filter bubble may slowly be surrounding us in ways we don't recognize.[24] If we don't reach out beyond our immediate social-media circles, we may be listening only to people who think and look like us. Our biases are reinforced when our information never reaches beyond what we already know. So Narcissus begins to dote on himself, mesmerized by his own appearance and observations. Social media can devolve into an echo chamber, with news outlets and headlines parroting what we have already agreed with. Narcissus and Echo both perish—unheard, unseen, and unnoticed.

Jesus recognized our tendency to stick with what we know. He started so much of his teaching with the preface "You have heard it said . . ."

before shifting perceptions with the corrective "but I say . . ." Jesus came to pop our filter bubbles, to burst our echo chambers. It may mean engaging with people from different races, cultures, languages, or religions. It may mean crossing borders, entering foreign countries with a willingness to learn rather than a predisposition to judge. It is a humbling experience, submitting to others' customs, tastes, and traditions. We may look ignorant or foolish. We may be laughed at or mocked. But with such humility comes freedom, a release from the burden of controlling others, conforming them to our image and likeness. As we accept their differences, we may suddenly learn to embrace our own limits and failings. Putting aside a war with others may allow us to stop wrestling with ourselves.

The prophet Jeremiah railed against "foolish and senseless people, who have eyes but do not see, who have ears but do not hear" (Jer. 5:21). Without the proper perception, we might miss the point of Jesus's parables. Hearing the words doesn't always mean we will understand the stories. Our eyes may stare at something, and yet it fails to register in our brains. The key to discipleship is an awareness of what's happening beyond ourselves, paying attention to our friends, our neighbors, our city, our schools. What are the headlines and needs of our neighbors overseas? When we feel tempted to begrudge our situation, we may be lifted out of our self-pity party by seeing how others live. Our boring life may actually look remarkably robust next to refugees fleeing war-torn homelands. Perhaps gratitude regarding our own conditions will also result in us reaching out and caring for others. Eyes to see how others are faring and ears to hear the stories of our neighbors' suffering or triumph are essential to long-term discipleship.

Narcissus also failed the first test of what makes us human. Self-consciousness is what allows the psalmist to proclaim humanity as a little lower than God (Ps. 8:5). It is what places humanity atop the hierarchy of creation in Genesis. We were created on the sixth day, alongside animals. We share an innate creatureliness. Yet we are also called to a seventh day of rest, reflection, and worship, in which we imitate God in gaining perspective over creation.[25] God put us in charge of the animals and the plants because we could allegedly see the bigger picture. We could superintend the situation. We are called to steward creation, to take care of it, to recognize when things are going awry, to bring order to chaos.

Ancient Wisdom: Know Thy Selfie

When it comes to crucial decisions, where do we turn for advice? A Google search may settle an argument and offer a lightning-fast fact. We may consult our friends, our parents, our peers. For big decisions, we may turn to the Bible for wisdom or to God in prayer. The ancient Greeks sought answers in Delphi. The oracle at Delphi could be found in the Temple of Apollo. She would get caught up in a reverie, with her ecstatic utterances, which were translated by the temple priests. The oracle was thought to channel the wisdom of the Greek god Apollo. She was a source of light, of poetry, of music, of healing.

The most enduring and widely embraced aphorism inscribed in the temple was *gnothi seauton*—"know thyself." This simple phrase has served as a clarion call for countless philosophies that have followed. In Plato's *Dialogues*, Socrates repeatedly stresses the importance of knowing ourselves before we proceed with additional investigations. Self-knowledge is seen as foundational to any pursuit of knowledge or wisdom. To know thyself, one must begin to develop self-consciousness: a recognition that we can identify. This basic starting point eluded Narcissus. He didn't know himself, so he couldn't recognize his own reflection in the pond.

The two-word challenge to "know thyself" ratchets up in adolescence. We begin to wonder, Who am I? How did I get here? What is my purpose? We take a wide array of classes in high school and college in an effort to sharpen a sense of calling. We may take aptitude tests to determine our strengths. For Socrates, all of these vocational-based activities may miss the larger point of contemplation. To know thyself is not a means to an end (like finding a job we love) but it is the end itself. Self-knowledge is the goal. It may help us find a satisfying career, but it is primarily a process of lifelong learning that shifts and twists and deepens over time. Self-awareness is an antidote to self-absorption. It is a long-term goal, an evolving art.

Contemplating our selves—who we are, where we are, what we are called to be—has a long and positive history. Narcissus showed how dangerous it can be to stare at our reflection, but other Greek myths affirm the power of mirrors. For Perseus, a mirror was a shield to protect him from the devastating stare of Medusa. It provided him with enough perspective to slay a mortal enemy. We may need a mirror to figure out how to deal with a monster (especially if that monster resides within us). Staring at our reflection can be beneficial when it is accompanied by thoughtful reflection.

Mirrors can also be a tempting snare. They may offer a skewed or even false perspective. To "know thyself" is to learn to recognize how or when our perception has been warped. We may think we will not be blinded by our own beauty, unlike Narcissus, but we are all too easily wrapped up in our own private world. The challenges of commuting to work or school, completing assignments, and keeping up with the demands of laundry, cleaning, yard work, and cooking can leave us too tired for contemplation. We may need a nap more than we need self-analysis. If we get too wrapped up in basic life management, we can miss the larger purpose in living. Narcissus's failure to even recognize his appearance cut short the process that Socrates encouraged. Narcissus keeps reaching out for something that cannot be grasped. He is fundamentally disconnected from reality, unable to distinguish a reflection from his own embodied self. If he didn't know he was looking at himself, how could he engage in even a surface-level reflection on his place and purpose in the world?

Postmodern French philosopher Michel Foucault attempted to bridge this merging of ancient ideals and practical daily matters. In his essay "Technologies of the Self," Foucault suggests that the Greek dictum to "know thyself" also meant knowing how to take care of yourself. Foucault notes, "The precept of the 'care of the self' was, for the Greeks, one of the main principles of cities, one of the main rules for social and personal conduct and for the art of life."[26] Narcissus becomes so enraptured with his own image that he fails to eat or sleep. Echo stopped taking care of herself as well. A little more self-care would have allowed both of them to take care of each other and ultimately serve the greater good. Self-awareness and self-reflection that lead to self-care translate into a healthier society. The Greek notion of democracy is built on responsible citizens contributing to the social good. It depends on everyone playing their part.

After work, we may drop that persona and put on clothes that reflect a different role—athlete, coach, dancer, cook, parent. We may have a disconnect between our true self and the roles we play in society, as a student or working professional. In ancient Rome, the state conferred the status of "person" to those who performed their role in society. Your recognition as a person began in your persona.[27] Your worth, your personhood, was defined by and conferred by the empire. Extending legal rights and status to individuals was a bold innovation. But it did not mean that people were free to follow their own bliss. Your value as a person began and ended with the state, with "playing" or "performing" a useful role in society.

Performance Anxiety: Acting in Ancient Greece

The problem with the performance-based self begins when the role-playing ends. The rush that comes from affirmation can be intoxicating, but when the audience leaves, what is the actor left with? To define our worth via applause (or likes or loves or followers) places us in a precarious position. We have surrendered our selves and our worth to the crowd. As long as they are paying attention, stroking our ego with shouts and hosannas, then we retain a sense of importance. We are not alone. We matter. But what happens if they fail to notice our performance? How big must the crowd be for us to feel loved? It is easy to get addicted to status updates that tell us exactly how people have responded to our posts. We may game the system with attention-grabbing stunts that keep the affirmations coming for a while. But what if we grow weary of performing in public?

Those who've spent time in the working world know how slippery such performance-based affirmation can be. A favorable annual review may be followed by rising expectations. As we expand our budgets, we also expand the management challenges that accompany them. Pastors who have grown a congregation face the daunting task of maintaining it. Students also get an early taste of performance anxiety. Genuine fear and panic may overcome students facing their first B or C. What happens to our self-worth if we are not used to anything less than excellence and affirmation? And what if it is not always possible to meet external expectations? Our performance may sometimes fall short due to the limitations of humanity. We get tired. We need a break. Our dog really may have eaten our homework (or, at least, our computer really may have frozen or locked up). No one and no thing is perfect. Our brains and our bodies are not always tuned for peak performance.

The early Christian community arose from within the Greco-Roman world. Statues celebrating an idealized form of beauty dominated the marketplace. The ancient world was well acquainted with performance-based anxiety. They were familiar with the capricious gods like Nemesis who enacted judgment toward those who disappointed them. Temples to

Apollo and Dionysus dominated the skyline. There were constant reminders of what was demanded or expected of a person. Religions have a way of heaping burdens upon weary people. The demands for sacrifices to appease the gods were steady and potentially overwhelming. Those who couldn't muster proper sacrifices to the gods were expected to hire priests to do it right.

The countercultural teachings of Jesus arrived as a balm to a weary people. His gracious invitation undercut social pressures: "Come to me, all you who are weary and burdened, and I will give you rest. Take my yoke upon you and learn from me, for I am gentle and humble in heart, and you will find rest for your souls. For my yoke is easy and my burden is light" (Matt. 11:28–30). What a sharp rebuke to performance-based anxiety. Jesus invites his followers to cease striving, to take a break, to cut loose the burden. Jesus presents an alternative God who dignifies us regardless of our performance. We are more than our social role. With Jesus, we can remove our masks and stop the exhausting, marathon performance.

Jesus entered into a Greco-Roman culture that had newly affirmed the rights of individuals. But he expanded the notion of who deserves recognition and dignity. Yes, people had a valuable role to play in the polis as voting members of a democracy in Greece or a burgeoning empire in Rome. But Jesus extended dignity to those who hadn't been given the right to vote. In his defense of a woman caught in adultery (John 8:1–11), Jesus leveled the field, questioning who has the right to cast aspersions (or stones). In Jesus's eyes, we are united not in our strengths but in our weaknesses. We have all sinned and fallen short of the glory of God (Rom. 3:23). To "know thyself" is to know one's limitations and shortcomings. So the game of spiritual (or professional) one-upmanship is upended. In God's kingdom, the old categories of righteous and unrighteous, clean and unclean, get blurred. Jesus sides with those who feel judged, unworthy, and cast out. He heals the sick, touches the contagious, and dares to reach out to the lepers.

Scholar Joanna Woods-Marsden puts the radical implications of such teaching into context. She writes, "To this notion of a 'person' with citizenship and other rights, Christianity later added the concept of an inner conscience and inner life. Even the slave, albeit not in possession of his own body, was given a soul. The foundation then of the modern individual is this notion of a 'person,' bearing on the one hand a civic identity derived from Roman law and on the other a conscience and soul bestowed on it by Christianity."[28] We start to see the social implications of Jesus's radical inclusion in Paul's Letter to the Galatians: "So in Christ Jesus you are all children of God through faith, for all of you who were baptized into Christ have clothed yourselves with Christ. There is neither Jew nor Gentile, neither slave nor free, nor is there male and female, for you are all one in Christ Jesus" (Gal. 3:26–28). What a welcome message of unity despite our differences. The hierarchy isn't just redefined in Christ; it is dismantled. We are not valued because of what we can contribute. We are precious and equal in God's sight regardless of our social status. This becomes the starting point for a new kind of society, rooted in equal rights for all. It is a project we are still working on.

Yet what about critics like Foucault, who see Christianity as requiring a repudiation of our selves? While affirming those on the margins of society, didn't Jesus also call his disciples to restrict and restrain their desires? In the Gospel of Luke, Jesus issues a radical call to potential followers: "Whoever wants to be my disciple must deny themselves and take up their cross daily and follow me. For whoever wants to save their life will lose it, but whoever loses their life for me will save it. What good is it for someone to gain the whole world, and yet lose or forfeit their very self?" (Luke 9:23–25). Could this kind of self-denial veer toward the unhealthy path of Narcissus? When Narcissus fails to see himself, he also fails to feed himself. The way of Jesus seems fraught with danger. He speaks in high-stakes paradoxes involving the loss of life. What kind of life is Jesus promising for those who deny themselves? And what does it mean to "lose or forfeit their very self"?

The call to follow Christ does involve casting off certain hindrances. On the shores of the Lake of Gennesaret, Jesus called Peter, James, and John to follow him and become fishers of people. They leave their nets and their livelihoods behind (Luke 5:1–11). For a rich young ruler, the call is to sell his possessions and give the money to the poor so he can follow Jesus unfettered (Mark 10:21). Jesus speaks of leaving home and the comforts of siblings and parents to follow him (Mark 10:29–30). The radical road to discipleship involves a question of fealty. Whom have we cast our lots with? Who or what is the focus of our worship? The Greeks constructed temples for all kinds of gods (and occasions) from Apollo, the sun god, to Dionysus, the god of the vine. What temple did Narcissus reside in? The borders of his temple did not extend beyond the pond. His world began and ended in his reflection.

Christianity arrived as a correction, an invitation to worship in a temple dedicated to a less capricious God. The God of Abraham, Isaac, Jacob, and Jesus was set apart as a generous God who doesn't tie dignity or worth to performance. In Christ, we are more than a social role; we can take off the mask. Contrary to Foucault's critique, Christianity is about more than just renouncing the self; it is about truly seeing who we are called to be. Awareness of our imperfectability is a great starting point. We acknowledge how far we've fallen short of God's divine perfection. We are released from the burden of performance-based spirituality. With salvation and the forgiveness of sin comes a freedom that can propel us forward on a lifelong pursuit of spiritual maturity. Hans Urs von Balthasar sees how Socrates's philosophy can be married to theology in a manner that frees us from perfectionism. Balthasar writes, "Knowing of the house built up in grace for him with God, [a person] can cheerfully inhabit his tumbledown hut and free himself through time."[29] I may not fulfill Greek notions of athleticism or beauty, but I can surely embrace my body as a tumbledown hut! Following God and progressing toward divine character becomes a grace-driven, lifelong project.

Redeeming Narcissus

The Bible arose within an ancient culture where competing gods demanded fealty. These self-interested deities expected to be doted and gazed upon. The Jewish prophets challenged such idolatry. Jesus modeled a self-emptying God rather than a self-promoting idol. Christianity offered a radical alternative, a different kind of emperor. This God in the flesh shares and even surrenders power. He is set apart not by beauty but by sacrifice. Jesus is known for how he shared rather than hoarded, gave rather than conquered.

How might the tragedy of Narcissus serve as a bridge between Greek paganism and Christianity? If Narcissus can be snapped out of his self-obsession, then surely we can all be redeemed from our skewed self-perception. Professor Julie Kristeva sees Narcissus as the first modern antihero, the non-god par excellence whose "murky, swampy, invisible drama must have summed up the anguish of a drifting mankind, deprived of stable markers."[30] Kristeva argues that his despair arises from the realization that there is nothing beyond himself. We may have this feeling when our post on social media does not generate the response we seek. We are confronted with a sense of loneliness that can be crippling. Do I have any real friends? Does anybody really care? Narcissus commits suicide in such a haunting moment.

Inspired by Plotinus, early Christian leaders sought to redeem Narcissus, to emphasize the potential within such moments of isolation and reflection. They reframed ascetic solitude as a gift and an opportunity. To gaze into one's soul could become a spiritual discipline. Being alone with oneself was a prerequisite of prayer. Instead of gazing into a pool, the early church fathers advocated clasping our hands before God in prayer. Narcissus could be an exemplar of how to go deeper with God, by withdrawing from distractions. Julie Kristeva marvels how "mythic tragedy has been changed into meditation and introspection. Henceforth, there is an *inside*, an internal life, to be contrasted with the *outside*."[31] The early church fathers saw the navel-gazing of Narcissus as the beginning of a taking stock of our soul, of communion with God rather than gazing down a self-obsessed rabbit hole. Staring at our reflection need not be dangerous when the pool is God.

Could selfie making lead to a revival of contemplation, a rediscovery of self-reflection rooted in prayer? The constant companionship of our phones may draw us away from such moments. We often take up our phone to defend ourselves against contemplation. We ponder how many responses there are to our Snapchat Stories rather than face our fears of being alone. Our existential crises are avoided by another update on Facebook or Instagram. Rather than looking within, we gaze out to our friends and followers in an effort to escape the gnawing questions of life. So our phones may serve as that sparkly surface, the steady distraction to keep us from recognizing ourselves in the mirror. We may devolve like Narcissus into suicidal thoughts that come from isolation, or we may instead rise up in prayer to a new Object of love beyond ourselves.

Studying ourselves, taking stock of our lives, need not be inherently sinful. In fact, strong self-reflection may be a prerequisite to responsible discipleship. People of faith must always aspire to purify our lives and straighten out our motives. There are powerful possibilities in reflection. We aspire to present ourselves as resplendent before God, shining with virtue even while living under the promise of Christ's grace.

Kristeva places such self-assessment in context, noting how "Christianity, particularly with Thomas Aquinas, involved taking up again the reflexive, specular, speculative, and intimist Narcissian *dynamics*, while at the same time considering the narcissistic *event*—his love—as a mistake in viewpoint."[32] Where did Narcissus go wrong? Not in staring at himself, but in failing to properly identify his place within the pond. He fell in love with a projected image and failed to recognize the source of his beauty. Kristeva suggests, "If Narcissus had known that he was not the source of the illusion, but that he himself was already a reflection of essential Unity, he could have loved himself with impunity, hence loved his image, within the orbit of essential, divine unity beyond which one cannot go."[33] We can look in the mirror, see our imperfections, and obsess over how to become perfect. Or we can see ourselves as so beautiful that we fail to recognize the Author of our beauty. We must be freed from both of these illusions. To a culture obsessed with the body and image the Bible offers an alternative: "Let the one who boasts boast in the Lord" (1 Cor. 1:31). Or as poet/priest Gerard Manley Hopkins wrote, "Give beauty back, beauty, beauty, beauty, back to God, beauty's self and beauty's giver."[34]

What is the good news arising from this cautionary tale? Our illusions can be redeemed: "Henceforth, love of self is an error only to the extent that one forgets one is the reflection of the Other (the Lord)." Christ snaps us out of the spell of self-delusion. The ripples on the pond created by his sacrificial love wake us up. Salvation creates "a space of love that takes into account the illusion, the seeming, and the impossible settled at the very heart of supreme reality."[35] Jesus introduces a new ground for our reality, beyond our own image. We are beautiful because we are created by God. We are valuable not because of what we do but because of who (and whose) we are.

Our understanding of beauty must expand beyond appearances into actions. Womanist theologian Shawn Copeland connects beauty to authentic ethics, asserting, "Beauty is living up to and living out the love and summons of creation in all our particularity and specificity as God's human creatures made in God's own image and likeness."[36] We are called to serve more than ourselves. We attend the temple not to bribe an angry God but to serve a community. We can still incorporate the wisdom of the Greeks. We can examine our lives. It is important to know thyself, to care for ourselves and our community. We must get past gazing at our own reflections. Don't fall in love with a reflection. Be reflective. We learn from those moments of reflection to recognize our error. We fall in love with the Source of the pond rather than with our reflections. Empowered by that Wellspring of life and beauty, we can turn toward Echo and engage with the community around us. As Jesus said, "love your neighbor as yourself" (Mark 12:31).

Questions to Consider/Discuss

1. Do you still have the first picture you drew or photo you took of yourself? What does it look like?

2. What can we learn from Narcissus and Echo's story? Whom do you relate to?

3. What do you see when you look in the mirror? Do you enjoy looking at yourself? What stands out when you start to #knowthyselfie?

Selfie Challenge

Make a photo of yourself using water. It may be at a fountain, a sink, a lake, a pool. Before you snap, pay attention to your reflection and study the water. How do they interact? What fresh perspectives might they reveal? Think especially about how you might reach out and serve others via selfies.

Color me in

3

Mastering the Mirror

A Renaissance of the Self

> Art is the representation not of the body but of the forces which created the body.
>
> —Nikos Kazantzakis[1]

W HAT'S THE ORIGINAL SYMBOL for the App Store? An "A" greets us whenever we want to upgrade the applications for our iPhones. What elements comprised the original "A" (prior to iOS 11)? Three ancient technologies—a pen, a brush, and a tablet—united, inviting us to explore the power placed in our hands. Our smartphones serve as our paintbrush. Thanks to these magical devices, the power of self-presentation previously reserved for the ruling classes is now available to almost everyone. With cameras in hand, we are reveling in the art of self-fashioning and self-representation. Disseminating our image is now a literal "snap."

Portraits of ourselves have always communicated status. Selfies are a more democratic form of that enduring artistic tradition, the self-portrait. They communicate "I was here" and "My life mattered." The commissioned portraits that now hang in the world's finest museums were a sign of wealth, a luxury that only a few could afford. But what about those who couldn't pay for their portrait or didn't have the brush in their hands? Some were rendered as objects or not depicted at all. Art history can be the study of (mis)representation.

This chapter will connect the rise of self-portraits in the Renaissance era to changes in technology, to rising social classes, and to a newfound acceptance of status symbols. The widespread production of mirrors enabled artists to experiment with self-images. They could study and render themselves with a detail previously unimagined. Court painters gradually came to be revered even more widely than their subjects, with Michelangelo and Albrecht Dürer becoming the first "celebrity" artists. The finest Renaissance artists, like Rembrandt, leaned into their social cachet to critique the pomp and circumstance surrounding self-portraits. They found freedom via self-incrimination rather than self-promotion. We celebrate these artists as geniuses while critiquing today's posts as narcissistic. Might the truth reside somewhere in between?

We will study the rise of self-portraits in painting as a way into contemporary questions. What kinds of power and prestige are we pursuing via selfies? Is the backlash against them a way to disempower those who finally have the ability to craft their own image? To what degree does image making spring from our roots as people created as the image and likeness of God? Self-imaging can be a spiritual discipline, an opportunity for us to grow closer to God.

Despite warnings in the Bible regarding idolatry, people of faith have not shied away from image making. Consider portraits of Jesus or the saints. We don't view these icons as a form of self-promotion because they serve a different kind of function. Their image offers a form of solidarity and solace. The Savior or the saints gaze directly at the viewer, inviting us into the painting not merely to revere but also to commune with the icon. The icon tradition allowed church patrons to paint themselves into heaven, to portray themselves in prayerful devotion. But it also allowed others to see themselves in the painting, to imagine a glorious gilded future. As a "mere" saint modeled Christian virtues, so others could aspire to a similar level of devotion. Icons bridge the gap of time and space, inviting us to adopt an eternal perspective. They reflect our heavenly aspirations. Could we shift from immortalizing ourselves via selfies to creating portraits that draw us nearer to our divine nature?

Holding Up a Mirror

Imagine a culture with limited social mobility, where people are locked into particular roles, their ambitions checked by a fixed class divide. No, I am not talking about Americans' contemporary revulsion at the 1 percent; I am talking about the medieval world of feudal lords and their vassals. While landowners presided over fiefdoms, serfs were pledged to serve the lord of the manor. Tapestries lined the walls of these great halls, memorializing noble hunts and revered battles. Royal families interested in preserving their social standing commissioned portraits that fixed their affluence in time and place. If they hired the right artist, they could secure their importance for centuries to come. The painters were viewed as tradesmen, performing a service with a sense of artistry and craft, but not necessarily with an individual style. The patron mattered far more than the painter.

Only as mobility and trade increased during the Renaissance did individuals begin to imagine a better life. With economic possibilities came more social fluidity. Joanna Woods-Marsden notes how it wasn't until the Renaissance that the word "self" came into its own, as combinations like "self-praise, self-love, self-pride, self-regard all entered the language."[2] Technological innovations fueled artistic and cultural breakthroughs. Art historian Maria Loh notes how "the development of new media, such as oil paint (with its mimetic potential) and print (with its capacity for rapid distribution), enabled a mid-sixteenth century boom in portraiture. The portraitist Leone Leoni announced enthusiastically, 'Everyone is now having a portrait made.'"[3] (Selfies have been fashionable before.) As the materials needed to make portraits spread farther and wider, so did the complaints about the expanding range of subjects. Giorgio Vasari complained about the rise of "lowly types," and "the self-aggrandizing Italian poet Pietro Aretino lamented, 'How is it your shame, oh century, that you allow even tailors and butchers to appear living here in paintings.' Anyone, so it seemed, could become somebody through the powers of portraiture."[4] We have seen a similar backlash in the selfie era. When seemingly "anyone" can become "somebody" through the democratizing force of self-portraiture or a YouTube channel, critics are bound to pounce on the flattening of culture. Provinces that used to be reserved for princes have now opened to "common people."

What technological breakthrough fueled the rapid rise of self-portraits? Innovations in the production of mirrors increased the incidence

Portrait of a Man, Jan van Eyck, 1433

of self-portraiture. The Gallo brothers perfected the production of glass mirror on the island of Murano, giving Venice a monopoly for years to come. While the Greeks had warned of the mesmerizing power of mirrors, in the Renaissance mirrors were associated with such positive virtues as "Veritas, truth, and Scienza, knowledge, symbolizing the truthfulness and verisimilitude that Renaissance painters claimed as their achievement."[5] The most accomplished artists depended upon this shimmering innovation.

Jan van Eyck may have painted the first independent self-portrait, in 1433.[6] *Portrait of a Man* juxtaposes the bright red *chaperon* on the subject's head with the piercing gaze in his eyes. It can be read as an anthology of reflections. We can see the light in his eyes. They reflect the window in the room in which he was painting. The eye serves as a mirror.[7] The dark background provides a sharp contrast, making the man's appearance pop. The painter is identified in two signatures intended to appear as etchings in the wood frame. Is this detailed study of a common man (with dashing headgear) a self-portrait? It could be an advertisement for what Van Eyck can do (for whoever hires him). The skill and care lavished upon a subject who clearly is not a member of a royal family communicates what a different cultural milieu we are entering. So how might Van Eyck have made this portrait, which showed what he could do? It was enabled by the magic of a mirror. He studied his appearance in a mirror in order to render it on canvas. The portrait is Van Eyck watching himself at work.

Art historian James Hall notes how "the self-portrait proves you are a mirror-owner, and [shows that you] know how to use them. The mirror-assisted self-portrait perpetuates your fame and—by its perfection—proves that your fame is merited."[8] Van Eyck has the skills, and he knows how to highlight his accomplishments. His signature is a form of advertising: "If you're impressed by these results, hire me." He sets himself apart from the competition, promising to deliver results "as only I can." Woods-Marsden points to Leonardo DaVinci's facility with mirrors, "acting as a mediator between Nature and himself. The painter, he thought, should keep his mind as clear as the surface of a mirror, so that ultimately, he became his own mirror."[9] Consider these masters as early adopters, employing the latest and greatest technological innovations for the sake of their art.

Perhaps the most conscious and brazen use of mirrors in Renaissance painting was by a twenty-year-old Italian known as Parmigianino ("the little one from Parma"). With his *Self-Portrait in a Convex Mirror* (1524), now at the Kunsthistorisches Museum in Vienna, Parmigianino plays with perspective, placing his right hand in the foreground of the circular canvas.

Self-Portrait in a Convex Mirror, Parmigianino, 1524

His hand is elongated and distorted. The entire room seems to bend around his head in the center of the circle. Rather than disguising the technology that allows him to render his appearance with such dramatic verisimilitude, Parmigianino embraces his source, creating a canvas that resembles a convex mirror. At only nine and a half inches wide, the miniature canvas could have potentially passed as a portable mirror. It was a visual trick, maybe even a publicity stunt designed to open doors. Parmigianino proved that he could render images comparable to the visual purity of the most polished mirror. This was a brazen visual calling card.

Parmigianino is celebrated for his youth, his inventiveness, his embrace of technology. And yet aren't these the same conditions that precede our critique of selfie-obsessed teens? Modern teens are projecting their self-image, using what's available, to communicate who they are and what they're capable of. They know that social media is a form of unfettered self-promotion. Aren't they just experimenting with their looks, their self-image, their public presentation?

Renaissance fascination with mirrors extended to the way they rehabilitated the reputation of Narcissus. Writing in the fifteenth century in his treatise *On Painting*, Renaissance man Leon Battista Alberti shifts the focus from the subjects to the artists. He connects painting to the act of creation, where artists "see their works admired and feel themselves to be almost like the Creator." Alberti celebrated Narcissus as the first artist (even though I don't recall him actually making anything). Alberti goes on to say, "I used to tell my friends that the inventor of painting, according to the poets, was Narcissus, who was turned into a flower; for as a painting is the flower of all the arts, so the tale of Narcissus fits our purpose perfectly. What is painting but the act of embracing by means of art the surface of the pool?"[10]

Narcissus became an exemplar as the Renaissance began to associate artists with beautiful boys arising as fully formed geniuses. Consider Michelangelo's idealized statue of the biblical king David, erected in Florence in 1504. David may be young, but his muscles are already well developed, his gaze quite clear. The massive scale of the marble statue makes David look more like a Goliath, capable of knocking off all challengers. *David* was undertaken when Michelangelo was only twenty-six years old and confirmed him as a boy genius, a sculptor without peers. As in David's victory over Goliath, youth triumphs over experience. The adolescent male is elevated rather than denigrated. Michelangelo's artistic triumph is so complete that it seems to defy our rational capacities. Such mastery and skill could not arise from practice. We are left to assume it is an innate, God-given talent bestowed on youth in an unequal manner. The myth of the artist / boy genius might arise from the myth of Narcissus but takes full flight in the Renaissance.

Albrecht Dürer leaned into the rising confluence of youth, beauty, masculinity, and divinity in his self-portraits. Dürer's luscious, curly hair cascades down past his shoulders in his *Self-Portrait at Twenty-Eight Years Old* (1500). He wears a luxurious coat with a fur collar rendered with remarkable detail and facility. Dürer stares from the canvas with a gaze quite comparable to iconic portraits of Jesus. His hand clasps his coat with a gesture that recalls a divine blessing by Jesus. Even the "AD" signature monogram on the left side of the painting makes conscious connections to

Alte Pinakothek, Munich

Self-Portrait at Twenty-Eight Years Old, Albrecht Dürer, 1500

Christ. Is this an effort to claim a godlike status for himself, or a conscious nod to Jesus as the source of his creative abilities? Hall describes Dürer as "the most celebrated, prolific and inventive creator of self-portraits during the Renaissance. . . . He believed that great artists had 'a creating power like God's. For a good painter is inwardly full of figures.'"[11] An exquisite self-portrait could be a form of praising God or blatant self-promotion—or a complicated mixture of both impulses.

A popular catchphrase that arose during the Renaissance was "every painter paints himself." The wisdom of the era suggested that artists were engaging in an unwitting form of self-portraiture whether they acknowledged it or not. Rather than disguising himself within the painting, Dürer may be consciously embracing the philosophy of his epoch. He does not obscure or hide his appearance whatsoever. Dürer's "selfie" may be an unabashed effort to connect the dots between his attractive physical appearance and his inner spiritual purity. By painting himself in an iconic religious style, Dürer could be advancing himself as a substitute for Christ. But it seems more likely that he portrayed himself as beautiful in an effort to celebrate the enduring beauty of Jesus. Dürer seems to be saying, "If you can see Christ in me, then perhaps you can begin to see Christ in you as well." When we dismiss selfies as acts of self-aggrandizement, we may be short selling adolescents' efforts to acknowledge how fearfully and wonderfully we're made (Ps. 139:14).

It is tough to sort out the motivations that may drive our self-portraits. They could be a way to say "I look good" or "I love who I am." They can be flagrant self-promotion, a desire to get our face out there (both for now and for eternity). An effort to commemorate ourselves at a particular age or stage can also be an important opportunity for reflection. It fixes what we looked like at a specific juncture in our lives, similar to the way getting a tattoo may be a form of commemorating an important life event. It can also provide a mirror—something with enough distance that we can use it to reflect on who we are or who we are becoming. Couldn't our selfies, at their best, operate on these simultaneous levels as a celebration of our creative capacity and as a mirror upon which we can ponder the state of our soul?

Social Climbing via Self-Portraits

While we may decry the self-promotional aspects of selfie culture, the Italian artists who ushered in the Renaissance embraced self-portraiture to climb the social ladder. The autonomous self-portraits invented in the fifteenth century expanded in sixteenth-century Italy. Woods-Marsden notes, "The images projected the aspirations of their creators for a change in the status of art and hence a change in their own personal social standing."[12] While we may be obsessed with fame, people in the Renaissance era were obsessed with social status. Renaissance court culture featured daily opportunities to rise or fall in social standing, from arranged marriages to seating charts at dinner. In a courtly world of "see and be seen," a renowned self-portrait could raise the social standing of both the artist and their art (and their subsequent commission rates). We did not invent the temptation to monitor our daily rankings in terms of posts liked, pictures loved, and followers gained. Court painters and artisans had to navigate shifting social dynamics as well.

During the Renaissance era, clothes were an important symbol of social status. Consider the crushed red velvet robe of Pope Leo X painted by Raphael.[13] While the pope is flanked by two cardinals in their own red robes, the sheen of their apparel pales in comparison to that of Leo X. The brocade on Leo's sleeves and the ermine fringe on his velvet cape communicate wealth and power. Artists could impress their clients with their attention to detail. They could also burnish their own legend in how they dressed themselves in self-portraits.

As the queens and kings of today's selfies depend on publicists to multiply their fame and followers, so many Renaissance artists were promoted by biographer Giorgio Vasari. Loh writes, "With the publication of the first edition of Vasari's *Lives of the Painters, Sculptors, and Architects* in 1550, the narrative of fame was opened up to a new social category of men and women who were capable of transcending their class position and gender restrictions through the sheer force of their ambition and talent."[14] She describes Vasari's collection as a "Renaissance Facebook" that contributed to the glamorization of the profession and the "celebrification" of artists as people who were not only famous but whose faces were subsequently recognized widely.[15] Artists' images became fixed by an appearance in Vasari's book.

With their newfound social status, artists no longer needed to resort to imitating kings in their poses and regalia. They began to paint themselves as craftsmen in their workshop, plying a trade.[16] We do the same today, communicating our mastery via a #healthyselfie at the gym, on a bike, on the court, atop a mountain, in the kitchen. These various forms of self-fashioning communicate a sense of self-mastery, as if insisting, "Quiet—genius at work."

Museo del Prado, Madrid

Las Meninas, Diego Velázquez, 1656

Among the most famous self-portraits of artists in their studios is Diego Velázquez's monumental *Las Meninas*, or *The Maids of Honor* (1656).[17] As a court painter in Spain, Velázquez stages the scene within the Alcazar palace of King Philip IV and Queen Mariana in Madrid. Their image is reflected in a mirror on a distant wall (in the center of the painting). Velázquez has essentially flipped the canvas, offering us a behind-the-scenes peek at the Spanish court (and studio) he inhabits. He has created a picture about reflections, made possible by the magic of mirrors. Martin

Gayford considers it "a picture of a reflection of a picture."[18] He sees it as a meditation on the questions, What is reality, and what is appearance? Velázquez tantalizes the audience (and his patrons) with a visual riddle: "What *are* we looking at?" It is a picture about mirrors made by mirrors. By playing with viewers' perspectives, the painting invites us to question our judgment and ponder, "What is truth?"

Velázquez captured the legacy of the king and queen by including their daughter, destined for their throne. He fulfilled the commission, performed his role. But Velázquez demonstrates his own mastery by capturing (and containing) the swirling world of the Spanish royal family in a single moment. He has made time stand still. Artists are becoming like gods, not just creating the image but inhabiting it as well.[19]

By placing the royal family within his studio, Valázquez makes his own image an essential part of the painting. He offers viewers a sneak peek of his studio and of his own creative process. His fame grows even as he is commissioned to celebrate the royal family. Pascal Bonafoux suggests that "the self-portrait is always an implicit acknowledgment of the painter's place of work."[20] Crowds clamor to get a peek into artists' and musicians' studios today. Self-portraits dominate the gallery of the historic Rembrandt House in Amsterdam. Tours of Elvis Presley's Graceland Mansion continue to draw fans to Memphis. The untimely death of Prince resulted in the conversion of his Paisley Park Studios into a memorial in Minneapolis. Fans jump at the opportunity to observe artists in their studios, to have a sense that magic happens in this creative space. We are graced by the opportunity to see "geniuses" in their element.

What about Her World?

We've heard so much about boy geniuses and the famous men that created the Renaissance. But what about the women who dared to enter a man's world of image making? Women in the Renaissance were assumed to be inferior. Even the rare female painters were thought to be incapable or unworthy of religious subjects or mythological narratives. Shut out of the regal portrait commissions, they polished their skills via self-portraits instead, like pioneering painter Sofonisba Anguissola. Most of these groundbreaking women, including Lavinia Fontana, Marietta Robusti, Barbara

Longhi, Catherina van Hemessen, and Artemisia Gentileschi, were the daughters of artists. They learned to paint without a formal education by watching their fathers practice their craft. In creating self-portraits, they had an opportunity to claim their own seat at the table, to be taken seriously by the academy.[21]

They had to combat social conventions that considered women suitable solely as subjects, not as artists. As subjects, women were often reduced to objects. Emma Hope Allwood notes how "the female nude in Western painting—hairless, buxom, invariably with skin as white and unblemished as a pearl—was there to feed an appetite of male sexual desire. She did not have desires of her own. She existed to be looked at, posed in such a way that her body was displayed to the eye of the viewer, there only to be consumed."[22] In *The Ways of Seeing*, art historian John Berger spelled out how male artists would often cover up their own selfish desires by placing the blame for temptation on women. Berger wished they would admit, "You painted a naked woman because you enjoyed looking at her. . . . Put a mirror in her hand and you called the painting 'Vanity,' thus morally condemning the woman whose nakedness you had depicted for your own pleasure."[23] How could women escape such a double bind? A few dared to craft and thereby control their own image.

During the Renaissance, if women dared to paint a man, they were not allowed to be alone with their subject. There are numerous renderings of male painters in their studios, studying their subjects closely, yet Sofonisba Anguissola (1532–1625) had to have her father present while she painted. She also had to acknowledge that social fact on the painting itself. Anguissola skirted the social pressures by painting domestic scenes (like girls engaged in the seemingly masculine game of chess).[24] She painted her sisters, Lucia, Europa, and Minerva, gathered around a chessboard, enjoying each others' company. The warmth of the scene contrasts with so many formal portraits of the era. Her attention to detail, from the sisters' ornate clothing to the tablecloth under the chessboard, demonstrates her mastery.

Italian painter Artemisia Gentileschi (1593–1653) dealt with issues of exploitation by unmasking the objectification of women. Her first signed painting comes from the biblical story of Susanna and the lecherous elders in Daniel 13. Included in the Catholic and Orthodox canon, Susanna's plight (and Daniel's defense) is considered apocryphal (and therefore omitted) in Protestant Bibles. In the story, Susanna has finished bathing and has sent her attendants away, when two Hebrew elders who have been spying on her engage in blackmail. They will publicly accuse her of a secret meeting with a young man unless she agrees to have sex with them. Susanna refuses to be blackmailed and is arrested and sent to trial. Only Daniel dares to challenge the elders' testimony. He ferrets out their falsehood and saves Susanna's life. The creepy sexual harassers are exposed and defeated.

This provocative story about the male gaze (and its deadly consequences) became a popular subject during the Renaissance, especially for painters longing for an excuse to depict a female nude. Spying on an unsuspecting woman sets the drama in motion. Yet Gentileschi's portrait of Susanna departed from convention. Susanna is depicted not as a seductress but as a victim, pressed in on by conspiring lechers. Susanna attempts to repel their advances and stop this traumatic event well before it gets to court.

One year later, Gentileschi's life began to mirror the horrors endured by Susanna. Seeing the early promise in his daughter's work, her father, Orazio Gentileschi, a renowned painter, hired one of his collaborators, Agostino Tassi, to tutor her. Gentileschi was raped by Tassi while under his tutelage. The resulting trial put Gentileschi to the test, as she was subjected to gynecological examinations and asked to prove her virginity prior to the sexual assault. The rapist was sentenced to a year in jail but never served the time. Gentileschi was married off in an effort to quell the public furor and to ensure the possibility of a new life.

In her subsequent paintings, Gentileschi continued to depict women in the Bible who had been abused by men. In her paintings of Bathsheba, Gentileschi places David far in the background, on a balcony, spying on the woman and her attendants. Her subject is Bathsheba, not the man who compromised his kingdom to possess her (and have her husband murdered). Gentileschi also draws upon the apocryphal story of Judith, who beheads Holofernes to protect the Israelites. A woman invades the Babylonian general's bedroom. For once, he is surprised and defenseless. Gentileschi's artistic accomplishments resulted in her becoming the first woman accepted into the academy in Florence.

She was eventually invited to England by Charles I. The king commissioned her to create "an allegory of painting" in 1630. She followed the standard conventions of the era with a painting described as "a

Self-Portrait as the Allegory of Painting, Artemisia Gentileschi, 1638–39

beautiful woman with dark black hair, disheveled, and twisted in various ways, with arched eyebrows that show imaginative thought." Yet in other ways she deviates from emblems of the era. Traditionally, the painter is shown with "the mouth covered with a cloth tied behind her ears, with a chain of gold at her throat from which hangs a mask, and has written in front 'imitation.'"[25] Gentileschi depicts herself wearing the gold chain but does not include the gag. She drops the mask. To her, painting is neither mute nor dumb. It also isn't an imitation; she doesn't need to copy anyone. Instead, she turns the allegory of painting into a self-portrait of a strong woman in control of her craft, balancing her brushwork with her colorful palette. All the tools she needs to portray herself are within her hands. Like the democratizing power of a smartphone camera, her brushes and paint allow her to control the narrative. She does not hide the mirror that enabled her to pull off this trick. Instead, Gentileschi places herself in the center of the long history of self-portraits. This is an artist that history attempted to ignore and forget, yet her creative force carries through. Controversial in its time, *Self-Portrait as the Allegory of Painting* now hangs in the Hampton Court Palace outside London.

One can imagine Gentileschi painting for all the women who have been asked to defend themselves, who've been placed on trial in literal and figurative ways every single day, who declare #MeToo. Allwood places the plight in contemporary context: "It comes with adolescence—maybe the first time a man yells at you from a moving car—and is the sense of living life one step removed, living as your own spectator. You are never yourself, you are yourself as you appear to others. To men, yes, and to the women with whom you are supposed to compete for their attention." When we dismiss selfies as inherently vain, we are failing to acknowledge this struggle that resides behind them. Yes, plenty of modern women still turn themselves into objects online. They pose for their audience rather than for their own self-worth. "To grow up a woman in a Western patriarchal society is to be constantly analysing and critiquing your own appearance, constantly struggling with the reality of your body and the ideals with which you have been presented, measuring yourself up—not for your own pleasure but for the eyes of men."[26] In Gentileschi, women and men have a rare model for how to retain their power, how to preserve their self-worth. Her women may be on the verge of victimization like Susanna and Bathsheba, but they are capable of exacting remarkable revenge (like Judith). Placing the power of self-depiction in their hands, Gentileschi inspires a new generation of women who are learning what it means to become a living allegory of painting and beauty.

Different Faces / New Colors

There were scant artistic role models for women or people of color during the Renaissance. More diverse figures have emerged since. It is still not easy for women who pick up the paintbrush. The physical and emotional travails of Frida Kahlo (1907–54) manifested some of the most original and charged self-portraits of the twentieth century. Despite a life cut short by failing health, Kahlo generated 143 paintings, including 55 self-portraits. Kahlo allegedly said, "I'll paint myself, because I am so often alone, because I am the subject I know best."[27] She has been embraced as a heroic symbol of hope by feminists, indigenous peoples, and the LGBTQ community. She did not hide her pain. She merged her body with her art. She engaged in countless self-portraits that expressed what she was feeling at the time. Kahlo has shown us how powerful and profound even the most deeply personal selfies can be.

A wave of diverse and original artists have followed in Kahlo's considerable wake. Andy Warhol (1928–87) turned self-promotion into art. He drew upon the Byzantine church icons that surrounded him during his upbringing in Pittsburgh to canonize celebrity culture. He understood the iconic power of images to make even the most mundane actor into a "superstar." Warhol embraced an array of outcasts from the margins of society. He discovered that by focusing his lens on himself, his fame and reputation grew. In his garish *Self-Portrait* (1966) located at the Museum of Modern Art, Warhol prints his image nine times on the silk screen.[28] The colors are altered in each frame. Warhol questions to what degree we are manufacturing our selves, human as machine. He turned his life in the studio, "the Factory," into its own art form, a kaleidoscopic trip.

Japanese artist Yayoi Kusama (1929–) caught the same spirit of the sixties, staging happenings and painting her subjects' bodies in dayglow colors. She burst into international fame with her installation at the 1966 Venice Biennale, *Narcissus Garden*. She placed fifteen hundred mirrored plastic spheres on the lawn outside the Italian pavilion. Kusama added a sign that said, "Your Narcissism for Sale." She tried to sell the shiny balls to passersby (until she was asked to cease and desist). *Narcissus Garden* is a scathing commentary on how we market and sell our self-interest, and its commentary has only grown more prescient with time. Kusama has battled various forms of mental illness throughout her long life and career. Art historian Jody Cutler places her oeuvre "in dialogue with the psychological state known as narcissism," as "narcissism is both the subject and the cause of Kusama's art, or in other words, a conscious artistic element related to content."[29]

The autobiography of Jean-Michel Basquiat (1960–88), like Kahlo's, became entwined with his artistry. His fame arose from the streets of New York City, from his first forays as a graffiti artist using the moniker SAMO to his rapid rise in the highbrow Manhattan gallery scene. In *Self-Portrait* (1982), the black figure on the left side of the canvas holds out his arm, brandishing an arrow.[30] Yet isn't that arrow also the painter's brush, his weapon of choice? Basquiat hoped his art would provide "a springboard to deeper truths about the individual."[31] He borrowed a page from Warhol's self-mythologizing handbook to magnify his name. Basquiat's self-portraits explode with ideas and fractured images that reveal some of the dissonance that ultimately resulted in his tragic death from a heroin overdose at age twenty-seven.

Chinese artist Ai Weiwei (1957–) also learned from Warhol how to self-promote. Ai moved from Beijing to New York City in the 1980s. He took a photo of himself in front of Warhol's self-portrait at the Museum of Modern Art in 1987. His performance art—smashing antique pots—commented upon what was happening in China's rapidly expanding economic culture. Nathan Smith notes, "While Warhol used the form to comment on the increasingly arbitrary and blurred relationship between the original and its duplicates in a world of mass production, [Ai] Weiwei's self-portraits are more concerned with national identity and issues of censorship and autonomy."[32] Ai's fame (and power) expanded once he began blogging in 2005. He posted silly selfies on bad hair days, covered his eye to "see only half the evil," and took photos of himself eating from a bucket of Colonel Sanders' fried chicken.[33] Ai mastered the art of a cheeky Instagram.

When a 2008 earthquake leveled an elementary school in Sichuan province, Ai crossed over from artist to activist. As authorities sought to cover up the damage, he launched a "citizens' investigation," creating an online forum for parents to add the names of their deceased children. The list grew to over five thousand names. Ai was arrested and beaten by Chinese officials in Chengdu. He snapped a photo of himself surrounded by the police. He holds his phone up in the center of the frame, a flashbulb pops above his head. Ai called the selfie *Illumination* (2009). The allusions to the halos found in sacred art are underscored. Nathan Smith observes, "The selfie is thus imbued with a political dimension: it is a kind of defense, an attempt at self-documentation that not only underlines [Ai's] pacifism but also circulates images of arrests and seizures the Chinese government would prefer to hide."[34] He followed this selfie by documenting his surgery for a cerebral hemorrhage (caused by the beating). Politics and the self blur in Ai Weiwei's performance art.

Kerry James Marshall (1955–) aspires to nothing less than covering the walls of the world's most esteemed art museums with the missing images of Africans and African Americans. The traveling retrospective *Mastry* documents his evolution from modest self-portraits to massive canvases that counter the historical portraits of European lords and ladies. In *A Portrait of the Artist as a Shadow of His Former Self* (1980), Marshall renders himself as barely visible and nearly a cartoon. His bugged-out eyes and gapped tooth evoke many stereotypes. What inspired this almost embarrassing portrait? Marshall says, "Until I read Ralph Ellison—his description, in the introduction to *Invisible Man*, of the condition of invisibility literally changed everything for me. What I was reading there, the notion of being and not-being, the simultaneity of presence and absence, was exactly what I had been trying to get at in my artwork."[35] By registering his face as barely there and pushing it toward cartoon versions of blackness, his self-portrait raised big questions about representation "because white figures in pictures representative of ideal beauty and humanity are ubiquitous."[36] He demonstrates his mastery of the Renaissance forms (vanishing points, regal bearings, attention to detail) but introduces characters that museums have rarely seen (or affirmed).

The most riveting of Marshall's portraits I saw at the Museum of Contemporary Art in Los Angeles features a black woman, brush in hand, preparing to finish a self-portrait. In *Untitled* (2009), the artist prepares to fill in a paint-by-number canvas. Her originality and vision have been limited (though she chooses paint from a massive palette). The color of black is noticeably absent. How can she portray herself without any black paint? The undertaking is absurd—she literally has not been given the tools to complete the task. Critic Lanka Tattersall notes how Marshall exposes the two-pronged problem for artists who are black and female: "Self representation is, if we follow the conceit, a foreclosed impossibility in this image."[37] The only consolation resides in her fingernail, decorated with the colors of the Pan-African flag. It is easier for her to paint her physical body than to paint the fill-in-the-blank canvas. Marshall has accomplished his goal of repainting history and populating the world's finest museums with beautiful and unapologetically black bodies. Photographic reproductions cannot do his work justice. His subjects (including himself) are nearly invisible. But for those with eyes to see, the wonders of their creation are deeply rewarding. He turned the paintbrush into a potent weapon for social transformation.

The Paintbrush in Our Pockets

So what do we do with this potent paintbrush in our pockets? How might we depict and define ourselves in the twenty-first century? I challenge my film students to re-create a masterpiece. This assignment forces them to consider what constitutes an artistic masterwork. Who decides what belongs in the canon? What kinds of images (and subjects) do they have to choose from? Who is included (or excluded)? They also have to think about lighting, costume, mood, and composition. If they choose to create a self-portrait, then they are automatically experimenting with acting. Will they re-create the role? How do they communicate an attitude of assurance or self-satisfaction? It is a great opportunity to stretch themselves, to think about what cameras (and performers) can and cannot do. They may struggle with how to capture the sublime. What role does mystery play in their portrait? This process of thinking through a single image heightens their perception. It deepens their understanding of power and expands their empathy for those treated as subjects. Regardless of the final image, they are almost always empowered by the process.

Rembrandt was the rare artist who used his self-portraits as a form of teaching. In depicting himself, Rembrandt was teaching patrons how to pose and portraitists how to paint. He saw art making as a pedagogical possibility. Martin Gayford calls him "the supreme painter of the inner life" because "he brings you close to the people in his pictures and to what they are feeling." David Hockney notes how "Rembrandt puts more in the face than anyone else ever has, before or since, because he saw more." Rembrandt depicted himself as a young man full of curiosity and as an elder still burning with a creative light. Hockney writes, "The Chinese say you need three things for paintings: the hand, the eye, and the heart. . . . Two won't do. A good eye and heart is not enough, neither is a good hand

Self-portrait (after Rembrandt)

and eye. It applies to every drawing and painting Rembrandt ever made. His work is a great example of the hand, the eye—and the heart. There is incredible empathy in it."[38] Can we develop a similar sense of empathy in our selfies? A frank self-appraisal will enable us to see the image of God in our selves as well as our finitude and shortcomings.

Some of the most accomplished artists dared to mock themselves. Italian masters like Giotto and Michelangelo dared to reveal that nature "has frequently planted astonishing genius in men of monstrously ugly appearance."[39] In an honest selfie we may dare to reveal ourselves as less than perfect. Hall notes, "For Caravaggio, self-portrayal was an occasion for self-incrimination, and an assertion of his own unheroic status. His biographer, Giovanni Pietro Bellori, said, 'Caravaggio's style corresponded to his physiognomy and appearance; he had a dark complexion and dark eyes, and his eyebrows and hair were black; this colouring was naturally reflected in his paintings.'"[40] Bellori suggested that "he gave himself up to the dark manner, and to the expression of his turbulent and contentious nature."[41] Caravaggio knew he wasn't a role model; he played up his reputation as a "bad boy." He cast himself in his paintings of Bacchus and Medusa. In a painting of David, the volatile and tortured artist dared to depict himself as the beheaded Goliath, still in grisly shock.

The social embrace of youth and vitality is widespread, but what about images of aging? Will we resist the ability to photoshop and airbrush our images? Will we remove wrinkles and blemishes prior to our posts? Is there a maturity in accepting our age a la Rembrandt even in our selfies? During the Renaissance, the ideal portrait age was thought to be thirty-three. Painters like Rembrandt and Michelangelo dared to "depict themselves as old, ugly, no longer in control."[42] In his monumental *The Last Judgment* for the Sistine Chapel (1536–41), Michelangelo pushed his self-mockery to unprecedented extremes. He literally sheds his own skin. Hall says, "This flayed self-portrait is the grisly apogee of the penitential self-portrait."[43] At the apex of his artistic mastery, Michelangelo dared to depict himself as an empty skin. What can we learn today from the wisdom of such artistic elders?

Snapchat's lenses offer users numerous ways to mock themselves and play with self-image. We may reduce our tongue to a rainbow-hued barf or attach a demon filter to communicate the darkness in our soul. While Snapchat's lenses are mostly played for laughs, they allow users to place themselves in different contexts and eras. We may not all become android robots someday, but we will have ample opportunities to see what we look like with wrinkles. Thanks to Snapchat, we may be able to get used to our older selves early. While there is a healthy degree of self-mockery available through Snapchat's filters, the ease with which they can be applied may keep them from rising to the level of a classic self-portrait. We may want to save our finest disappearing images on Snapchat, just in case.

Early Orthodox Church leaders challenged us to consider our lives as a painting and to follow the lofty role of creator in how we apply virtues to our self-imaging. The Cappadocian Fathers' notions of how we craft our lives sprung from God's declaration in Genesis 1:26, translated in contemporary language as "Let us make humans in our image, in our likeness" (God's Word). In his essay "On the Origin of Humanity,"[44] Basil of Caesarea infers that God grants us the divine image in our birth, but it is only via active choices and free will that we come to resemble the likeness of God. Basil challenges us to rise to our calling: "In giving us the power to become like God, he let us be artisans of the likeness of God, so that the reward for the work would be ours. . . . For I have that which is according to the image in being a rational being, but I become according to the likeness in becoming a Christian."[45] We are born into the image of God, but how and when we conform to the likeness of God depends upon the life we paint.

Basil's younger brother, Gregory of Nyssa, extends the metaphor by declaring, "Every person is the painter of his own life, and choice is the craftsman of the work, and the virtues are the paints producing the image."[46] In his essay "On Perfection," Gregory challenges us to copy the masterpiece of Jesus's life, for "if we paint well, we become an image of Christ, who is the image of the Father."[47] He describes how God adds virtues as if they were colors. The glory of Jesus is not rendered via red or white or a touch of black that a painter uses to render an eyebrow, "but instead of these, purity, freedom from unruly emotion, blessedness, alienation from all evil, and all things like these, through which the likeness of God is formed in the human being. With such hues the Fashioner of his own image stamped our nature."[48] How interesting to discover that "self-fashioning" is actually an ancient concept tied to the original Fashioner.

While painters hone their craft over years of careful study, technologies place the tools for instantaneous electronic makeovers in our hands starting at earlier and earlier ages. Self-portraits previously reserved for the rich and powerful are now available to nearly all, regardless of gender, class, or ethnicity. When we try the latest Snapchat filter, we are engaging in a time-honored tradition of portraying and presenting ourselves in a new light. What a profound gift to alter our appearance and try on fresh personas with the push of a button. The apostle Paul assures us, "If anyone is in Christ, the new creation has come: The old has gone, the new is here!" (2 Cor. 5:17). The challenge is to bring the same depth of observation and reflection to self-portraiture that has elevated art across the centuries. While we need to pay attention to form, lighting, structure, and design in selfies, our calling as Christians is to, in addition, hone the inner virtues of patience, endurance, and compassion. Artists have paid attention to how their subjects are clothed and coiffed. Let us remember also to clothe ourselves "with tenderhearted mercy, kindness, humility, gentleness, and patience. . . . Above all, clothe yourselves with love" (Col. 3:12–14 NLT).

Questions to Consider/Discuss

1. What paintings attract or inspire you? What images would you like to see more of?

2. Have you ever painted your portrait? What painting or selfie are you proudest of?

Selfie Challenge

Pick a masterpiece, something that moves you or disturbs you. Study the light, the color, and the composition. Now try to re-create or reimagine it (using yourself as the subject) with your camera. Take your time to get the look, the feel, the pose, just right. What did you learn through the process?

If I'm Zelda

4

Reframing Memories

The Literary Self

I believe there are visions that come to us only in memory, in retrospect.

—Marilynne Robinson[1]

WHETHER I SHALL TURN OUT to be the hero of my own life, or whether that station will be held by anybody else, these pages must show." "What are you looking at me for? I didn't come to stay." "I am an invisible man." "Call me Ishmael." Recognize the sources of these quotations?[2] These memorable opening lines usher readers immediately into characters' hearts and minds. We are invited to step into their shoes, to follow their journey, to share their struggle. Writing is a form of reaching out, of sharing an experience, of letting others know they are not alone. It is celebrated as a brave endeavor, with the finest novels lauded as a lofty art form. Yet writing is also one of the most self-centered activities imaginable. It involves hours and hours of isolation, left alone with our thoughts, staring at a blank page or screen. If novelists stared into a mirror, they would be vilified as narcissistic. Instead, our most acclaimed are accorded awards, prizes, and hefty contracts for more. Why do we consider composing literature a noble endeavor but posting a photo of oneself as vain?

Many of the finest novels are autobiographical. They arise from reflecting on and rearranging our fragmented lives into a meaningful and portable tale. What novels begin with these famous opening lines? Although written in 1849, the heroic questions posed by Charles Dickens in *David Copperfield* feel quite contemporary. How will David respond to the grim circumstances (like being born six months after his father died)? Young David faces challenges from his stepfather, his boarding school, and the nefarious schemes of Uriah Heep. He writes, "I am thankful for myself, at any rate, that I can find my tiny way through the world, without being beholden to anyone; and that in return for all that is thrown at me, in folly or vanity, as I go along, I can throw bubbles back."[3] What a great social media strategy—throw bubbles at bullies! In *Moby-Dick* (1851), Herman Melville immediately places readers inside the mind and motivations of his narrator, Ishmael, who was so poor and uninspired by his surroundings on shore that he sets out to "sail about a little and see the watery part of the world."[4] He didn't necessarily expect to be serving Captain Ahab in pursuit of an elusive white whale. Ralph Ellison spells out his nameless protagonist's dilemma. Although he is "a man of substance, of flesh and bone, fiber and liquids,—and [he] might even be said to possess a mind," he remains an "invisible man," unseen, unnoticed, unacknowledged, "simply because people refuse to see [him]."[5] Published in 1952, *Invisible Man* gives readers an unprecedented glimpse into the harrowing experience of far too many African Americans in pre–civil rights America (and even now). On Easter, dressed for church in her Sunday best, Maya Angelou cuts short her recitation of a poem with "I didn't come to stay."[6] In the autobiographical novel *I Know Why the Caged Bird Sings* (1969), Angelou and her brother Bailey are shipped off by their estranged parents from New York City to Arkansas to St. Louis to San Francisco. Where will young Maya feel at home? After being raped by her mother's boyfriend at age eight, Maya will render herself mute. These opening lines announce the struggles at hand. Will we succumb to the forces that may overwhelm us, from abusive parents to bullies at school to mind-numbing factory work? Despite such trauma, can we also experience healing and become heroes of the story we are writing, the story of our lives?

So many literary classics are rooted in the authors' life experiences. Like Ishmael, Herman Melville did take to the sea. When his father was sent to debtors' prison, twelve-year-old Charles Dickens had to leave school and begin working ten-hour days at Warren's Blacking Warehouse in London. The struggles of David Copperfield are rooted in trials of a young Charles Dickens. Ralph Ellison described what it was like to grow up as an African American man in an indifferent and even hostile white Anglo world. The silent young Maya Angelou eventually found her voice, becoming a renowned singer, poet, and activist. Would we call their act of turning their personal challenges into (barely) fictionalized struggles self-indulgent or solipsistic? Isn't that what we expect our finest writers to do? We want them to mold moments that might have broken them into life lessons we all can learn from. Perhaps our finest self-images contain similarly powerful potential.

Good writing begins in our memory of fond or fearsome experiences. It may begin with a smile or a scar, a question or a longing to understand. Over time, those memories are filtered through our imagination and forged into something more, maybe delusions or digressions, but also hopefully art. Writing is a form of time travel, snapping back to scenes we may have forgotten (or wish we could forget). When we close our eyes, we may suddenly recall how a room looked or a river sounded or a meal smelled. The images flash on the screen playing in our mind's eye. We extract meaning from those events through the gift of space and time. The results may range from the horrific, as in Franz Kafka's *Metamorphosis* (1915), to the fantastic, as in J. R. R. Tolkien's *The Hobbit* (1937). This chapter will focus primarily on the realistic and will include the epistolary and the autobiographical. Given enough perspective, failures may become life lessons. Heartbreaks may heal. Regret may move toward relief. Painful moments may be recovered, rewritten, and even redeemed. The act of writing and reflecting can offer us a valuable sense of perspective, a way to (re)frame our world. As Nobel laureate Nadine Gordimer says, "Writing is making sense of life."[7]

Selfies and social media are becoming the record of our sojourn on earth (mostly via pictures instead of words). Taking a selfie is easy (or at least, it can be). One click and we're done. Taking time to reflect on the memories generated by those selfies is tougher. Do we apply the writer's craft to our social media posts, adding reflection and analysis before weaving a particular image or series of scenes into a meaningful whole? From a casual Snapchat Story may arise a singular image that constitutes something worthy of a public post for all to see. Might we even approach these social media platforms as a daily diary, an occasion for spiritual reflection and maybe even a form of prayer?

Are Selfies Literary? How to Read a Selfie

I see selfies as a contemporary form of literature. They are a series of scenes and vignettes on a time line, attempting to convey the meaning of a life. They can be edited and remixed into a commentary on our life and times. In literature, the authors disguise their own journeys behind fictional characters and carefully outlined plots. But the impetus behind selfies and serialized novels like *David Copperfield* is remarkably similar: "Here is my life—what I've seen, heard, and learned. I hope it will prove useful to you." The posting of a selfie is an invitation for others to follow our journey. It comprises the elements of everyday life—what I had for breakfast, what I saw, who I met, what stood out. Similarly mundane moments occur in, for example, *Swann's Way* by Marcel Proust. For Swann, intense memories arise from a bite of a madeleine cake dipped in tea. The commonplace and everyday can lead to strong associations, feelings, and remembrance of things past. Out of such common actions as eating a cookie or dipping a cake can come profound insights.

Why did I invest so much time analyzing opening lines? In a world of fractured attention, first impressions matter. We have such a limited window in which to capture people's attention, to get them to notice our words, our stories, our selves. Selfies are a kind of opening line. Our Facebook profile photo is akin to "Call me Ishmael." It establishes who we are in a fast, clever, and often unvarnished way. We may labor over the impression we are making. We may change that profile picture on a regular basis, never quite satisfied with such a singular image to identify us to the world. At the end of the day, we have to simply put ourselves out there: call me Ishmael or Moisés or Grace or Ji-woo or Sherrod. Selfies are also an effort to overcome our invisibility. Social media is crowded. As we scroll through our feeds, we are reading hundreds of faces and their notes and concerns every single day. We can take Facebook's name literally; it is an endless book of faces. We couldn't number our friends and acquaintances in an earlier era. But now we know how many relationships we may be competing against in an effort to capture our friends' attention. It may take a new hairstyle, a fresh pair of glasses, or multiple personas to establish ourselves as a character worth following. We need a big opening line. However, as with novels, the real challenge arises beyond the opening line or the first selfie on our profile.

It is tough to pick out the highlights of our life while we're in it. We have so many images and scenes to choose from. Facebook started doing the work for us. I'm struck by how many moments, which felt significant at the time, end up slipping my mind until Facebook recycles them. Its algorithms recall photos and posts that earned the most likes. Is that how we determine what matters, what stood out in a given year? When my wife was battling Hodgkin's lymphoma, her chemotherapy treatments were not exactly social-media friendly. We may not have wanted to share those vivid and horrible memories on Facebook. Yet those lowlights are among the most life-changing months we've encountered. The care lavished upon us by friends and family was humbling. The meals brought to our home communicated so much more than a like button. We knew we were loved. But none of those moments would have been captured by Facebook's year-in-review video. The algorithms assume that the photos that generated the most chatter and biggest response must have been most memorable. Do we want to outsource our memories to Facebook's clever code? Are we too busy to assemble our own highlight reel? What if my most powerful memories don't conform to a time line?

Instagram allows us to curate a particular version of our lives. We can edit our photos and videos into a select highlight reel. The focus is often on beauty. Our shots may be united by color, by season, by themes. Our aesthetic is a reflection of who we are, how we see the world. It may lean more orange or more blue. We may filter out certain pictures if they no longer reflect our evolving aesthetic. These filtered results may present an idealized version of our lives. They may constitute peak moments that communicate what our best selfie looks like. But good literature and memorable stories also spring from the messiness of life. It is when our feelings are raw or unfiltered that our true character may emerge. Not every experience is camera ready, sunny and bright.

The disappearing nature of Snap Stories makes them primed to inspire literature. Because the photographs disappear on Snapchat, they don't quite get fixed. We don't fuss over them like an Instagram photo that has to communicate a certain level of perfection. With vanished photos, we can see ourselves as something more in our mind. In our memories, we can change the color of our shirt, the temperature of the day, the look in our beloved's eyes. Snapchat's ephemeral quality makes space for art and mystery to enter in. "I remember that day. It felt important. But what was really going on? It is a bit fuzzy, but the essence of it was . . ." That essence is usually the starting point for literature—getting at the nature of things, both the external details and particulars as well as the internal struggle, the moments of insight. These are moments noted, reflected upon, mined for deeper meaning. They are not merely preserved for posterity via social media ("this happened three years ago") but are placed into a larger context of what was happening in my life, what I was struggling with, aspiring toward, hoping and praying for. Literature invites us into the story behind the photograph, the psychology behind the post. It plunges beyond the surface into the larger reality residing behind the smirk or smile.

The Gospels of Mark, Matthew, Luke, and John also draw upon moments in time. They are a unique and original literary genre—biography as divine revelation. The Gospels are a carefully arranged chronology that highlights particularly resonant moments in the rather short time span (three years) of Jesus's public ministry. Some may read the Gospels as a highly polished highlight reel—Jesus's greatest hits. The stories are laden with beautiful moments of caring for widows and feeding the hungry that are so compelling. Jesus's divinity (literally) rises above the most murderous aspects of our humanity. I marvel at his patience, his endurance, his love. The Instagram aspects of the Gospel are utterly perfect. Yet I'm also intrigued by the background characters, the disciples' failure to understand the miracles or see the big picture. I can see the connection with the messiness of my own life. When the disciples bicker about who is the greatest among them, I see a reflection of our pettiness on social media. When they fail to duplicate Jesus's miracles, I picture the silly moments of failure we post and then dispense with on Snapchat. Enduring stories are formed via transcendent highs and depressing lows. May we see how God meets us in both places.

The Gospels reveal that Jesus had a remarkable ability to spot teachable moments amid everyday life. He calls his first disciples while they are fishing (Matt. 4:18–22). Frustrated by their meager catch, Jesus challenges the fishermen to do it his way, follow his instructions, and enjoy a massive haul (Luke 5:1–11). Simon Peter leans on his experience, knowing full well that nighttime is the right time to fish. But he indulges Jesus's wishes (which probably felt a bit like a fairy-tale wish) until the boat is nearly swamped with fish flapping in the nets. Years later, the fishermen are once again beleaguered (John 21). Their master and teacher has been mowed down by the Romans, locked in a dark grave. They have returned to the Sea of Galilee, the sight of their original calling, to fish. And once again, they have had a frustrating night that yielded nearly nothing until Jesus shows up on shore. He challenges them to try again, tossing the net over the right side of the boat. The massive haul results in a moment of recognition. I imagine them whispering, "We've been here before. We've done this before. And the same person, with the same instructions, has made the difference, both times." The ordinary suddenly becomes extraordinary, not just because of the 153 fish in the net but also because of their understanding of who they are and whose they are. Jesus is still calling them to the same bold mission. Similarly, great writing reveals the higher purpose behind seemingly mundane moments. Whether in tasting a madeleine or embarking on a fishing trip, we may be surprised by how quickly tangible objects and experiences can morph into transcendent moments.

Literature: What Is It Good For?

> Imagination, working at full strength, can shake us out of our fatal, adoring self-absorption and make us look up and see—with terror or with relief—that the world does not in fact belong to us at all.
>
> —Ursula K. LeGuin[8]

Great literature expands our empathy, placing us inside the minds of people not like us, forcing us to spend an extended amount of time considering their plight. In Ralph Ellison's *Invisible Man*, I was plunged into the basement hidden from the white residents above, with illumination provided by the Monopolated Light & Power Company. *Invisible Man* expanded my young mind. I had never been a student at a historically black college or university, but, thanks to Ellison, I had a much greater sense of how shielded a well-meaning white trustee might be from the students' reality. After reading *Invisible Man*, I could imagine how one might fall in with communists or black nationalists or anyone who offered hope in a painfully fallen world. The "invisible" narrator endures a shock treatment that also alters readers' minds. By the conclusion, I could recognize the blinding Optic White paint that seemed to cover everything in the novel *and* in my hometown. Ellison wrote a prescription for a new pair of glasses that I could never remove (even if I wanted to!). That is the power of my all-time favorite novel, *Invisible Man*.

Maya Angelou revealed her horrific experience of rape in *I Know Why the Caged Bird Sings* so that victims of sexual abuse could be assured that they are not alone. We come to understand why a student may withdraw from the limelight or be too ashamed to speak. After walking in Angelou's shoes, we are emboldened to break the cycles of racism, ignorance, and abuse that marked her life. Stories can provide comfort (my struggles are similar to their struggles). Novels can serve as a wake-up call (my life isn't like their life). In the opening line of *The Great Gatsby*, the author's intent shines through. F. Scott Fitzgerald writes, "In my younger and more vulnerable years my father gave me some advice that I've been turning over in my mind ever since. 'Whenever you feel like criticizing any one,' he told me, 'just remember that all the people in this world haven't had the advantages that you've had.'"[9] Fitzgerald may have written about people with remarkable wealth and style, but the overriding purpose behind the tragedy of Gatsby may have been to expand our empathy.

To feel invisible takes a terrible psychic toll. Mexican poet Octavio Paz declares, "Solitude is the profoundest fact of the human condition." In a celebrity-obsessed culture where our friends and followers can literally be numbered, we can easily feel alone, invisible, unnoticed, and unimportant. Paz further asserts, "Man is the only being who knows he is alone, and the only one who seeks out another."[10] Documenting small moments via photos, poems, and stories becomes a way of justifying our existence, affirming our value, fighting that ache. Perhaps selfies provide a way to escape loneliness and isolation, comparable to how the words of Ellison helped the invisible navigate a cruel world. The selfie can be an affirming and artistic cry of recognition: "I am not invisible. I am a human being. Please see me." Jill Walker Rettberg notes how "feeling misrepresented by the camera is one common reason for beginning to take selfies instead of being the subject of other people's photographs."[11] It is a way to take back the narrative in our own lives, to assert our own power and ability to define ourselves. Great literature (or a brilliant selfie) makes us visible, enabling us to see and be seen.

Shadows

Jesus recognized and affirmed individuals within crowds. Early in Jesus's public ministry, he was already being called upon to heal. Jairus, a synagogue leader, implored Jesus to come to his home to heal his twelve-year-old daughter. News of an impending miracle attracted considerable attention. Luke writes, "As Jesus was on his way, the crowds almost crushed him" (Luke 8:42). A woman who had suffered from twelve years of bleeding without a cure came up behind Jesus and touched his cloak. Immediately, her bleeding stopped. Jesus halted his journey and asked, "Who touched me?" (v. 45). Perhaps out of fear, no one answered. Peter pointed out the chaos of the scene, "Master, the people are crowding and pressing against you." Jesus insisted, "Someone touched me." The Gospel account says, "Then the woman, seeing that she could not go unnoticed, came trembling and fell at his feet" (vv. 46–47). What kind of public shaming or even stoning was she about to endure? She explained why she had reached out and how she'd been healed. Jesus offers an affirmation, "Daughter, your faith has healed you. Go in peace" (v. 48). Instead of judgment, Jesus offers peace and release.

When Jesus entered Jericho late in his ministry, another throng greeted him. Zacchaeus, a wealthy tax collector, wanted to see Jesus, but his small stature was a handicap (Luke 19:1–3). The size of the crowd actually prevents Zacchaeus from getting a good look at Jesus. Sometimes the daily distractions of social media can inhibit our ability to focus. We can fail to see the face of Jesus amid such a crowd. Zacchaeus climbs a sycamore tree to get above the crowd, to see Jesus. And there, in the tree, Jesus calls him out, "Zacchaeus, come down immediately. I must stay at your house today" (v. 5). The incident stands out because Jesus singles him out. Within a large crowd, Jesus recognizes individual people. The book of faces on social media does not overwhelm Jesus. People who may have considered themselves nobodies were considered somebody significant in Jesus's sight.

Great literature crosses borders and builds bridges. Stories allow us to leap across time and space, to enter worlds far removed from our experience. So many new authors have emerged from distant corners of the globe to tell their communities' stories. Many focus on the plight of widows and orphans. Khaled Hosseini's *The Kite Runner* (2003) introduced millions of readers to Amir and his friend Hassan, growing up amid upheaval in Afghanistan. In *Snow Flower and the Secret Fan* (2005), Lisa See documents the travails of Lily as she endures foot-binding and an arranged marriage in nineteenth-century China. Nigerian author Chimamanda Ngozi Adichie recounts the Biafran War through the eyes of thirteen-year-old Ugwu (and others) in *Half of a Yellow Sun* (2006). In *In the Country of Men* (2006), Hisham Matar follows the struggle of Suleiman and his family under the Qaddafi regime in Libya. Aravind Adiga's debut novel, *The White Tiger* (2008), explains how the dire conditions in the streets of contemporary Bangalore can turn a boy from an entrepreneur into a murderer. These riveting social reform stories would make Charles Dickens proud. They embody the ethic of Jesus when he began his public ministry by reading from the scroll of Isaiah. Jesus announced good news to the poor, freedom for prisoners, and recovery of sight for the blind (Luke 4:18). To people suffering under an oppressive Roman occupation, Jesus announces the year of the Lord's favor, a jubilee that cancels all debts. These fresh voices of contemporary literature extend the prophetic tradition that Jesus lifted up—fighting for the poor, the marginalized, the victimized.

Social media offers us an opportunity to enter the experience of people outside our everyday circle. Online, we can meet people from around the world. Residents of seemingly closed countries like China or Pakistan can find ways around electronic firewalls. Organizations like Kiva can connect us with entrepreneurs trying to raise a small but significant bit of capital to feed their families. Once they've established their small business (sometimes on as little as twenty-five dollars), they will repay the microfinance loan that we provide, allowing us to support another fledgling entrepreneur. Thanks to the internet, we can exchange letters and photos and understand the stories of those we're giving to. We can choose to follow people on Instagram or Twitter who present alternative viewpoints and perspectives. When students in Hong Kong challenge oppressive policies coming from the mainland Chinese government, we can follow the young leaders via Twitter. When I want to understand more about shootings of African Americans in Ferguson, Missouri, and in Baltimore, Maryland, social media allows me to hear directly from local leaders. In the digital world, we may not walk in another person's shoes, but we can at least follow their steps and marches.

The inherent but unspoken social contract in literature (and social media) includes the question, "What did I learn along the way?" When we show off our outfit of the day (#ootd), we are asking, "What do you think?" But we are also offering a recommendation: "This is what I put together." "These are the elements that satisfy my eye." "Try this." It is the opening of a conversation, the revealing of our character, our values, our taste. The same goes for our food shots on Instagram. It is an opening line of a conversation that follows: "Does this look good to you? It looks delicious to me." Or alternately, "This place is definitely one to avoid." As with novels, we are often saying, "Here's what I experienced and learned and recommend to you." Sometimes we are meant to admire the character's (or, in the case of social media, our) choices. In other instances, the selfie can serve as a cautionary tale. "Look at how my car got wrecked." "Avoid this mechanic." Or even more poignantly, "Look at the wreck I've made of my life." Isn't that the core of social media? It is one giant, unending recommendation engine—a book of people to admire and emulate and of fools to avoid.

Literature is an invitation to empathy, to see the world through the eyes of someone in Bangalore or Buenos Aires. It is a ticket for time travel, to snap back to the pre–civil rights era, to learn old lessons that still apply today. Those too selfie-obsessed may miss the opportunity to walk in the shoes of another. But great books challenge us to rise above our judgmentalism. Jesus approached people with compassion. He was angered by injustice. He embraced widows and let the children come to him. Jesus reached out to Samaritans shunned by his own people. He also condemned the religious phonies who heaped burdens upon those they were purporting to serve. Wisdom comes in identifying the flaws of our community without cutting ourselves off completely. In reflecting on our selfies and ourselves, may we recognize our blind spots. Great literature challenges us to correct ourselves before we call out others. The finest stories appeal to our better selves.

Honest Letters to God

> I think it pisses God off if you walk by the color purple in a field somewhere and don't notice it.
>
> —Alice Walker[12]

The Color Purple (1982) opens with a sobering warning: "You better not never tell nobody but God."[13] Celie's subsequent letters to God take on the tone of the imprecatory biblical psalms where David complains about his enemies: Celie pleads with God to defend her from the advances of her stepfather, Alphonso; to protect her younger sister, Nettie, from his sexual violence; to be released from the arranged marriage to the abusive Mr. ___. What happens when God doesn't answer her letter or hear her prayers? She takes stock of her deplorable situation and concludes, "You must be [a]sleep."[14] Celie endures so many trials and heartbreaks that it is easy to see why she would give up on religion.

The Color Purple wades into that messy space of theodicy, asking why such bad things can happen to good people. Celie's opening letter to God begins with her struggling to even introduce herself. Walker has her cross out the words "I am" on the page. She manages to write, "I have always been a good girl." While Celie questions some of her actions, the readers definitely question the cruelty of the men in Celie's life. The glamorous singer Shug Avery becomes Celie's conduit for hope and love. Avery tells her, "God is inside you and inside everybody else. You come into the world with God. But only them that search for it inside find it."[15] But that doesn't change the harsh reality, she says, that "all my life I had to fight. I had to fight my daddy. I had to fight my brothers. I had to fight my cousins and my uncles. A girl child ain't safe in a family of men."[16]

By the conclusion of *The Color Purple*, Celie and Nettie are reunited after thirty long years and a continent between them. Celie addresses her final letter with "Dear God" but also, "Dear stars, dear trees, dear sky, dear peoples. Dear Everything. Dear God."[17] Walker acknowledges how Celie has shifted in her understanding of God as a "patriarchal male supremacist" to "the realization that she, like Nature itself, is a radiant expression of the heretofore perceived as quite distant Divine." For Celie, that is radical and freeing progress; these are essential theological shifts made for mental health and physical survival. Walker goes on to say that writing this story was "a chance for me as well as the main character, Celie, to encounter That Which Is Beyond Understanding But Not Beyond Loving."[18]

I come away from *The Color Purple* challenged by Walker's testimony. I may hope that a more traditional Christian notion of God could emerge for Celie. But given the suffering inflicted by the men in her life, I don't see how she could ever be comfortable addressing or approaching what she understood to be a patriarchal God. It is understandable how Alice Walker initiated a womanist movement that made more room for African American women to affirm their beauty and calling and culture.[19] In Judith Butler's "ethics of relation," we are not expected to empathize or identify with everyone. Maybe it is more respectful *not* to draw parallels, for "no matter how much you are similar and consonant, says this ethic, your story is never my story. No matter how much the larger traits of our life-stories are similar, I still do not recognize myself *in* you and, even less, in the collective *we*."[20] Attempts at solidarity ("I know how you feel") can actually trivialize others' traumatic experiences. There is plenty of God talk on the internet, theological ideas floating around social media. I might caption a mountaintop experience as #blessed, and yet to those viewing my post, this hashtag only adds to their pain. They may want to be happy for me, but it is tough if they're enduring a season of suffering and silence. My testimony of answered prayer with a joyous selfie may not be received with the same encouragement that I intend. Social media is so much about broadcasting our own status updates and celebrating our own accomplishments that it can be overwhelming and depressing to those in a fallow period of life.

How might taking selfies deepen our relationship with God? We can start by documenting our true feelings, getting in touch with both praise and petitions. The epistolary form of literature—letter writing—may be an instructive starting point. People of faith are steeped in the epistles of Paul and Peter, James and John. They are addressed to early Christian churches in need of counsel and advice. They are instructive in nature, often correcting errors in church practices or teaching. The Psalms are another form of letters to God. Within the same psalm, David both laments his situation—"LORD, how many are my foes! How many rise up against me!" (Ps. 3:1)—and lavishes praise upon God: "You, LORD, are a shield around me, my glory, the One who lifts my head high" (v. 3). Grievous lows in one Psalm—"My God, my God, why have you forsaken me?" (22:1)—are followed by calm confidence in the next: "The LORD is my shepherd, I lack nothing" (23:1). The Psalter was the Hebrews' original songbook, brought out for times of national celebration, like when the king came marching in. But it also expresses feelings of abandonment and betrayal. As a musician, Bono, lead vocalist for U2, resonates with these ancient songs: "What's so powerful about the Psalms are, as well as [their] being gospel and songs of praise, they are also the Blues. It's very important for Christians to be honest with God, which often, you know, God is much more interested in who you are than who you want to be."[21] We've all had days that begin with a sense that "I will sing of the LORD's great love forever" but devolve into questions like "How long, LORD? Will you hide yourself forever? How long will your wrath burn like fire?" (Ps. 89:1, 46). Celie discovers that letters are a safe place to bring our burning questions to God. What about social media?

Reflecting on the Daily Me

How can our selfies become a form of autobiography—not just where we've been and what we've done but also what it all means? Introspection is required to transform photographs of events into autobiography. It requires discipline and determination and honesty. Do we consider our Facebook, Instagram, or Snapchat memories a form of diary? There are plenty of

Camille Tucker

#NewYear #NewSlate #MovingForward

apps that will remind us to take a "selfie a day" or a "dailyme." The Everyday app offers prompts at a set time or a random time. PhotoChron will crunch all those daily selfies together into a seamless time-lapse video.

I am intrigued by the photos and videos of England's Rebecca Brown.[22] In her most popular video, "She Takes a Photo: 6.5 Years," Rebecca documents the awkward experience of her adolescence from ages fourteen to twenty-one without airbrushing her acne or anxieties. The photos reveal dramatic change in locations, clothes, and especially hairstyles. At the end of the four minutes of time-lapse, Rebecca appears with a simple message.[23] Viewers who wonder what happened to her hair and why she occasionally appeared almost bald find out it was because she has trichotillomania. I wasn't familiar with this condition but through Rebecca learned that it is an impulse-control disorder characterized by the pulling out of one's hair.[24] What courage and bravery she has to make her face and her condition so public. For those wrestling with self-harm, obsessive-compulsive disorders, and the bullying that may follow, Rebecca's videos offer life-giving empathy and solidarity. They communicate, "You are not alone."[25] Her story has reached over fifteen million viewers (comparable to a literary best seller). Rebecca writes, "Beauty is more than what we see with the eyes. People are more than their conditions. I am more than my hair and skin. This only shows my exterior; I hope that people will check out my videos to see more of the girl inside." To those who wonder how she can smile during seasons in which this disorder literally attacked her head, Rebecca concludes, "When you see the smiles in this, especially after the baldness happens . . . those smiles are genuine. I'd rather look back and see a project filled with honesty than seeing two thousand photos of fake smiles."[26] Daily selfies have been transformed into an autobiography of a teenager engaged in an ongoing battle, demonstrating dignity, creativity, and grit.

People of faith have often been at the forefront of diary keeping, adopting it as a form of spiritual reflection. *The Confessions of St. Augustine*, written between 397 and 400, is generally recognized as the first Western autobiography.[27] Augustine's starting point was the mistakes he made, the regrets he had, how long it took him to find God. His frankness paved the path for the unflinching ways that Maya Angelou chronicles her youth in *I Know Why the Caged Bird Sings*. Autobiographies have proven to be a remarkably compelling literary genre. In America, these range from *The Autobiography of Benjamin Franklin* (1791) and *Narrative of the Life of Frederick Douglass* (1845) to the poems of Emily Dickinson and *The Autobiography of Malcolm X* (1965).

Autobiographies like Mahatma Gandhi's *The Story of My Experiments with Truth* (1925–29), Che Guevara's *The Motorcycle Diaries* (1993), and Nelson Mandela's *Long Walk to Freedom* (1994) chronicle how political leaders were forged in life's crucibles. The traumatic events of World War II only hinted at in Adolf Hitler's *Mein Kampf* (1925) prompted Anne Frank's brave and heartbreaking *The Diary of a Young Girl* (1947). The shadow of the Holocaust prompted autobiographical reflections like Viktor Frankl's psychological strategy for enduring Auschwitz in *Man's Search for Meaning* (1946), Elie Weisel's recollection in *Night* (1956) of his adolescence in concentration camps, and Corrie ten Boom's chronicle of her family's work with the Dutch underground resistance in *The Hiding Place* (1971). Memoirs of challenging childhoods have been turned into best sellers like Anchee Min's *Red Azalea* (1994), Frank McCourt's *Angela's Ashes* (1996), and Jeannette Walls's *The Glass Castle* (2005). Jean-Dominique Bauby blinked his autobiography, *The Diving-Bell and the Butterfly* (1997), into existence after suffering a stroke. Marjane Satrapi drew upon her experience growing up amid the Islamic revolution in Iran to pen her graphic novel *Persepolis* (2000). Bob Dylan's *Chronicles* (2004), Patti Smith's *Just Kids* (2010), and Keith Richards's *Life* (2010) offer artful and compelling examples of a burgeoning subgenre, the rock-and-roll autobiography. We are quite eager to hear celebrities' confessions.

How might we reconnect with the roots of autobiography as a form of confession and engage in diary keeping as a spiritual discipline? Augustine grew up in Hippo, North Africa, which we know today as Algeria. He was from a wealthy, upper-class Berber family. *The Confessions* brims with lived wisdom that has been handed down across the centuries, like "Thou hast made us for thyself, O Lord, and our heart is restless until it finds its rest in thee."[28] Augustine's long road to conversion became a template for spiritual autobiographies that followed.

So why weren't more autobiographies written in the centuries that followed? Technological limitations kept many from writing. Paper was an expensive luxury, as was education. Until two hundred years ago, most people were illiterate. Most early autobiographies were written by priests and nuns because they were among the educated class who knew how to read and write.[29] They had to wrestle with self-centeredness even as they engaged in self-reflection. Scholar Rodger Payne notes how "the self was a problem at the center of the spiritual autobiography. It was viewed as the source of pride, egotism, and conceit, yet the spiritual autobiography required people to talk and write about themselves. In order to renounce themselves, authors still needed to reflect upon and write about themselves."[30] The first autobiography in the English language, *The Book of Margery Kempe*, wasn't written until almost a thousand years after Augustine, in 1373.[31] As the art of accounting expanded in the Renaissance, English Puritans began to adopt a spiritual bookkeeping. Keeping a daily account with God became a religious expectation. Believers examined their conscience on a daily basis. While Roman Catholics confessed to priests, Puritans turned to their diaries.[32]

John Beadle, an English minister, published a guidebook in 1656 titled *A Journal or Diary of a Thankful Christian*. Beadle outlined why "to keep a Journal or Diary, especially of God's gracious dealings with us, is a work, for a Christian singularly."[33] The Puritans pointed back to the biblical book of Numbers as a guide. In the preface "To the Reader" of Beadle's guidebook, publisher John Fuller suggests, "The spiritual diary was to become a great autobiographical account book, a 'divine arithmetic' to which diarists were expected to 'bring in your tallies of old, if you look for new mercies to be put upon your account.'"[34] People of faith were expected to take stock each and every day, keeping record of their sins.[35] Beadle traced the source of the spiritual diary back to God. He wrote, "God himself seems to keep a journal by him of all the care he hath of us, the cost he bestows upon us, and the good things he gives to us. He hath a book of remembrance of every passage of providence that concerns us. And indeed, the Scripture for a great part is little else but a history of his goodness to his people."[36] The Bible was read as a spiritual diary with God as the author/accountant. Scholar Rodger Payne concludes, "God, in other words, was the first spiritual diarist, and the Bible was his paradigm for all the elect to follow."[37] Similarly, the act of posting pictures falls into the ancient tradition of keeping account of our lives—the blessings, the trials, our failings, and our hope for forgiveness.

The Puritans kept spiritual diaries to sharpen their spiritual lives, to root out habits that hampered their efforts to follow God. One big difference between the spiritual diary and our Instagram accounts is this: the Puritans expected their diaries to remain private. Those spiritual diaries that survived the Puritan era were not expected to become public. Their records survived by accident and sometimes even in contradiction to the authors' wishes. Rodger Payne notes, "Whatever help the diary might offer was intended only as an aid to the author, not as a model for others."[38] When we begin to think about our audience, we shift the focus from communion with God to communicating with others. Do we need to recover the private aspect of spiritual diaries? When we pause to think about who we are, where we are, and who God remains, we reset our spiritual dials. It could be in a prayer diary or an accounting of our day or thoughts that we capture in a photo. It is tough to turn a selfie into a letter to God. Would we engage in daily picture taking if we knew that nobody (but God) was watching? What pictures might we take solely for God?

Ann Voskamp challenged her readers to practice gratitude in *One Thousand Gifts* (2011).[39] Gratitude begins to take hold when we slow down long enough to find the beauty in everyday life. She writes, "I want to see beauty. In the ugly, in the sink, in the suffering, in the daily, in all the days before I die, the moments before I sleep."[40] The impact of her words snuck up on me via the pervasive hashtag #1000gifts. I saw it applied to so many posts on social media, everything from food to flowers to family. Voskamp encourages us to literally count the blessings that surround us every single day in a gratitude journal. We are invited to list every good and perfect gift from above (James 1:17). Perhaps living on a farm predisposes Voskamp to slow down, to appreciate the subtle changes in the seasons. Or perhaps she is simply modeling the kind of careful attention to the details of life that we're all invited to observe.

Practicing gratitude could begin with silent introspection. It might involve taking our camera on a long walk. I've been inspired by Christine Valters Paintner's challenge to approach photography as a Christian contemplative practice. In Paintner's approach, "Photography as a spiritual practice combines the active art of image-receiving with the contemplative nature and open-heartedness of prayer. It cultivates what I call sacred seeing or seeing with the 'eyes of the heart'" (Eph. 1:18).[41] Every day is an opportunity to recognize the gifts of God. We may respond with a poem, a song, or a photograph that praises God, thanking him for the gifts revealed to and received by us. Instagram strikes me as a perfect platform for gathering one thousand gifts. We can take as long as we need. We may have days where only one thing strikes us as a blessing. Other occasions may result in a flood of gratitude. When we pause before a beautiful meal to take a photo of the food on the plate, we are engaging in a form of thanksgiving. Prior generations may have prayed; we pause with our smartphone in hand, admiring the bounty before us, and snap an artistic shot. The act of reverence is remarkably similar.

When we keep a journal, whether in written or visual form, we are engaging in the imitation of God. As we've seen, to the Puritans, God was the original spiritual diarist, and the Bible was his autobiography, a model for his people to follow. To keep a daily spiritual journal (or even video diary) isn't just a pastime to draw us closer to God. It reflects God's creative activity.

The Bible can be read as God's letters to us. It also includes our response in the psalms of ancient Israel and the letters of Paul, Peter, James, and John. These songs and letters may take the form of confessions and complaints, praises and petitions. They reflect a dynamic relationship between Creator and creation, a tumultuous lovers' quarrel, divine give and human take. In blinding moments of divine revelation, we may fall to our knees, take off our shoes, shield our eyes from the glory before us. We may emerge from these encounters with our faces shining or by walking with a limp. We may be humbled by the sacrifice before us or befuddled by a resurrected friend. The proper response may be to burst into song. It could be to fall on our face or to serve people at a homeless shelter. The Bible offers so many portraits of ordinary people caught up in extraordinary situations, called to rise above their own sense of limitations. God the Father, Jesus, and the Holy Spirit emerge as heroes. But we are given moments when the divine spotlight hits us. Hopefully, we're ready to act.

Where selfies and literature diverge is in the act of self-reflection. Selfies often document an external event: "I was here, I did this, I saw that." We need not reflect on the meaning of the occasion. We can just post and move on. Literature arises via a profoundly internalized process—probing our hearts, feelings, motivations, memories, triumphs, and regrets. How can we incorporate more thoughtful reflection and memory making into the selfie production process? In taking stock of our life journey (both the foibles and the triumphs), we are following the ancient Greek aphorism to "know thyself." We can snap photos without posting. The confessional aspect of literature invites us to track our own journey, whether in regret or in gratitude. The promotional aspects of social media may undercut our attempts to turn inward. We may have to sign off for a day, a week, a holy season of seeking God.

In Exodus, God appears to Moses as a flame that does not consume matter and that reveals a personal name: "I AM WHO I AM" (Exod. 3:14). What an intriguing moniker. God's name seems to answer itself, like a Buddhist koan. It has a present, a past, and a future embedded within it. "I am" is the starting point for how we address others when we initiate a relationship. We identify ourselves with our name: "I am Craig." "I am Michaela." "I am Deepak." (On social media, we are often reduced to our name, a photo, and the briefest of descriptions. It is tough to reduce ourselves into a thumbnail sketch.) We round out that introduction with additional self-definitions, using the words "I am" in so many ways: "I'm a student." "I'm a police officer." "I'm a baker." We have so many identifiers in our families, from child and sibling to spouse or even grandparent. And as we go further in a relationship, we reveal more, using "I am" to describe our state of mind. "I am thankful." "I am regretful." "I am lonely." "I am sorry." "I am loved." Only God says, "I AM WHO I AM." And that makes all the difference.

Our anthropology begins with theology—God's initiating action. We lose the narrative thread if we make ourselves the center of the story. In the Lord's Supper, Jesus invites us to remember whose we are (created by God, bought with a price) and who we are (a new community, united across cultural, racial, gender, economic, and other barriers at the base of the cross). Psalm 100 spells it out simply: "Know that the LORD is God. It is he who made us, and we are his" (v. 3). When we are literally beaten down by life (like the Invisible Man or Celie or Rebecca Brown), it is easy to forget this. We may have horrendous experiences with men or women who claim to speak on behalf of God but who make us feel worthless. Jesus knows what it is like to be judged, rejected, cast aside, left for dead by religious and political authorities. When we struggle to define ourselves, to fill in the blank of "I am _____," God steps forth with an answer that transcends time and circumstances. It may be tough to address ourselves to God, but we can be confident that the one who initiated our lives and made us in his image is ready to receive our questions, our complaints, our doubts, our fears, our devotion. "I am tired, I am scared, I am lonely" are all well within his realm. Jesus says, "Come to me, all you who are weary and burdened, and I will give you rest" (Matt. 11:28).

The best literature offers robust gifts: a sense that we are not alone, an expanded empathy to those not like us, a recognition of injustice (aka calling out the phonies), a resolve to take up the fight and reform the current situation. How can selfies deepen and grow, perhaps even rise to a literary level? We must astutely observe and record significant moments in time. We must make space for reflection regarding ourselves, our surroundings, our era. We must return to those moments with fresh eyes of wisdom and insight and commitment to share what we've learned along the way.

A healthy selfie recognizes the beauty and pain of what's happening. A smart hashtag puts a moment in context. A mature person then takes the time to go back and put that moment into a larger story. We think about what it meant then and realize what it means now, with the benefit of hindsight. Is the moment wistful? Wrapped in a gauzy haze? Or perhaps tinged with bitterness and regret? We elevate the selfie when we recognize how our failures and triumphs fit within a larger story and use that recognition to help someone else navigate the way.

Questions to Consider/Discuss

1. Who are your favorite literary heroes? What do you admire about those characters?

2. How often do you reflect on your self-portraits? What patterns do you see? What kind of story is being formed and potentially written?

3. If you had to limit your life to just three or four photos or scenes, what would they be? Do you have a selfie that fills in the blank, "I am _____."

Selfie Challenge

This selfie challenge may take the focus off ourselves. Take a walk with your camera in hand. Proceed with a prayerful attitude, ready to receive images as a gift. What photo would you give to God as an act of praise or gratitude?

Untitled film still #58, 1980

5

Seizing the Light

Photographing Ourselves

Man is a creature who makes pictures of himself, and then comes
to resemble that picture.

—Iris Murdoch[1]

CONSIDER HOW MANY IMAGES we're tasked with processing. New
York University professor Nicholas Mirzoeff states, "Every two minutes, Americans alone take more photographs than were made in the entire
nineteenth century. As early as 1930, an estimated 1 billion photographs
were being taken every year worldwide. Fifty years later, it was about 25
billion a year, still taken on film."[2] What a great time to be the Eastman
Kodak Company, creating the film that recorded those images. Alas, the
digital revolution of pixelated images arose and undercut Kodak's business.
"By 2012, we were taking 380 billion photographs a year and nearly all
digital. One trillion photographs were taken in 2014."[3] We need a robust
visual theology to sort through the avalanche of images.[4]

Selfies date from the beginning of photography itself. The word *photographie* was coined in 1832 by French scientist and artist Antoine Florence. He combined the Greek words for "light" and "writing" to describe his experiments with light-sensitive paper. Scientists understood the properties of light but struggled to find a way to capture it. In prior centuries, churches in Paris and Florence were encouraged to poke a hole in their ceiling so the movements of the sun could be studied on the floor below. Artists employed devices like the camera obscura to trace natural vistas that they hoped to paint. The camera obscura was also employed in the creation of dioramas. One of the most renowned showmen in Paris, Louis Daguerre, specialized in dioramas. Photography has roots in the stage, putting on a show.[5] We've been acting for the camera ever since.

Since the advent of the medium, there have been competing claims about who invented photography. In January 1839, François Arago spoke of the breakthrough technique of Daguerre to a joint meeting of the Academy of Science and the Academy of Fine Art in Paris. How appropriate that art and science merged in the photochemical process documented by Daguerre. The curious properties of light projected through a pinhole had long been discovered. The challenge facing nascent photographers was how to permanently capture and fix the images projected into a light box. The daguerreotype was created on a highly polished, silver-plated sheet of copper, sensitized with iodine vapors, exposed in a large box camera, developed in mercury fumes, and stabilized (or fixed) with salt water or "hypo" (sodium thiosulphate). It took over a decade of chemistry experiments to achieve this photographic miracle. Writing to a friend, Daguerre exclaimed, "I have seized the light. I have arrested its flight."[6] Fixing. Seizing. Freezing. Photography attempts to stop time and capture light in a box. It is a possessive art.

This is the promise and limit of photography. It can capture a moment, freezing light (and us) in place, but it cannot stop the tyranny of time. Photographs are an effort to hold off our inevitable sense of loss (of time, youth, innocence, etc.) by fixing it, offering us a chance to cherish it. Unfortunately, the gift of life does not stop making us almost instantly nostalgic even while we're enjoying a day, a friend, a family moment. We want to hold precious moments for an eternity (or at least for an extended moment of bliss). And yet, the second we try to capture that holy or celebratory moment by fixing it in a photograph, we inevitably lose it (or at least sully it). How do we embrace the beauty of key moments without immediately embalming them in a photochemical bath? Can we appreciate the ability to capture moments in time without robbing ourselves of the genuine, spontaneous joy contained in those moments? We may need to shift our understanding of time from linear and progressive to eternal and theological. The author of Hebrews suggests we fix "our eyes on Jesus, the pioneer and perfecter of faith. For the joy set before him he endured the cross, scorning its shame, and sat down at the right hand of the throne of God" (Heb. 12:2). How does that kind of focus square with the photographic images that surround us?

This chapter will cover the history of photography as a struggle between artifice and authenticity, between arranging objects (including ourselves) to make a statement and standing apart from the situation before us in an effort to tell the truth about a predicament. All too often we have treated others as strange curiosities rather than as children of God. We may have even turned ourselves into objects, acting for the camera, approaching life as a game. The finest photographers have often unmasked the artifice that informs our "objective" pictures and challenged us to find a more authentic self than what we've projected for the camera. Can we develop a more sacramental approach to photography and toward life, dignifying others and ourselves in how we give and receive images?

The First Selfie

From the beginning, photography has been an effort to capture reality as it glides by, to hold on to nature (and our lives) while the world keeps turning. The early photographs focused on buildings because the daguerreotype process took from three to fifteen minutes to form an image on the copper plate. It required subjects to stand still. Inspired by reports of Daguerre's breakthrough, American lamp maker and amateur chemist Robert Cornelius took a camera into the yard behind his family's store in Philadelphia. He must have held quite still to capture the crisp daguerreotype that resulted. Cornelius stares straight at his camera, perhaps wondering if his experiment would work. On the back of the resulting self-portrait, he wrote, "The first light Picture ever taken. 1839."[7]

While Cornelius may have created the first selfie, Hippolyte Bayard added the self-conscious artistry and commentary we have come to expect in our selfies. Having heard about Daguerre's complex method involving nitrate and copper, Bayard began experimenting with light-sensitive paper. Bayard displayed thirty of his direct-positive prints on paper a month before Daguerre's techniques were officially lauded (and purchased) by the French academy. Bayard was convinced to keep his own breakthroughs quiet, lest the academy become confused by competing claims and techniques. Angered that his own process was ignored, Bayard staged an artistic protest. In *Le Noye* (*Self-Portrait as a Drowned Man*) (1840), Bayard portrays himself as a corpse rotting in the morgue. He is surrounded by a few modest possessions, his body essentially unclaimed, his life unnoticed. On the back of the photo, Bayard lodged his complaint: "The government, having given too much to M. Daguerre, said it could do nothing for M. Bayard and the unhappy man drowned himself. Oh! The fickleness of human affairs! Artists, scholars, journalists were occupied with him for a long time, but here he has been at the morgue for several days, and no-one has recognized or claimed him. Ladies and Gentlemen, you'd better pass along for fear of offending your sense of smell, for as you can observe, the face and hands of the gentleman are beginning to decay."[8]

Bayard launched so many breakthroughs in this one photograph. *Le Noye* is likely the first staged photograph intended to fool the public. In the early days of the medium, Bayard already understands how the alleged reality of a photograph can be used to manipulate an audience, to make viewers think Bayard has committed suicide out of despair. His selfie is a fakey. It may also be the first practical joke captured via photography (a century and a half before Snapchat!). He captures people's sympathy by faking his own death (and thereby undercutting his wealthy and celebrated rivals like Daguerre). He makes people think they're looking at a pitiful sight—an unclaimed corpse in the morgue. But the joke is on the audience, like a magician playing a trick on the "ladies and gentlemen" in an auditorium. Bayard is laughing at us, the unsuspecting public.

Le Noye is also the first photographic protest. This selfie plays on viewers' emotions, seeks to invoke sympathy, and calls upon people to correct a social and economic injustice. Like so much photojournalism that has followed, it is an invitation to outrage. How else can he turn the public tide against the claims of Daguerre already affirmed by the academy? These are shock tactics, a shot of slumber designed to wake the audience up to improprieties. Even more so, *Le Noye* is physical proof that Bayard created a method of fixing photos on paper that Daguerre did not. The photograph is evidence of Bayard's marvelous results. While Daguerre requires a copper plate to fix light, Bayard's more nimble methods can be captured on paper—cheaper, lighter, portable. Daguerre may have won the initial battle for recognition, but in this photographic "trick," Bayard attempted to demonstrate his own mastery and sleight of hand.

Bayard's self-portrait is among the first *memento mori* in photographic form. Pausing to remember death and the fragility of life was a way to be grateful for today and to resist the allure of earthly things. Like the symbol of a skull and bones, this *memento mori* was intended as a wake-up call to the fleeting nature of fame and fortune. Bayard casts himself as a cautionary tale.

This multilayered experience is made possible via the combination of word and image. Bayard's note on the back of the photograph harkens forward to the hashtags we attach to our Instagrams or Snapchats to frame our self-images in a particular way. We now understand how easily photographs can be misread. Images we intend as a joke may be taken seriously. And selfies that are intended to invoke sympathy can sometimes backfire by turning us into a joke. So we attempt to signal when our image is ironic or satirical. We prompt our friends to react with words of admiration and support. Bayard staged this selfie to get people thinking, to stir up emotions, to call attention to his plight.

Bayard's subversive work resembles so many of our selfies today: aggrieved, attention seeking, positioned as a joke, but inspired by painful realities as well as a desire to be noticed, to stave off death, to have our life matter, to have our contributions confirmed. Bayard put so much work into plotting his visual revenge. Yet we also fuss over our appearance, engaging in repeated photos en route to choosing a single image that proves worthy of Instagram. Daguerre's and Bayard's inventions (with all the developments that have come since) placed tremendous power in our hands. With the rise of digital photography, we now have endless possibilities for appropriating and editing others' images. Our ability to distribute our photos far and wide has also made us susceptible to editing and repurposing. A medium that was hailed for offering evidential proof of certain facts and events has now become as fluid and fractured as our own shifting self-image.

What Is Photography For?

Only with effort can the camera be forced to lie: basically it is an honest medium: so the photographer is much more likely to approach nature in a spirit of inquiry, of communion, instead of with the saucy swagger of self-dubbed artists. And contemporary vision is based on an honest approach to all problems, be they morals or art. False fronts to buildings, false standards in morals, subterfuges and mummery of all kinds must be, will be scrapped.

—Edward Weston[9]

What kind of potential and pitfalls are inherent in photography? Astute essayist Susan Sontag writes, "The history of photography could be recapitulated as the struggle between two different imperatives: beautification, which comes from the fine arts, and truth-telling."[10] We have similar tensions in our understanding of human nature. We have our glorified position as sons and daughters of God, partakers of the divine nature. And then we have the trail of blood that often accompanies our decision making. Who are we? We can point to majestic canvasses, inspiring symphonies, and noble scientific breakthroughs as a celebration of our potential. We can also point to the invasion of countries, the dropping of bombs, and the blowing up of our marriages and families as horrific evidence of our collective and individual sin. At times, we rise to our lofty calling. In other instances, we descend into the most primal self-destructive tendencies. Our potential is glorious: "'For I know the plans I have for you,' declares the LORD, 'plans to prosper you and not to harm you, plans to give you hope and a future'" (Jer. 29:11). But we still need sobering daily reminders to remain vigilant in our attention to God's creation. Photographers have shown us the glory of the natural world and how easily we can destroy it.

Not everyone was immediately enamored by the possibilities of photography. It has not always been taken seriously as an art form. As Roland Barthes noted, "Photography has been, and is still, tormented by the ghost of Painting."[11] While painting is a slow and potentially painstaking process, photography seemed to arise more from a chemistry lab than from an artist's vision. Painters understandably feared what this invention might do to their art. The French poet Charles Baudelaire lamented how photography might replace painting because of its superior ability to record the natural world. In his review of the paintings from the Salon of 1859, Baudelaire lamented how "the idolatrous mob demanded an ideal worthy of itself and appropriate to its nature. . . . A revengeful God has given ear to the prayers of this multitude. Daguerre was his Messiah."[12] Baudelaire described the public embrace of photography as "a madness," saying, "an extraordinary fanaticism took possession of all these new sun-worshippers."[13] Baudelaire compared photography lovers to the self-destructive Narcissus, gazing into Daguerre's silvery emulsion. He wrote, "From this moment on this vile society rushed, like a single Narcissus, to contemplate its trivial image on the metal. . . . The love of obscenity, which is as perennial in the natural heart of man as is his love of self, did not escape such a fine occasion of satisfaction."[14] Baudelaire's warnings sound remarkably similar to parents' initial concerns about Snapchat.

For most people, photography is neither an art nor a social revolution but merely a convenience. Thanks to the innovations of George Eastman and the introduction of his No. 1 Kodak camera in 1888, photography became something remarkably easy. The first Kodak cameras were loaded with a roll of film containing one hundred exposures. When customers finished the roll, they were instructed to send the entire apparatus back to Kodak for developing. The company slogan promised simplicity: "You press the button—We do the rest."[15] Susan Sontag notes how the camera was no longer "a cumbersome and expensive contraption—the toy of the clever, the wealthy, and the obsessed." Perhaps it is appropriate that an American company like Kodak would make photography affordable, allowing us "to democratize all experiences by translating them into images."[16] Photography may be the most democratic of art forms. Thanks to the self-correcting nature of electronic cameras, most of us can get what we want into the frame.

Photography has always been about documenting rituals, from baptisms and graduations to weddings and funerals. For holidays and anniversaries, we may return to the same settings each year. For special occasions, we have always felt the need to memorialize them. We want to mark achievements like the birth of a child. Barthes notes how "photography began, historically, as an art of the Person: of identity, of civil status, of what we might call, in all senses of the term, the body's *formality*."[17] It is a form of proof, perhaps even superior to a birth

5 years

certificate, of sheer existence. We pull out a camera when we gather as an extended family, often when we're dressed our best. These early, faded photographs now look so formal, so stiff. Everyone seems to feel the pressure to present their best self on such sacred occasions. Barthes suggests, "Every photograph is a certificate of presence (or at least it used to be)."[18]

During these celebrations, several generations are often reunited. In taking pictures at the same occasions, over time we begin to assemble a family history that allows for comparisons. We can compare our baby picture to a grandparent's baby picture, our wedding to their wedding. Barthes points out how photographs may offer better genetic evidence of family heritage than legal documents. We can study resemblances and traits across time: "You have her eyes, his hair, her body."[19] Snapshots are often the only thing we will hand down from one generation to the next. We may toss out old furniture and give away old plates, but family photographs are usually cherished. They have replaced the family Bible as the bearer of ancestry.

How intriguing that the camera often accompanied religious rites. Perhaps the rise of photography has corresponded to a reduction in ecclesiastical authority. What used to be a sacred ceremony blessed by the church has become instead a camera-ready event. We stage church weddings for the photographs. The need (or right!) to document supersedes the sacred occasion itself. Churches that fail to provide the proper lighting and backdrop are often eschewed for more "photogenic" settings. Consider how wedding photography has changed over the past fifty years.[20] Static shots focused upon the bride, groom, attendants, and family have now morphed into an artistic take on the entire day of preparation. The (formerly) sacred rite is the setup for the real artistic shots taken on- and off-site, of the couple in profile, with close-ups of hands, rings, and table settings. A religious ritual has become the jumping-off point for an eminently Instagrammable album.

We use photographs to do what the church used to do—provide meaning at significant signposts along our journey. It is so much cleaner, simpler, even more emotional to flip through a photo album than to drive to a gravesite. (Those gravesites have also been outsourced, moved to funeral parks rather than church grounds.) Holding on to a photograph may feel much more comforting than pausing before a tombstone. Barthes notes how "the Photograph does not necessarily say *what is no longer*, but only and for certain *what has been*."[21] As long as we can point to the photograph, we can say in a sense, "They are still with us." Barthes notes the strange ironies in our attachments: "For Death must be somewhere in a society; if it is no longer (or less intensely) in religion, it must be elsewhere; perhaps in this image which produces Death while trying to preserve life."[22]

How does a photograph produce death while trying to preserve life? Consider how we document our children's lives. When our children graduate from high school (or even elementary school!), we put together slide shows of their childhoods, trying to hold progress and adulthood at bay. We try to stop time via photos. But if we don't let our children move on, we may kill them slowly, strangling out their aspirations, frustrating their maturity. We take pictures to prove we existed, but now we may stage so many events for the camera that we cannot recall what makes certain occasions special or sacred. As Jill Walker Rettberg notes, "Photography is no longer about documenting social rituals but about documenting the everyday."[23] The rise in convenience has corresponded to a loss of the sacred and set-apart.

Objectivity and the Other

> I am a camera with its shutter open, quite passive, recording, not thinking.
>
> —Christopher Isherwood[24]

While families embraced the camera for special occasions, scientists and anthropologists employed photography to enhance their study of nature and humanity. Photographic historian Mary Warner Marien notes, "The camera image was thought to be like the picture on the retina of the human eye, confirming an eighteenth-century proposition that the retinal image is completely independent of the subject's thoughts and feelings."[25] It was perceived as an objective device. Photography could be used "in weather forecasting, astronomy, microbiology, geology, police work, medical training and diagnosis, military reconnaissance, and art history."[26] Courts began to accept photographic evidence in trials. The Parisian police submitted photographs to build their trumped-up case against Communards in 1871, an early example of how surveillance could be used as a tool for social control.[27] Those with the cameras often exerted power over those who could not afford this new technology. Fascism may not have arisen without the power of the camera to coerce. The myth of objectivity allowed a Nazi regime to galvanize the German people. Seeing could lead to all kinds of strange believing.

Otoe Delegation, 1881, by Charles Milton Bell (American, 1848–93)

Cameras accompanied Western economic and colonial expansion to the far corners of the globe. Photographs recorded stirring vistas and documented disappearing tribes. In 1864, the future prime minister of England Robert Cecil wrote, "The noblest function of photography is to remove from the paths of science in some degree the impediments of space and time, and to bring the intellect of civilized lands to bear upon the phenomena of the vast portion of the earth whose civilization has either not begun, or is passing away."[28] A camera was an essential companion to the anthropologist and explorer. While Anglo guns and westward expansion pushed Native Americans off their tribal lands, some attempted to capture these displaced peoples on film. The pioneering photographs of Edward S. Curtis could ennoble the Native Americans he found in the West, or they could be used to distinguish Anglo cultures from such "savages." Charles Milton Bell photographed representatives of the Otoe tribe (*Otoe Delegation*) on their visit to Washington, DC, in

1881 for "negotiations" regarding their tribal lands.[29] Bell profited from the photographs, but his subjects were not paid. In a sense, photographs *were* stealing Native American souls, reducing them to objects or curios.

Photography also revived pseudosciences like physiognomy and phrenology. Physiognomy insisted that a person's character could be determined by studying their face. Phrenology focused more on the skull as revealer of the inner person. According to German philosopher Arthur Schopenhauer, "That the outer man is a picture of the inner, and the face an expression and revelation of the whole character, is a presumption likely enough in itself, and therefore a safe one to go by; borne out as it is by the fact that people are always anxious to see anyone who has made himself famous. . . . Photography, on that very account of such high value, affords the most complete satisfaction of our curiosity."[30] Thanks to photographs from far-flung lands, contrasts could easily be drawn between us and those "not like us" in the West.

In 1852 American doctor James W. Redfield published *Comparative Physiognomy, or Resemblances between Men and Animals*. The table of contents of this "scientific study" compares "Germans to Lions, Negroes to Elephants, Arabs to Camels, Englishmen to Bulls, Chinamen to Hogs, Yankees to Bulls and Turks to Turkeys."[31] As the camera traveled, photographers cast women from the Middle East and Asia as "exotic," often in sexually suggestive poses. Such "Orientalism" has resulted in "the wholesale social labeling of non-Western peoples as passive, rather than active; childlike rather than mature; feminine, rather than masculine; and timeless, that is apart from the progress of Western history."[32] The snap judgments we make of others' selfies today are connected to these visual stereotypes handed down throughout the history of photography. Do we view people with God-given lenses of dignity and equality or via social lenses blurred by preconceived notions of gender, race, and culture? Thank God for the ubiquity of today's smartphones that allow people to take control of their own images.

A photograph's ability to transport us is reflected in the founding of the National Geographic Society in 1888. Their original goal "to increase and diffuse geographic knowledge" has expanded to include "a passionate belief in the power of science, exploration, and storytelling to change the world."[33] Such noble and inspiring goals must be chastened with an understanding of how pointing a camera at someone or something alters the dynamic. In a 1909 address to the National Child Labor Committee, pioneering cameraman Lewis Hine addressed the question of photographic truth. Hine warns that "an unbounded faith in the integrity of the photographs is often rudely shaken" because, "while photographs may not lie, liars may photograph."[34] When we point our lens at someone (including ourselves), we assume a great deal of moral responsibility. Susan Sontag writes, "To photograph is to appropriate the thing photographed. It means putting oneself into a certain relation to the world that feels like knowledge—and, therefore, like power."[35] She celebrates how the death of objectivity has resulted in a different kind of agency. Sontag suggests, "Photographers made seeing into a new kind of project: as if seeing itself, pursued with sufficient avidity and single-mindedness, could indeed reconcile the claims of truth and the need to find the world beautiful."[36]

This is approaching the world with a sacred perspective, comparable to the original calling in Genesis to cultivate the garden. We are called to plant, to nurture, to grow. Yet we won't all approach that calling with the same emphasis. We will perceive different needs and priorities. Most of us are blessed with the gift of sight, but that does not mean we see things the same way. Photography can be used to point out how we are physically different and remarkably diverse. Perhaps it is even more interesting as a study in how differently we perceive the world around us (including each other).

A Unifying Force

> The camera is an instrument that teaches how to see without a camera.
>
> —Dorothea Lange[37]

Photographs can take us places and show us faces we've never seen before. While some study photographs to discern the differences between us, others have embraced photography as a way to unite around our common humanity. During the Great Depression, the Farm Security Administration (FSA) hired photographers such as Walker Evans, Arthur Rothstein, Gordon Parks, and Dorothea Lange to gather and document the good works accomplished by President Franklin Delano Roosevelt's New Deal. Rothstein's evocative photo *African-American Family at Gee's Bend, Alabama* (1937), raises many questions about poverty, property, and resettlement.[38]

Metropolitan Museum of Art, Purchase, Alfred Stieglitz Society Gifts, 2001

African-American Family at Gee's Bend, Alabama, 1937, by Arthur Rothstein (American, 1915–85)

To retain dignity within a sharecropping situation, perhaps even on a former plantation, took much resolve and determination. Dorothea Lange took up photography out of a burning sense of injustice. Her subject matter ranged from labor demonstrations and breadlines in San Francisco to the forcible internment of Japanese Americans in Manzanar.[39] She focused her camera upon the poor and marginalized in an effort to reveal inequality. Her compassionate images of migrant workers and Okies fleeing the Dust Bowl still resonate. They evoke biblical stories of wandering in the desert. Lange's famous photo *Migrant Mother* (1936) taps into our visual memory of the Virgin Mary holding baby Jesus.[40] Perhaps photographs could soften a hardened heart, expanding empathy toward the suffering of others. This social realism movement underwritten by US government agencies became a significant part of the history it was documenting. It found its fullest expression twenty years later.

As head of the Museum of Modern Art's photography department, Edward Steichen organized a 1955 exhibition titled "The Family of Man." The show was organized around the universal themes of birth, work, and love.[41] It drew upon 503 photographs by 273 photographers from sixty-eight countries—a comprehensive, encyclopedic approach. Alfred Stieglitz had the images cropped and printed with a consistency that highlighted the similarities of the subjects. The overriding purpose of the exhibition was "to prove that humanity is 'one' and that human beings, for all their flaws and villainies, are attractive creatures. The people in the photographs were all races, ages, classes, physical types."[42] Staged in the wake of atrocities in World War II, "The Family of Man" was intended to convey a sense of global unity. There is a dignity and beauty in each and every person. Historian of photography Helmut Gernsheim summed up the optimistic spirit behind the exhibition: "Photography is the only 'language' understood in all parts of the world, and bridging all nations and cultures, that links the family of man."[43] Consider it a visual Esperanto.

While Stieglitz and friends attempted to demonstrate how the humanity that unites us supersedes the politics that often divide us, other photographers leaned into the distinct cultural differences that still remained.[44] Sociologist Pierre Bourdieu's book *Photography: A Middle-Brow Art*, published in France in 1960, raised questions about who and what is photographable. Following the rise of the advertising age, the public had already seen many ads and images that implied who or what is beautiful and worthy to be recorded. Even then, the average person might come away from a fashion magazine utterly depressed. Bourdieu could admire the aspirations of "The Family of Man" project but still point out how it ignored or disguised the substantial social and economic gaps between the subjects. The exhibition failed to tell the whole truth. What we photograph, how we frame people, and who is worthy of being published and promoted are all rooted in social norms. Stieglitz and his team of photographers were still in the position of power, deciding who was "in" and who was "out."

Our discomfort and even outrage toward selfies may stem from remnants of these social standards regarding who is worthy to be photographed and displayed. Jill Walker Rettberg writes, "Perhaps much of the discomfort we see surfacing around selfies is related to this: we are still bound by these social norms, but technology allows us to photograph so much more than when the social norms for photography developed. The technological filter has changed, but the cultural filters are still in the process of changing."[45]

The camera phone bypasses previous power dynamics. Social media acts as a leveling agent. Now almost anyone anywhere can control and disseminate their image.

Humanity at its best celebrates our differences rather than seeking to blot them out. We should not crop out the social conditions that form us. If poverty surrounds us, then why shield others from our reality? We may be embarrassed by our affluence, but it undoubtedly forms a huge part of who we are. I can readily affirm the nobility and dignity inherent in the FSA and "The Family of Man" photographs. But I also acknowledge the massive gaps that still separate our life experiences (and forge us into who we are). We are created by God with inherent beauty and worth. But social structures can make our lived realities shockingly different. The compassion expressed in Rothstein's and Lange's photographs affirms the dignity of their subjects (regardless of their struggle). They took up photography to bridge those gaps, to spark us to action. Perhaps this universal language demonstrates not how alike we are but rather how much we all deserve a life we like.

Technology altered aesthetics. In the 1950s and '60s, photographers took to the streets with smaller and lighter cameras to capture the lived experience of everyday Americans. This next wave of photographers explored the moods and feelings that family photos of celebratory moments like weddings and birthdays ignored.[46] Photographer Lee Friedlander focused on small towns. His framing cropped people in or out in disorienting ways. Friedlander would capture his subject's reflection in a store window, perhaps with an American flag trapped in the corner of the frame. In response to accusations of being too heavy-handed in his commentary on American life, Friedlander countered by including himself in the frame. The image may be about absence, but the photographer is clearly present.

The recently discovered photographs of Vivian Maier also feature her shadow looming in the frame. Maier lived a quiet life as a nanny but also took thousands of photographs of people on the streets of Chicago during the 1940s and '50s. She catches people in moments of isolation and contemplation, alone with their thoughts even amid a bustling city. Occasionally, Maier focuses the camera on herself. She may be framed in a mirror, in a reflection, as a shadow. But she is invariably alone in the world. She portrays herself as a specter or ghost, unperceived by the masses passing by. Anonymity is reserved not only for the subjects she captures on the street but for the photographer as well. How intriguing that Maier's life and over one hundred thousand photographs came into the public eye only after her death.[47]

Thank God for compassionate photographers like Arthur Rothstein and Dorothea Lange, who uphold our dignity. Thank God for honest photographers like Lee Friedlander who unmask our loneliness. Thank God for the "amateur" photographers and selfie-makers like Vivian Maier who reveal a remarkable eye for beauty, even though no one recognized their gifts in their lifetime. We may feel isolated, but God stands with us in our loneliness.

Spontaneous Absurdity

With scientists and journalists claiming that a camera lens captures objective truth, artists were bound to poke fun at such seriousness. The gravitas of photographs from the Dust Bowl and the Great Depression was quite sobering. In the 1920s and '30s, photographs were being reproduced in newspapers, magazines, and professional periodicals with increasing frequency.[48] Advertising executive and avant-garde artist Kurt Schwitters noted that "modern man hears and sees such an enormous amount of impressions, that already he is accustomed to unconsciously turn off."[49] How to wake people up? The surrealists approached photography as a playful and highly malleable endeavor. Industrialized images became an occasion for artists' subversive collages. The avant-garde experimented with this new art form, turning photography into a fun house. Manipulating one's self-image was an essential part of their game.

While inventors had experimented with photo booths for years, Anatol Josepho, a Siberian immigrant to America, patented his Photomaton in 1925. It was an immediate hit on Broadway, attracting crowds of up to 7,500 customers a day.[50] For twenty-five cents, patrons would get a strip of eight photos. Advertisements suggested that getting your picture taken was "no longer a chore—now it's a game."[51] Enthusiasm and interest in the Photomaton was so great that Josepho's patent was purchased for one million dollars. That's a lot of quarters, even today. The invention of the photo booth made it easier than ever to create a self-portrait.

The surrealists embraced the photo booth with childlike glee, adopting "goofy faces, questioning gazes, and grimaces." They called it "a system

Jarred Hammet

Rotary selfie

of psychoanalysis via image."[52] The ease and economy with which the photo booth created images allowed for loose experimentation. Marien notes, "Making photographs could be the visual equivalent of free association, and other methods of side-stepping the monitoring rational mind."[53] Pioneering art photographer Henri Cartier-Bresson was drawn to Surrealists' theories of the irrational. He focused on "the role of spontaneous expression . . . and of intuition and, above all, the attitude of revolt." We long to capture those moments when spontaneous joy bursts forth from our expression. Cartier-Bresson devoted himself to a lifetime of capturing "the decisive moment" in a single photo frame. He defined the moment as "the simultaneous recognition, in a fraction of a second, of the significance of an event as well as of a precise organization of forms which gave that event its proper expression."[54] Isn't that the perfect selfie—both simultaneous and free, yet somehow formal and artistic in its composition?

This sense of playfulness suggests the fun we find on Snapchat. Teens feel free to be goofy, to poke fun at themselves, to alter their self-image with all kinds of absurd captions and cartoons drawn on the photo. It has the disposable and spontaneous feel of a photo booth. Snapchat is a bit of a game. We can keep score, but nobody is really paying attention to the numbers. Snapchat is not meant to be taken seriously, but consciously subverts the studied presentations of Instagram. It invites us to simply be ourselves.

We lose the gift of freedom and spontaneity when we focus too much on editing ourselves. We fret over Instagram photos but post more random photos on Snapchat. Why do we enjoy playing with our self-image? Rettberg suggests that "perhaps the reason we feel the need to take another, and yet another selfie, is in part that we, as the surrealists wrote in 1928, never seem able to create a photo that will 'fully correspond to what you want to see in yourself.'"[55] We acknowledge the absurdity of trying to contain our complex self within a single image. On Snapchat, we can change our moods and our looks by the minute and certainly by the day or the hour. Subverting ourselves, taking the air out of our own tires, is part of Snapchat's social media game. Those who refuse to laugh at themselves become the biggest joke.

Photography can offer the gift of "surprise," capturing a spontaneous moment when the subject was not aware of the camera (like the decisive moment espoused by Cartier-Bresson).[56] Yet with selfies, we are sometimes too painfully aware of the camera. We are the operator and the subject (en route to becoming an object). Too many selfies are predicated on a loss of surprise. It can be posed, frozen, unspontaneous. Acting is innate to the process. Yet the spirit of the surrealists encourages us to act up, to have fun. Like Snapchat, the surrealists encourage us to be as goofy as we want to be.

Photography as Performance: Puncturing Perfectionism

How do we overcome the conundrum of acting for the camera, even while we're taking a selfie? How do we forge a more authentic image of ourselves? It begins with recognizing how the act of being photographed alters our behavior. We begin to pose, maybe even preen, when we realize the lens is aimed at us. And when we're the photographer, pointing the camera at

Cindy Sherman, untitled film still #21, 1978, gelatin silver print, 8 x 10 inches / 20.3 x 25.4 cm (MP# CS-21)

Untitled film still #21, 1978

ourselves, we are engaging in an even stranger bit of acting: performing for ourselves. Roland Barthes described the process of turning from a subject into an object. He wrote: "In front of the lens, I am at the same time: the one I think I am, the one I want others to think I am, the one the photographer thinks I am, and the one he makes use of to exhibit his art. In other words, a strange action: I do not stop imitating myself, and because of this, each time I am (or let myself be) photographed, I invariably suffer from a sensation of inauthenticity, sometimes of imposture."[57] Where does authenticity reside? How do we resist the tendency to become an imposter, to project a false image of ourselves for a perceived audience?

It begins, perhaps, by recognizing the artificiality of photographing ourselves, of trying to act like we don't notice the camera we're pointing at our face. The curators of an exhibition of photographic self-portraits at the Los Angeles County Museum of Art acknowledged how, "ultimately, every self-portrait is a fiction, a portrait of someone else, and an arena in which another is confronted or an alter ego encountered."[58] When we recognize the acting we're engaged in, we suddenly become more capable of being authentic. That doesn't make us liars; it makes us self-aware. Celebrity and fashion photographer Richard Avedon recognizes that self-portraits are a form of performance. Like any performance, the portrait will ultimately be judged as good or bad, compelling or off-putting. Avedon says, "I can understand being troubled by this idea—that all portraits are performances—because it seems to imply some kind of artifice that conceals the truth about the sitter. But that's not it at all."[59] Perhaps in recognizing the artifice, acknowledging the ways we're projecting an image, we can begin to get at something more inherently human. We will never get in touch with our genuine, nonperforming private self until we embrace the ways in which we act for the camera (and our social media audience) on a daily basis.

Cindy Sherman's self-portraits call attention to the social roles we're preassigned. She focuses on the ways that women alter themselves to conform to preestablished notions of beauty. By dressing herself in tropes taken from classic films, Sherman reveals the roles we take on, whether consciously or unconsciously. In her *Untitled Film Stills* (1977–80), Sherman drains her face of emotion. She says, "In a lot of movie photos the actors look cute, impish, alluring, distraught, frightened, tough, etc. but what I was interested in was when they were almost expressionless."[60] She impersonates a character trying to play a role. Her blankness suggests that much more is happening behind the angst, but Sherman allows audiences to fill in the emotional gaps. When nothing is projected, we are invited to consider our own feelings about being pushed toward conformity. Sherman isn't necessarily acting like an actor. She says, "I don't feel that I *am* that person," but "the one thing I've always known is that the camera lies."[61]

In re-creating the look and feel of Hollywood's Golden Age, Sherman invites us to consider how these older images have shaped our consciousness. We judge women according to the glossy photos and body standards established in the 1940s and '50s and rarely consider the cost of such comparisons. Women cast themselves in such glamour shots without realizing the emotional weight of trying to compete with an airbrushed perfectionism of an earlier era. Sherman's are cold, joyless glamour shots re-created for every woman who has ever tried to live out that ideal and been shamed or frustrated by her shortcomings.

Sherman's consciously artificial scenes are a form of protest, railing against the unrealistic standards we've projected onto women's bodies. Yet

Sherman acknowledges her own conflicted feelings about these idealized images: "Even though I've never actively thought of my work as feminist or as a political statement, certainly everything in it was drawn from my observations as a woman in this culture. And a part of that is a love-hate thing—being infatuated with makeup and glamour and detesting it at the same time. It comes from trying to look like a proper young lady or look as sexy or as beautiful as you can make yourself, and also feeling like a prisoner of that structure."[62]

She is both drawn to and repelled by the various guises she tries on. It is possible to unmask the ways in which women are forced to act for the camera, to perform for the male gaze. As both the subject/object as well as the photographer, Sherman rearranges the power dynamic. She puts the camera in women's hands and invites models of all types to reclaim their agency. Sherman wakes us up to these social pressures and gender stereotyping by failing to achieve perfection, by falling short of the glory that Hollywood projects.

Sherman insists that she is not shooting self-portraits, even though she almost exclusively casts herself in these tableaus. She is actively alienating herself, taking on a false self in order to reveal how we've disguised and costumed our true selves. She acts so that we don't have to. Her performance becomes a kind of sacrifice, holding up a cracked mirror for an exhausted audience.

Sherman's artful selfies offer alternatives to the millions of women and girls with self-facing cameras in their hands. Dressing up and playacting can be fun. It is definitely a social game. But do not get lost or confused by that process. Understand that those costumes you've been assigned are not innate. Her photographs empower women to say no.

Sherman unmasks the social pressures to perform by donning an artful mask. The real Cindy Sherman exists far apart from the images she has projected. Her artistry may be public, but her dignity and privacy are preserved far from the madding crowd on social media. Her provocative work echoes these words from Rosemary Radford Ruether: "What does promote the full humanity of women is of the Holy, it does reflect true relation to the divine, it is the true nature of things, the authentic message of redemption and the mission of redemptive community."[63] Thanks to Sherman, a new generation of photographers can freely explore what full humanity and the nature of things look like.

From Here to Eternity

> Perhaps more than any other artifact, the photograph has engaged our thoughts of time and eternity.
>
> —Errol Morris[64]

Why do we get attached to certain photographs? Why do particular images stick in our brains? How can we describe the mysterious process by which we fix special moments in our hearts and minds? Words may fail to convey all that an image stirs in us. Is that the power of photography, to capture sublime and eternal feelings that we struggle to articulate? Roland Barthes analyzed his attachment to a faded photograph of his beloved (and deceased) mother, Henriette. The "Winter Garden" photograph of Henriette as a young girl became the launching point for her eulogy and for Barthes's collection of essays on the nature of photography, *Camera Lucida* (1980). He suggests photography should be labeled not as a kind of darkness (*camera obscura*) but rather as *camera lucida*, offering clarity and light.[65] For the average viewer, the photograph of his mother does not evoke any particular feeling. We observe the facts of Henriette's life as spectators: she lived, she died. He called this objective approach to photography the *studium*. This is comparable to how we scroll through Instagram or Snapchat Stories. We may casually like an image with the "vague, slippery, irresponsible interest one takes in the people, the entertainments, the books, the clothes one finds 'all right.'"[66] The social contract is casual, our emotions weak.

Barthes approaches the photograph with a reverence befitting a son beholding his mother. He sees the image fixed in nitrate as a kind of magic, a physical trace of her soul. For Barthes, every photograph is "the chemical revelation of the object."[67] In holding her photograph, he can nearly touch her across time, in something approximating a resurrection, "the return of the dead." For Barthes, our grasp on the image resembles the moment when Thomas put his fingers through Jesus's wounds in an effort to confirm a miracle. This active form of engagement he labels the *punctum*. He compares the piercing nature of this punctuation to "this wound, this prick, this mark made by a pointed instrument."[68] His language echoes Christ on the cross, pierced for our transgressions. Some images evoke so much emotion that they literally hurt. The *punctum* is comparable to revelation. We do not necessarily seek out feelings from a photograph. They come to us. This revelation will likely be particular to each viewer. It may occur not in the moment of first encounter but rather in retrospect. Our eyes may open upon reflection.

Barthes employs overtly theological terms to describe his love and affection for the "Winter Garden" photograph. The details in a photograph that "pierce our consciousness, wake us up, move us in unexpected ways" are comparable to those religious breakthroughs, those moments when the Spirit reveals to us hidden truths about ourselves and our God. He compares the magic of photography to the appearance of Jesus's face on Veronica's veil. We receive it as a gift, not prescribed by human hands.[69] Barthes writes that the *punctum* "rises from the scene, shoots out like an arrow, and pierces me."[70] This sounds like divine revelation, comparable to Moses before the burning bush (Exodus 3) or the experience of Paul on the Damascus road, struck down and blinded by the light (Acts 9). Teresa of Avila described a piercing of her heart by a golden spear brandished by an angel. She wrote, "The pain was so great, that it made me moan; and yet so surpassing was the sweetness of this excessive pain, that I could not wish to be rid of it. The soul is satisfied now with nothing less than God. The pain is not bodily, but spiritual."[71] Barthes does not name a source for the *punctum*. "What I can name cannot really prick me," he says. "The incapacity to name is a good symptom of disturbance."[72] He preserves a sense of elusive mystery. Like the Jewish reverence for God's name, saying "Adonai" and not "YHWH," he leaves room for a power beyond words.

Sarah Sentilles notes how "Barthes's understanding of photography depends fundamentally on a sense of mystery, which when read alongside certain aspects of the Christian theological tradition rooted in thinking about and living with the unknowability of God, can be claimed as an ethical category."[73] This may be comparable to why God tells Moses through the burning bush, "Do not come any closer." In Exodus 3:5, God instructs Moses, "Take off your sandals, for the place where you are standing is holy ground." Moses hides his face out of deference and reverence, "because he was afraid to look at God" (v. 6). Moses may try to describe this overwhelming experience to others. He will write it down. But even if Moses took a photograph of the bush burning to show to his friends, some would only approach it with a sense of *studium*. Do we have eyes to see and ears to hear what God may be revealing? Are we open to experience the bush as *punctum*, a moment of piercing revelation?

What is our responsibility when it comes to divine encounters, these piercing moments? They cannot be manufactured, but they can be encouraged by an openness in our hearts and minds. Sentilles suggests that for Barthes, "The punctum depends upon the viewer—on how the viewer looks at the photograph, on what the viewer brings to the photograph, on the relationship of the viewer to those pictured in the photograph."[74] She applies the wisdom of Barthes to this discernment process. She notes how "an idol comes from humans toward God, while an icon comes from God toward humans; the *studium* comes from the viewer toward the photograph, while the *punctum* comes from the photograph toward the viewer."[75] We must humble ourselves and resist the temptation to *preconceive* things a certain way in order to *receive* the larger revelation that awaits.

This notion of seeing is comparable to a spiritual discipline. Barthes challenges us to not settle for the easy gaze of the *studium* but to be open to a *punctum*. We must not fixate on that image of the invisible God and make it into a bounded idol. We do not seize the light; the Light seizes us. In the same way that Barthes learns to hold loosely to that photograph of his mother, we also train our eyes to see the reality beyond the image of Jesus either in the manger or on the cross. Be open to receive. This is a sacramental approach to life, to seeing. Make a conscious effort to see through the image before us. As Orthodox Christians train themselves to worship *through* the icons, so we can hopefully learn to see through our selfies to the divine nature within us.

We must resist the urge to scroll past our friends' stories, to consume them (as *studium*) rather than receive them (as *punctum*). It takes time and patience to perceive why they post so many photos of their dog or cat on social media. Perhaps that animal is truly their best friend, their one constant companion. What kind of attention or affection are they communicating in their seemingly random choices on Snapchat? What do their carefully choreographed and curated Instagram photos communicate about their ideal version of themselves? What are they aspiring to? And how can I encourage them in that pursuit? If people long to be truly seen, then how do I train my eyes to see through their posts to the longings contained therein?

There is a degree to which everyone withholds or protects and preserves themselves in photographs. Why would we reveal our whole self to a plastic black box or a cell phone? We must learn to *see through* the look that people offer to the camera. We must not get caught up in the trap of physiognomy, judging people's character by their appearance. As the iPhone X unlocked the power of facial ID, so we must learn to recognize the unique appearance and dignity of every person. I advocate for a more spiritual, even transcendent, approach to art, imagery, and matter. What resides behind the gaze, the smile? We must humble ourselves in appreciating the mystery and complexity of another person. We approach that photograph, that seemingly silly selfie, with reverence. This is the prayer of David: "Show me your ways, LORD, teach me your paths. Guide me in your truth and teach me, for you are God my Savior" (Ps. 25:4–5).

Questions to Consider/Discuss

1. Do you have family photos of your relatives that you cherish? What's your favorite and why? Share it with someone.

2. Are there people that you've prejudged based on their appearance? What might we learn from having honest, face-to-face interactions with people whose experience (and appearance) differs from ours? Share a selfie of someone you've grown to respect and appreciate.

3. What would you say is the most natural photo you've ever taken of yourself? What's an image that makes you truly say, "That's me"?

Selfie Challenge

Cindy Sherman dresses up as characters to rebel against social pressures to conform. What kind of costumes and characters could you create to show who you don't want to be or how you don't want to be perceived? Dress up, and have fun! Post this #selfiechallenge and track your friends' responses.

Cloud of doubt

6

Behind the Mask

The Psychological Self

We wear the mask that grins and lies,
It hides our cheeks and shades our eyes,—
This debt we pay to human guile;
With torn and bleeding hearts we smile,
And mouth with myriad subtleties.

—Paul Laurence Dunbar[1]

I N DISNEY'S *SNOW WHITE*, when the wicked witch stares in the mirror, she asks a basic question: "Who's the fairest of them all?" It is a natural, human tendency to measure ourselves against others. But what if that mirror provides a cracked perspective? How do we resist the temptation to define ourselves externally, via comparison with others, and instead develop an integrated self, content within our own parameters? Are there feelings of frustration and inadequacy burrowed into our psyche that we may not even be aware of? We may have repressed our most painful memories, suppressed our shadow side. The rise of psychology via pioneers such as William James, Sigmund Freud, Carl Jung, B. F. Skinner, and Jean Piaget led to an intense focus on our selves, our happiness, and our identity. Our neuroses were diagnosed as psychological rather than spiritual in nature. Are we more whole, healthy, sane, and satisfied as a result? We know about the dangers of narcissism and pride, but can these vices also contain positive aspects to embrace? Where are our selfies headed or directed? Perhaps the ancient, religious roots of contemplation of the self and meditation on God can move us past our manias.

Psychology arose as a science while photography blossomed as an art. Perhaps one can enlighten the other. It is one thing to perform for someone else's camera, to submit ourselves to their timing and shutter. But what about when we turn ourselves into something resembling an object—a commodity that can be studied, forwarded, and judged across the internet? What goes through our mind when we take a selfie? We may have reached a destination we want to remember. We may be relishing a moment with friends we want to preserve. We may have a feeling of triumph or accomplishment we want to communicate far and wide. But where does that motivation, that hunger for affirmation spring from? We may not have reflected on why we take selfies. It is an unconscious act. In this chapter, we will attempt to probe the many feelings rumbling inside our self-promotional instincts. Our photos may spring from places of genuine joy and a desire to connect. But we may also be seeking to satisfy the most basic of childhood needs. Will that selfie satisfy the longings lodged deep within our hearts and minds? How many likes will it take for us to feel seen and heard, validated and loved?

Franz Kafka asserts, "We photograph things in order to take them out of mind. My stories are a way of shutting my eyes."[2] Perhaps in snapping a quick shot, we are thereby relieved of the responsibility of being fully present. We have evidence that we exist. We were present. We walked this corner of the earth at this moment in time. But do we have proof that we were accounted for? That we mattered? This is where social media steps in. With the advent of the like button, Facebook made it possible to take literal stock of our presence. When our photo is liked by a significant number of people (and what constitutes significance is a slippery proposition depending on how much social media status you seek), we feel noticed, affirmed, and maybe even loved. The expansion of Facebook's expressive options, from like to love and even sadness and laughter, further humanize social media. It reflects the broader palette of emotions that we all carry inside.

To be externally defined works while we're rising. But what if the public turns on us? Downfall is swift. We can lose a job, a marriage, or our reputation in an instant. In order to avoid such embarrassment, we have taught the next generation how to perform. We have made them change their names and scrub their Facebook profiles in anticipation of college applications and professional interviews. We have subjected them to performance reviews at early ages, forcing them to "grow up in public" in ways that we never endured. The social-psychological pressure to project a healthy, whole, and satisfied self is immense (and sometimes debilitating). In *The Principles of Psychology* (1890), William James considered how we alter the presentation of ourselves in different social settings. James writes, "Man has as many social selves as there are individuals who recognize him and carry an image of him in their mind. To wound any one of these images is to wound him."[3] How do we deal with those psychic wounds? Where does one take those dark days, those inchoate feelings? To Snapchat. Only in the comfort of disappearing photos can we let down our guard. We relish the opportunity to toss off images and opinions (almost) free of repercussions.

Donna Freitas warns us about "the happiness effect" that arises when we are always performing on social media. After extensive interviews with college students across America, she notes, "In always trying to appear happy, perfect, even inspiring and certainly enviable, we often neglect the very parts of ourselves that bring us true happiness, joy, connection, love, and pleasure." She notices how, "by putting up these facades, by convincing our 'audiences' not only that all is well but that all is *always* well, we sacrifice ourselves. When we feel pressured to project the best version of ourselves, we may lose touch with those more complicated feelings that are often excluded from our posts."[4] Sociologist Christian Smith worries about "the schizophrenic effect social media has on people's sense of self." He wonders what happens when "the problems and blemishes of real life are hidden behind virtual presentations of self that struggle, often obsessively, to be 'Liked.'"[5] When we measure worth via our social media performance, the stress to our psyches is considerable. Freitas concludes, "Our brave faces are draining us. We're losing sight of our authentic selves."[6]

How might we reconnect with or reclaim our authentic self? There is power in controlling our self-image. We can keep taking photos until we're satisfied. But that process of submitting ourselves to the four corners of the frame can also be belittling. We can end up submitting to the preestablished standards of the photographic models we admire. Our dress, our hair, our makeup may all conform to external standards of what is good, true, or beautiful. Roland Barthes recalls when a friend looked around a coffee shop (years before the invention of the iPhone) and bemoaned how "nowadays the images are livelier than the people."[7] Have we reduced our life to a series of photo opportunities that conform to a preestablished image repertoire? Our admiration for the carefully curated images of Instagram could soften the edges that make us most human and reduce our notion of ourselves. We may have suppressed our very necessary shadow side. Students labeled as narcissists are suffering from considerable performance anxiety. May a healing combination of psychology and practical theology liberate us from these social media canyons.

The Rise of Self-Analysis

Psychoanalysis was born out of the complex confluence of frustrated sexuality, misdirected love, and unsatisfied desire. When many of us think of psychology, we are referring to some form of psychoanalysis, whether via television talk shows we've watched or family therapy and counseling sessions we've experienced. We may talk about guilt, shame, repressed memories, free association, individuation, or an identity crisis without ever reading the work of Sigmund Freud, Carl Jung, or Erik Erikson. Nonprofessionals may apply diagnostic terms to their spouses, children, and coworkers. We may even attempt to diagnose our nation's president.[8] We brandish loaded concepts like narcissism in our everyday conversations. Is that a helpful starting point in our discussion of selfies? Karl Barth suggests that there is such a gulf between God and humanity that we will never find God by studying the human psyche. He writes, "It is evident that the relation to God with which the Bible is concerned does not have its source in the purple depths of the subconscious, and cannot be identical with what the deep-sea psychical research of our day describes in the narrower or broader sense as libido fulfillment."[9] Despite his pessimism, we will press on in search of integration.

Freud published *On Narcissism* in 1914.[10] For such a thin volume (approximately thirty pages), it has had an inordinate influence on how we think about our ego and its attachments. Freud started with Paul Nacke's clinical description of narcissism. In 1899, Nacke used the term "narcissism" to refer to a sexual attachment to ourselves (instead of others). Homosexuals were singled out as especially disordered (a stigma that would not be dropped by psychologists for sixty long years). Freud agreed that narcissism can be associated with an unhealthy autoeroticism. To Freud, we are all narcissists, but when our egos fail to attach to an object outside ourselves, we turn inward and our ego links to our libido. There is no satisfaction with self-pleasure because the object is really ourselves. To cover our insecurities and frustrations, we may develop a boastful and overcompensating personality. Freud suggested that the narcissist's inward turn could manifest as megalomania. This is how we primarily use the term "narcissist" today in reference to vain and self-centered people. Yet we often overlook how Freud also posits the possibility of escaping such fixation via love. We can rise above our narcissistic tendencies, or at least become mature narcissists, when we give ourselves to an object (preferably a person) outside ourselves.

Philosopher Martin Buber explored the dangers and limits of treating others as an object in *I and Thou* (1923).[11] We can approach the world and others as objects in an I-It relationship. This may involve studying a tree for its aesthetic beauty or analyzing its biological processes. We can admire and appreciate the science behind it. But when it comes to God and our fellow humans, we have an opportunity to enter into an I-Thou relationship. It is powerful, spiritual, communal, and full of mystery. We may develop a sense of being united with something far beyond ourselves. It can lead to feelings of transcendence. In pathological narcissism, we distance ourselves from others, treating others as objects. Social media may encourage us to think of our friends as followers, to measure their allegiance via likes. We begin to objectify others when we treat them as a faceless audience. "It" is only there to serve us. Buber challenges us to erase such barriers and invest in a more respectful and mysterious I-Thou relationship. We risk rejection by giving ourselves wholeheartedly to another. It is scary. Such commitment is rare. Yet so are the unquantifiable rewards. An infinite number of likes cannot compare to the abiding love of God.

Psychoanalyst Julie Kristeva upholds the biblical Song of Songs as an example of this transforming love. She notes that although rabbis (and later Christian priests) interpreted this dramatic poem as allegorical, "The enunciation of the Song of Songs is very specifically individualized, assumed by autonomous, free subjects, who, as such, appear for the first time in the world's amatory literature."[12] My wife and I had the dialogue of the two lovers read aloud at our wedding by our reverend and his wife. On our humid June wedding day, the lovers' passion came across as unabashedly steamy. It involves anticipation and a nighttime rendezvous. The descriptions are erotic and embodied. The Shulamite woman's attachment to her beloved is so strong that she says, "I am sick of love" (Song 2:5; 5:8 KJV). Kristeva describes the process of healthy attachment: "In amorous dialogue I open up to the other, I welcome him in my loving swoon, or else I absorb him in my exaltation, I identify with him. With those two motions, the premises of *ecstasy* (of one's going out of oneself) and of *incarnation*, insofar as it is the ideal becoming body, are set within the amorous incantation of the Song of Songs . . . sick and yet sovereign."[13] Kristeva embraces the subjectivity and individuality that arises from committing fully to the object of love.

Rather than focusing on the positive aspects of satisfying our ego via healthy attachment, as in Song of Songs, narcissism has become associated almost exclusively with a disorder. Freud's Viennese disciple Heinz Kohut introduced the term "narcissistic personality disorder" to America in 1968. It was soon listed within the *Diagnostic and Statistical Manual of Mental Disorders*. Fred Alford offers a summary: "DSM-III characterizes pathological narcissism in terms of an exaggerated concern with power and control, the result of which is interpersonal exploitativeness. Typical also is an orientation of entitlement, the notion that one is worthy of great admiration, respect, and reward regardless of one's achievements."[14] Grandiosity is coupled with a fragile self-esteem. These are the roots of the many epithets hurled at millennials as entitled and narcissistic.

While no more than 1 percent of the population is thought to have the disorder during some juncture of their lives, the term caught on and crossed over into common usage (perhaps because of the enduring power of the Greek myth).[15] A few disordered narcissists may lust for power at any price, but most of us will learn to edit ourselves and reign in our most aggressive impulses. So why do we label others (and even an entire generation) as narcissistic?

A sense of social responsibility and connectedness (I-Thou) pulled Americans together during World War II. In the postwar economic boom of the 1950s, jobs, cars, and housing were plentiful for those who had access to the opportunities. Amid the affluence, social critics worried that individuals were being swallowed up by the system.[16] We were becoming more outer-focused than inner-directed. Affluence enabled families to flee to the suburbs, where consumption became a new national pastime. By the 1970s, postindustrial conformity had congealed into rabid self-interest. Tom Wolfe dubbed it the "'Me' Decade." Daniel Bell's *The Cultural Contradictions of Capitalism* (1976) and Christopher Lasch's *The Culture of*

Narcissism (1979) bemoaned the sorry state of the American soul. Twenty years later, Robert Putnam announced that we were now *Bowling Alone* (2000). Our social capital and sense of community were depleted. What a precipitous fall for a formerly united nation. After our finest social critics had invested half a century in exposing our faults, it has become easier to see why many longed to "Make America Great Again."

Throughout these best-selling critiques of the American psyche, the authors focused almost exclusively on the destructive side of narcissism. Many saw psychoanalysis as contributing to our national problem. Christopher Lasch wrote, "People have convinced themselves that what matters is psychic self-improvement: getting in touch with their feelings, eating health food, taking lessons in ballet or belly-dancing, immersing themselves in the wisdom of the East, jogging, learning how to 'relate,' overcoming the fear of 'pleasure.'"[17] Despair regarding the future drove people "to live only for the moment, to fix our eyes on our own 'private performance,' to become connoisseurs of our own decadence, to cultivate a 'transcendental self-attention.'"[18] He decried how the therapeutic replaced the religious with the momentary illusion of "personal well-being, health, and psychic security" (rather than salvation).[19] To Lasch, our celebrities, politicians, and idols reflect our cultural values in frightening ways.

Christian critiques of modern culture have also been rigorous and pervasive.[20] I agree with Cornelius Plantinga Jr. that life is "not the way it's supposed to be." He offers this summary: "In an ego-centered culture, wants become needs (maybe even duties), the self replaces the soul, and human life denigrates into the clamor of competing autobiographies. People get fascinated with how they feel—and with how they feel about how they feel. In such a culture and in the throes of such fascination, the self exists to be explored, indulged and expressed but not disciplined or restrained."[21] Plantinga quotes theologian David Wells on how theology has been usurped by therapy: "The biblical interest in righteousness is replaced by a search for happiness, holiness by wholeness, truth by feeling, ethics by feeling good about one's self. The world shrinks to the range of personal circumstances; the community of faith shrinks to a circle of personal friends. The past recedes. The Church recedes. The world recedes. All that remains is the self."[22] These exercises in tough love have called us to confess our collective sins and own up to our personal responsibility in this shift from sin to psychosis.

This narrative of national decline describes "Americans as a people shifting from sturdy production to meaningless consumption . . . from the self-denying hysteric of Freud's day to the pampered and indulged narcissist of our own."[23] The shift from "we" to "me" has continued unabated, according to psychologist Jean Twenge, who blames baby boomers for raising what she calls "generation me."[24] The focus on self-actualization has become so widespread that narcissistic personality disorder was dropped from the American Psychiatric Association's fifth edition of the *Diagnostic and Statistical Manual*.[25] To some, this implies a simple diagnosis: we are all pathological narcissists. It has been so normalized (and even rewarded) that psychologists no longer call it a problem.[26] Are our socioeconomic problems a by-product of the sickness that dogged Narcissus? "Am I the lover or beloved? Then why make love? Since I am what I long for, then my riches are so great they make me poor."[27] It is easy to see why some have concluded that the only viable strategy is a monastic-like retreat.[28]

While I am firmly convinced that sin dogs us, I also recognize that grace abounds. We have a tremendous capacity for megalomania and narcissistic blindness. By some measurements, these may be the worst of times. But those who are just launching out sail with hopes that the best of times may yet be ahead. By focusing solely on the dark side of narcissism, these cultural critics miss the possibility still residing in our divine calling and nature. Those who snap selfies may be serving their worst instincts, or they may still be figuring out who they are and whose they are. While some may be sinking into a spiral of cynicism, they may yet be determined to forge a future that leans into their gifts, affirms their callings, and embraces their best selves.

The Positive Side of Narcissism

We have been schooled in the perils of narcissism, but could there possibly be a positive side to our self-seeking tendencies? Maybe we simply want to make a memory. Psychologist Elizabeth Lunbeck notes how Freud "conceived of narcissism as both normal (present in everyone and necessary to sustain life) and pathological (a state of self-love to be overcome in the course of development)."[29] She found that the social critics who got rich condemning our self-centeredness may have misused the groundbreaking work of Viennese émigrés and psychoanalysts Heinz Kohut and Otto Kernberg. In *The Americanization of Narcissism*, Lunbeck documents how "Kohut boldly reframed narcissism as a desirable, even healthy, dimension of mature self-hood. He consistently underscored narcissism's positive aspects, arguing that it fueled individuals' ambitions, creativity, and fellow-feeling." Lunbeck says Kohut even suggested that "the emptiness and fragmentation critics saw as a characteristic of modernity resulted not from too much narcissism but from too little."[30] In contrast, Kernberg "focused on narcissism's darker side, in precise and vivid prose describing narcissists' destructiveness, rage, and aggression as well as the masterful ways in which they exploited and enslaved their hapless victims. Kernberg's narcissists were charming and seductive, expert at eliciting admiration and tribute from those they would invariably devalue and discard." Kernberg described how "the most creative and intelligent of them enjoyed a level of worldly success that fueled the critics' complaint that the culture not only tolerated but rewarded narcissistic traits."[31]

To what degree have we applied the same filters to our understanding of those who take and post the most selfies? Best-selling books like *The Narcissism Epidemic* present easily recognizable figures of "the vacuous consumer, the 'ego-addled' brat, and the preening celebrity."[32] Lunbeck notes "the danger of assessing an entire generation based upon the Narcissistic Personality Inventory (NPI) like the research of Jean M. Twenge and W. Keith Campbell." Questions they asked (and perceived as narcissistic) actually "align with the positive traits of high self-esteem like 'psychological health, assertiveness, and confidence.'"[33] Statistics showing that the percentage of teenagers who agreed that "I am an important person" jumped from 12 percent in the 1950s to 80 percent in the 1980s are brandished as a sign of a narcissistic crisis. As a college professor, I've definitely dealt with students who couldn't imagine that their work would garner anything less than an A. Parents can place their children on too lofty a pedestal. Giving everyone a trophy doesn't make everyone special. It would be wiser to say "You did a good job" than to say "You deserved to win."[34] But is a rise in self-confidence and a stronger sense of self-worth a major problem? Corrosive narcissism springs from poor self-esteem. Campbell concludes, says Lunbeck, that "narcissism may be a functional and healthy strategy for dealing with the modern world."[35] Perhaps the expansion of a healthy self-image aligns with God's vision for us as his image bearers. Maybe more people are reclaiming their God-given power and potential, what it means to "participate in the divine nature" (2 Pet.

1:4). Yes, it could result in more self-obsessed people, but it could also inspire more active, engaged citizens.

Rest assured, I have not set out to write a defense of narcissism. Centuries of religious teaching rail against the deadly sins of vanity and pride. Proverbs warns us that "when pride comes, then comes disgrace" (Prov. 11:2). Esteemed kings from Jewish history, like Uzziah and Hezekiah, were brought down by pride.[36] Jesus railed against the Pharisees, who "accept glory from one another but do not seek the glory that comes from the only God" (John 5:44). James reminds us that "God opposes the proud but shows favor to the humble" (James 4:6). Psychologist Jessica Tracy studied the history of pride and found that "Saint Augustine, Thomas Aquinas, and Pope Gregory I characterized pride as the queen of sin, the beginning of all sin, and the root of all evil. Dante considered it the deadliest of all the seven deadly sins. Buddhists, Taoists, Greeks all warned against hubris."[37] We have been warned: pride is bad.

Fourth-century saint John Cassian chronicled the snares of vanity and pride in his voluminous *Institutes*. Cassian documents how vainglory attacks us from almost every angle: "For it tries to injure the soldier of Christ in his dress, in his manner, his walk, his voice, his work, his vigils, his fasts, his prayers, when he withdraws, when he reads, in his knowledge, his silence, his obedience, his humility, his patience."[38] We are under constant attack even when we are trying to be spiritual. Cassian describes vanity: "Like some most dangerous rock hidden by surging waves, it causes an unforeseen and miserable shipwreck to those who are sailing with a fair breeze, while they are not on the lookout for it or guarding against it."[39] In other words, be vigilant! As a monk, dedicated to a life of asceticism, John still wrestled with spiritual pride. He described how "the more thoroughly a man has shunned the whole world, so much the more keenly does it pursue him. It tries to lift up with pride one man because of his great endurance of work and labour, another because of his extreme readiness to obey, another because he outstrips other men in humility. One man is tempted through the extent of his knowledge, another through the extent of his reading, another through the length of his vigils."[40] Escaping the world doesn't mean escaping the pit of pride. It traps us even in our humility!

I was surprised to discover that Canadian psychologist Jessica Tracy suggests that there is an authentic and helpful pride that can supersede the destructive kind that bedevils even the finest Christian saints. She points to two divergent definitions of the English word "pride" in Merriam-Webster's dictionary: "The first is 'inordinate self esteem/conceit.' The second? 'A reasonable or justifiable self-respect.'"[41] This echoes the two sides of narcissism that Freud and his followers like Kohut and Kernberg outlined. To resolve the tension, Tracy turns to Italians, who have distinct words for two different kinds of pride. She goes on to say, "The pride that narcissists experience—a pride that's best summed up with words like *arrogance*, *conceit*, and in Italian, *orgoglio*—is not about feeling good; it's about *avoiding feeling bad*." This is the pride that craves the spotlight, demands attention, and needs to be applauded. Tracy highlights a different Italian term that aligns with self-esteem, the pride "represented by words like *accomplished* and *productive*, or even *confident* and *worthy*. It's the pride that Italians call *fierezza* and that the dictionary defines as 'reasonable or justifiable self-respect.'"[42] This pride has poise, presence, a rootedness that does not bend with the winds of change. Both *orgoglio* and *fierezza* will take a deep bow, but with different motivations.

For Tracy, pride should not be understood as one concept composed of competing impulses. It is two distinct things. *Hubristic* pride leads to arrogance, egotism, and smugness. These are the snares that the Bible repeatedly warns against. *Authentic* pride sparks feelings of achievement, accomplishment, and productivity.[43] This is the voice of God that pours forth from the heavens to declare, "This is my Son, whom I love; with him I am well pleased" (Matt. 3:17; 17:5). This is the loving affirmation of Jesus that announces, "Daughter, your faith has healed you" (Luke 8:48; see also 7:50). This is a divine sense of pride and accomplishment that goes all the way back to the garden, when the Creator assessed his work and called it "good." We know when we have done good. And we should never be ashamed of that. This is our calling, to cultivate God's glorious creation, to nurture the earth and our fellow humans.

How can we distinguish between these two distinct forms of pride? We judge them by their fruit. Tracy writes, "Authentic pride motivates us to do what's needed to become the best we can be—to achieve, create, innovate, and behave morally." This is humanity at its generative best. We've had moments when we are so flowing in our giftedness that we lose a sense of time or place. We are no longer working but simply playing. Tracy notes that while hubristic pride is also motivating, it results in a completely different set of behaviors. Hubristic pride "makes us aggressive, manipulative, and domineering; we become primed to do whatever it takes to get power and influence over others."[44] This may get results, but it almost always feels like work. It stresses everybody out (including ourselves).

Our selfies can be driven by either impulse. We may Snap when we are looking good, feeling good, doing good. Or we may post to snatch more power and popularity, to lord our likes over our peers. Tracy suggests, "When we lack a clear path for seeking authentic pride in our lives, we feel a void. The answer, instead, lies in knowing the difference between authentic and hubristic pride and maintaining—during every pride experience—an awareness of this distinction."[45] We check ourselves so we don't wreck ourselves. This is the spirit of reflection behind the wisdom of the apostle Paul: "If anyone thinks they are something when they are not, they deceive themselves. Each one should test their own actions. Then they can take pride in themselves alone, without comparing themselves to someone else, for each one should carry their own load" (Gal. 6:3–5). Paul makes room for what Tracy would call authentic pride, a part of human nature to be celebrated for bringing out the best of what we have to offer. But Tracy adds a similar caveat: "Our pride must be linked to actual successes or to morally good, empathetic, generous and compassionate behaviors. Our pride must be used to help each of us become the kind of person our societies want us to become *and* the kind of person that feels like an authentic part of who we are."[46] In other words, don't take selfies while on a service project in order to be praised. Don't engage in a "humblebrag" to cover up insecurities. Love and serve others, because that is the best of who we are and reflects the glory of the One who made us kind, compassionate, and generous.

Playing Roles: What about Our Off Days?

> We smile, but, O great Christ, our cries
> To thee from tortured souls arise.
> We sing, but oh the clay is vile
> Beneath our feet, and long the mile;
> But let the world dream otherwise,
> We wear the mask!
> > —Paul Laurence Dunbar,
> > "We Wear the Mask"[47]

Courtney Perry

Cinecitta selfie

We have talked about our best selves, about when we should feel a sense of authentic pride. That's easy when we're feeling good, at the top of our game. But what about the shadow side of ourselves, those times when we are down? We all have off days. I've had off *years*, seasons when I could barely summon the strength to carry on. Grief, disappointment, and depression are part of our human experience. Psychologists and pastors are trained to guide us through periods when we can no longer smile in our selfies. Behind closed doors, we can let our guard down, confess our darkest impulses, reveal our greatest aches and pains. We desperately need safe places to share our deepest longings and regrets. Professor Soong-Chan Rah notes how all too often in our churches "a triumphalistic theology of celebration and privilege rooted in a praise-only narrative is perpetuated by the absence of lament and the underlying narrative of suffering that informs lament."[48] We need room to grieve. Yet social media pressures us to perform, to present our best selfies. We may find ourselves playacting in public settings, putting on a brave face for weeks or even months at a time.

William James acknowledged the multiple faces we present in shifting social situations. Well before the advent of social media, he wrote, regarding the average person, "We may practically say that he has as many different social selves as there are distinct groups of persons about whose opinion he cares. He generally shows a different side of himself to each of these different groups. Many a youth who is demure enough before his parents and teachers, swears and swaggers like a pirate among his 'tough' young friends. We do not show ourselves to our children as to our club companions, to our customers as to the laborers we employ, to our own masters and employers as to our intimate friends."[49] When those settings were separate, it was easier to keep our public and private selves distinct. But with social media gathering work, family, and friends into the same arena, we may have difficulty keeping our selves straight. It is easy to see why teens retreat to Snapchat as a haven of authenticity (or at least as one place to be less than perfect). "Thank God that Mom and Dad and Grandma can't see my Snapchats!" All of us need a place to retreat, a backstage area where we can let down our hair, where we can take off the mask that we're forced to wear at school or in the workplace. Over time, the goal would be to find a job and calling that allows us to be our authentic selves, to align our real life with our online life in a manner that reduces the dissonance. But what do we do in the meantime?

Sociologist Erving Goffman published *The Presentation of Self in Everyday Life* in 1959, long before the advent of selfies. Goffman saw the individual as a *performer*, "a harried fabricator of impressions involved in the all too-human task of staging a performance."[50] In this social contract, we are perceived as a *character*, "a figure, typically a fine one, whose spirit, strength and other sterling qualities the performance was designed to evoke."[51] We are judged according to our performance, how well we played the role. While most submit to these rules of social engagement, that doesn't necessarily make the rules fair. We are placed onstage without always knowing the script or the setting. Goffman warns that this self, as a performed character, "is not an organic thing that has a specific location . . . ; it is a dramatic effect arising diffusely from a scene that is presented, and the characteristic issue, the crucial concern, is whether it will be credited or discredited."[52] We've all felt the pressure to play the part of "the oldest son," "the younger sister," or "the baby brother." What if we add expectations placed on the jock or the cheerleader or the brain? We may enjoying watching *The Breakfast Club* (1985), but few of us would want to be stuck in that kind of detention for life. These social roles may be shifting, but the call to perform arises early via social media. We are judged by our number of friends, our posts, and our likes. Adolescents are invited to platforms at the moment when their self-images are still in dramatic flux. They are forced to grow up in public. Impression management and profile curation can be exhausting.[53]

Goffman extends his acting metaphor by discussing the gap between our public profiles and our private selves. We may perform particular roles at work or at school. This is when we are onstage, performing. But what about when we're backstage, at rest, living our private lives? We all need time to rest. Goffman wrote long before the advent of social media and the distinctions between our Rinsta (Real Instagram) and Finsta (Fake Instagram) accounts. Would he find the time we spend offstage and online to be in conflict? How do we bring our projected selves (the Rinsta) into alignment with our private selves (the Finsta), with who we really are? Goffman talked about how "the expressiveness of the individual (and therefore his capacity to give impressions) appears to involve two radically different kinds of sign activity: the expression that he *gives*, and the expression that he *gives off*."[54] We are judged by what we say and what we do. The things we claim may not match up with our actions, creating dissonance for our audience (and for ourselves). The goal is an integrated personality, where our speech and actions are aligned. Goffman would challenge us not to engage in deceit (via false speech) or in feigning (via false actions). Jesus said, "Let your 'Yes' be 'Yes,' and your 'No,' 'No.' For whatever is more than these is from the evil one" (Matt. 5:37 NKJV). Keep your word. Fulfill your promises. Another simple test of integrity and alignment is this: "By this everyone will know that you are my disciples, if you love one another" (John 13:35)—both online and offline.

Goffman notes the ways we can engage in falsehood: "an individual may be taken in by his own act or be cynical about it."[55] We may project a false or idealized version of ourselves for so long that we begin to believe our own publicity. We may also engage in known falsehoods in order to get something, presenting one face for the sake of a larger goal. Interestingly, the wearing of a mask, particularly an aspirational one, can also have positive outcomes.

We see this played out in Scripture when the apostle Paul's letters challenge followers of Jesus to set aside their old selves and step into a new self in Christ. To Christians in Ephesus, Paul writes, "You were taught, with regard to your former way of life, to put off your old self, which is being corrupted by its deceitful desires; to be made new in the attitude of your minds; and to put on the new self, created to be like God in true righteousness and holiness" (Eph. 4:22–24). He offers a similar call to the church in Colossae: "Do not lie to each other, since you have taken off your old self with its practices and have put on the new self, which is being renewed in knowledge in the image of its Creator" (Col. 3:9–10). Putting on a new self, a new image, is a way to distance ourselves from deceit. We are called to see ourselves in a new way, to walk as people set apart for a lofty purpose. And where do we see that standard? When we look in the mirror, we can begin to picture ourselves in the image of our Creator. This is an aspirational "mask" that we can wear with pride, checking ourselves in relation to it, measuring our progress in living up to our highest potential.

How do we act out the part? Hans Urs von Balthasar suggests that God sets the stage for us in the original "theo-drama." God acted first, in creation. Balthasar notes that "God does not play the world drama all on his own; he makes room for man to join in the acting."[56] Jesus enters the stage and transforms what it means to act in truth and love. Jesus "plays" through human beings and as a human being. But he is not hiding behind a mask that he takes off just before the crucifixion.[57] He acts out his part on the cross. The role is so immersive and complete that one of those assembled declares, "Surely he was the Son of God" (Matt. 27:54). Transformed by the Spirit, we can now carry out the roles outlined in Scripture: to be loving, joyous, peaceful, forbearing, kind, good, faithful, gentle, and like any trained actor knows, in self-control (Gal. 5:22–23). Balthasar writes, "The *good* which God does to us can only be experienced as the *truth* if we share in performing it; we must 'do the truth in love.'"[58] What a role God reserves for us!

Healthy Projections

How might selfies contribute positively to this process of renewal (known throughout church history as sanctification)? During the Renaissance, Claudio Tolomei documented how seeing himself portrayed as noble by the painter Sebastiano del Piombo inspired him. Tolomei wrote, "Seeing myself vividly portrayed by your art will provide me with a continual stimulus to purge my soul of its many defects, and seeing therein the illuminating rays of your genius (*virtú*) will kindle in my soul a noble longing for glory and honor."[59] None of us are born perfect or immediately transformed into a holy person the moment that we decide to follow Jesus. It is a lifelong journey of faith, forged in a pattern of choices that slowly remakes us as virtuous, perhaps even Christlike. We may be buoyed by a selfie taken during a mountaintop spiritual experience, to remind us of our faith commitment. This image could serve as the backdrop on our phone, the anchor from which we start and end each day. What about when we encounter pitfalls and setbacks along the way? We may need to snap a selfie in disgust at who we've become, a marker of how far we've fallen. This could be a reminder of what we don't want to do, a side of ourselves we hate and hope to overcome. When we confess our sins and renew our vows, we remind ourselves whose we are and what we long to be. Another selfie may signify a fresh start, a restored sense of spiritual resolve. We may mark the day with a tattoo, a journal entry, or an Instagram post that communicates our best intentions. Eugene Peterson called this process of refinement "a long obedience in the same direction."[60]

We didn't have selfies when I was beginning my spiritual journey. We kept prayer journals. And we memorized plenty of Scriptures to bolster our spirit and strengthen us as temptations arose. This remains one of my favorites: "No temptation has overtaken you except what is common to mankind. And God is faithful; he will not let you be tempted beyond what you can bear. But when you are tempted, he will also provide a way out so that you can endure it" (1 Cor. 10:13). In writing this book, I flashed back to one "selfie" (taken with a camera set on auto-timer) that I sent as a Christmas card in 1987. When I decided to serve teenagers as a part of the Young Life staff, I had an image of what a youth minister looked like. I hoped to be loving, patient, kind, and fun. One of our founder's mottos was "It's a sin to bore a kid." Consequently, our Young Life gatherings tended to be a big, raucous blast that reflected adolescent energy. We played games, did skits, and sang—*loudly*. One of my responsibilities with Young Life was song leading. I could belt out a chorus with gusto, but what about leading a melody? I needed to learn how to play guitar. I didn't really have time to take lessons, but I bought a guitar and started to

Craig Detweiler

Christmas '87

teach myself chords. The learning curve was pretty steep. I wasn't necessarily born to play. Yet I persisted.

   With Christmas approaching, I thought about what I'd like to communicate to my friends, extended family, and supporters. How could I
put a face on my work with Young Life? Perhaps I could take a photo of
teens at a club meeting. Or maybe they'd enjoy a picture from a weekend
retreat at a beautiful camp. But neither of those captured the colors of
Christmas, so I decided to take a picture of myself playing guitar. I put on
a bright red sweater for the occasion, sat in front of the stockings hanging
from the fireplace, and picked up my Ovation. When my supervisor, Ken
Schultz, saw the card, he was quite surprised. Ken said, "You don't know
how to play guitar, do you?" I told Ken I was *hoping* to play it. Ken could
have judged me, maybe even challenged my deceit. Instead, Ken saluted
my faith and how I dared to project a version of how I saw myself and
who I aspired to become. This mentor affirmed my vision: "You dared to
show almost everybody you know who you intend to be." In projecting
an image of myself as a guitar player, I set a standard that I ultimately
lived into. My practices caught up with my belief. The projection became
a part I literally learned to play.

When we criticize those engaged in taking selfies, we may be cutting them off from their aspirational selves. The masks we wear in our selfies may not reflect who we are, but they are likely to communicate who we'd like to become and how we hope to be perceived. If we photograph ourselves dunking a basketball, it may be because we imagine making a breakaway shot in a big game. Sons and daughters may be affirmed for this positive visioning. But what if those self-images are sexy or alluring? The provocative self-portrait may not be the right way to experience self-worth, but it may spring from a remarkably pure place of longing and need. Photographing ourselves with a duck face, chin down, may reflect insecurities about our appearance and also our aspirational self. Rather than castigate the photograph or the person, we must adopt the patience of Jesus, who sees us as precious in his sight.

These concepts are not new. Pioneering social psychologist Charles Cooley coined the term "looking glass self" in 1902. We have been defining ourselves based on others' perceptions for a long time. The concept of peer pressure may have arisen in the century since, but people have always looked outward as a means of redefining how we perceive ourselves. Cooley affirmed the positive side of this process: "If we never tried to seem a little better than we are, how could we improve or 'train ourselves from the outside inward'? And the same impulse to show the world a better or idealized aspect of ourselves finds an organized expression in the various professions and classes."[61] We do not judge the aspiring lawyer who puts on a suit or the med student who wears a white coat. They are growing into their profession and role, trying it on for size. When we post selfies online, we may be casting ourselves as a jock, a brainiac, a chanteuse, a chef. We are testing whether others will affirm such callings and aspirations. Do these roles fit us? Social media makes the voting fast, easy, and occasionally painful. I hope readers will take the opportunity to create an aspirational selfie for themselves.

What about situations where we are engaging in the humblebrag? We may be posting photos of our new house, our new job, our new car. We are fishing for compliments in barely disguised ways. We can't wait to Instagram vacation photos of ourselves in the sun having fun. Do we ever pause to consider how our perfect images affect those back home? Maybe we do. And maybe we want to make others just a little bit jealous of our home, our family, our success. Doesn't such bragging run counter to biblical calls to humility? Absolutely. Paul challenges Christians in Philippi, "Do nothing from selfish ambition or conceit, but in humility count others more significant than yourselves" (Phil. 2:3 ESV). James teaches us, "God opposes the proud but gives grace to the humble" (James 4:6 ESV). So why are we so quick to share our newest toys and latest accomplishments online?

Goffman reminds us that our fascination with potent signs and symbols of material success are grafted into our social fabric. In 1959, he wrote that American society "seems to have been singled out as an extreme example of wealth-oriented class structure—perhaps because in America the license to employ symbols of wealth and financial capacity to do so are so widely distributed."[62] Those who flaunt their wealth, like the Rich Kids of Instagram, are merely following the social codes handed down from one generation to the next. We may need to actively resist these cultural idols. But these temptations are not new. Jesus addressed the inequities he saw in the Pharisees' guest lists. He challenged his followers to rearrange the seating at the table. At God's heavenly banquet, "All those who exalt themselves will be humbled, and those who humble themselves will be exalted" (Luke 14:11). This doesn't mean that we cannot celebrate a victory or be thankful for a new job in a quick photo. There are definitely times when hard work and persistence deserve recognition. We tread a fine line in social media and must be aware of the temptations embedded in self-imaging. C. S. Lewis wrote that the truly humble person "will not be thinking about humility; he will not be thinking about himself at all. . . . If you think you are not conceited, it means you are very conceited indeed."[63]

Developing Integrity

How to put all of these thoughts in action? Psychologists and philosophers have long ruminated on the mind-body problem. Theologians ruminate on the dual nature of humanity as body and soul. Others counter that we are tripartite in nature: spirit, soul, and body. These rigorous (and ancient) debates overlook a more vexing problem: our *dueling* nature. We are often at odds with our selves, our families, our workplaces, and our communities. Our inward struggles manifest themselves in external conflicts. There is so much drama on (and off) social media. We lash out, get short-tempered, sever relationships with those who've known us longest and cared about us most consistently. Self-sabotage is a universal problem.

The King James Bible refers to this as "the mystery of iniquity" (2 Thess. 2:7). God describes it to Cain in almost animalistic terms: "Sin is crouching at your door; it desires to have you, but you must rule over it" (Gen. 4:7). This struggle can also be expressed in psychoanalytic terms. Moral psychologist C. Fred Alford writes, "Narcissism is neither sick nor healthy. It is the human condition. What is sick or healthy, regressive or progressive, is how individuals come to terms with their narcissism, understood as a longing for perfection, wholeness, and control over self and world."[64] Theologians and psychologists offer perspectives to help us unite and heal our dueling nature, to develop integrity. Sin is a hard habit to break. How do we move from lofty intentions into daily practices?

The lived wisdom of Saint Catherine of Siena (1347–80) may serve as a spiritual guide. The visions and insights she experienced in prayer connect self-knowledge to the knowledge of God. As a nun in the Dominican order, she practiced its core principle: to contemplate and to hand on to others the fruits of contemplation (*contemplari et contemplata aliis trader*).[65] Her great friend, confessor, and biographer, Raymond of Capua, recounts what Jesus told her when she was in prayer: "Do you know, daughter, who you are and who I am? If you know these two things you have beatitude in your grasp. You are she who is not, and I am he who is."[66] What a simple and profound answer to the question of who we are in relation to God. In her most renowned reflections, *The Dialogue*, Catherine peers into her soul as the way to discover God's goodness to us. She communicates God's challenge to those who "would come to perfect knowledge and enjoyment of me, eternal Life: Never leave the knowledge of yourself. Then, put down as you are in the valley of humility, you will know me in yourself, and from this knowledge you will draw all that you need."[67] From a place of humility, we have an opportunity for rebirth and renewal.

Being born again in Catherine's terms serves as an antidote to the blindness of Narcissus. She writes to Raymond of Capua about how the soul seeing "not self for self's sake, but self for God and God for self . . . is then moved to love self in God and God in self like a man who, on looking into the water, sees his image there and seeing himself loves and delights in himself."[68] This is where Narcissus got stuck—becoming fixated upon himself as the most beautiful object he ever imagined. Yet Catherine anticipates the positive side of narcissism, challenging us to push through the process: "If he is wise, he will be moved to love the water rather than himself, for had he not first seen himself, he could not have loved or been delighted by himself."[69] When we encounter our reflection in the water, the tendency is to obsess over ourselves and our appearance. Catherine dares us to first recognize and then embrace the water that provides the reflection.

Rather than turning to the phone in our pocket or purse, Catherine of Siena dares us, "Build yourself a spiritual cell, which you can always take with you, and that is the cell of self-knowledge; you will find there also the knowledge of God's goodness to you." She heals the (false) divide between knowledge of self and knowledge of God by reframing them as insepa-rable. She continues, "There are really two cells in one . . . ; if you dwelt in self-knowledge alone you would despair; if you dwelt in knowledge of God alone you would be tempted to presumption. One must go with the other, and thus you will reach perfection."[70] Studying only ourselves can be depressing. Psychology alone may not provide the relief and insight we seek. Studying only God can make us spiritually proud, impressed by our knowledge. We've all known a person who can quote Bible verses but who may not put those profound truths into practice. We need the knowledge of self (and our limitations) to soften the knowledge of God, which can puff us up. Catherine's concept of this united spiritual cell echoes the positive pride that balances the hubris that can undo us.

Psychology can help us analyze what inspires our selfies. We may Snap just because everyone else is doing it. We may be seeking affirmation that we've failed to experience in childhood via parents, teachers, or friends. We often act out of shadow sides hidden in our subconscious. We may be expressing the best side of ourselves, flowing in the talents and abilities God has given us. We may be fixated on needs or giving freely to those we love. St. Catherine challenges us to see self-inspection as a prerequisite to finding God. In fact, self-knowledge is the beginning of being born anew. Only when we recognize how little we bring to the table do we start to appreciate the generosity of God. When we study our selfies, we can admire our appearance like the beautiful Narcissus. But we must also see the Wonder that extends beyond the frame, unable to be captured within it, that has given us the gift of self-analysis. Admiration for our selves is rooted in the glory of God reflected in us. A clear assessment of our gifts and limitations, our strengths and our sin, is the starting point for swim-ming in the pool of God's grace.

Questions to Consider/Discuss

1. What do you think of the term "healthy narcissism"? What does that look like in your life?

2. How and where do you express your shadow side? Who gets to see it and when? In what ways might it be helpful to your psychological well-being?

3. How can we bring our thoughts and actions, our aspirations and our shortcomings, into alignment? How do you describe or picture integrity?

Selfie Challenge

Photograph your shadow side. Reflect your darker, hidden feelings and mood. You may want to use black and white. Consider how to portray the contrast (or even bridge the divide) between your public and your private self.

Cindy Sherman, untitled #463, 2007/2008. Chromogenic color
print. 68.6 x 72 inches / 174.2 x 182.9 cm (MP# CS-463)

Untitled #463, 2007–2008

7

Instapressure

The Selfie Today

> I try not to be too invasive into my personal life. When I was younger, I used to tweet a lot, everything I was doing and feeling. I can't do that anymore, because it's just giving people too much room to judge. I love posting a good picture, though.
>
> —Kendall Jenner[1]

THE COMPETITION IS BRUTAL at the top. In 2015 Kendall Jenner stole the crown for most-liked Instagram photo of all time from her older sister Kim Kardashian.[2] Kendall's heart-shaped hair unseated Kim's wedding picture with Kanye West. Kendall didn't set out to unseat her sister. On social media, sometimes lightning simply strikes. Kendall Jenner lies on the floor, in a white lace dress, her eyes closed like Sleeping Beauty waiting for a kiss. Her hair unfurls in seven hearts that encircle her head. The pattern echoes the black and white carpet pattern.[3] She appears blissful, transported by thoughts of romance that might even be divine. Kendall revealed the secrets behind the iconic photo to *Vogue*.

Kendall was on a yacht, anchored off Monaco with her sister Kylie, as well as Gigi and Bella Hadid and Hailey Baldwin. "I was having a bad day. I wasn't in the flow. I was like, Everyone sucks."[4] Her friends arranged her hair into hearts. Then came the photo. Kendall debated its merits: "I was lying in bed and messing with it. And I thought, Is this good? And I just posted it, and I remember looking at it right away and having a lot of likes and saying, '*Huh*.'"[5] Eventually, 3.6 million people liked her Instagram post (almost the population of her hometown, Los Angeles). Kendall's image reigned until she was unseated by Justin Beiber's grainy flashback photo of his better days with then-girlfriend Selena Gomez: 3.7 million people "hearted" their approval of Justin and Selena's kiss.[6] Beyoncé more than doubled those numbers with the veiled photo announcing she was pregnant with twins.[7]

Shakespeare wrote, "Uneasy lies the head that wears a crown,"[8] but these celebrities make it look effortless. Their Instagrams are supposed to come across as casual, authentic, and maybe even attainable. Inspired by Kendall, fans from around the world created their own "heart hair" photos. A graphic artist identifying himself as her "secret twin Kirby Jenner" even photoshopped himself into the iconic image (sporting his own hilarious heart hairdo). In the digital age, we all hold in our imaginative hands the tools to alter our appearance, to mirror what's fashionable. Sometimes we're the audience keeping score, watching the online drama unfold. But we're also playing the same social-media game—measuring our progress according to the same metrics of friends and followers, likes and loves. Outsourcing our sense of self-worth is a dangerous, high-stakes game.

We've placed so much faith in technology. Art historian Fred Ritchin writes, "We are busily reinventing media under the guise of what is essentially a marketing term, the 'digital revolution,' not daring to admit, in these perilous times, that what we are really reinventing is ourselves. Media have become, in their easy transcendence of previous limitations of time and space, nearly messianic for us."[9]

We have so much power concentrated in such a tiny and portable device. We can redefine ourselves by the hour and distribute our image across almost any border. Speed, ease, and audience are three distinguishing traits of the selfie that separate it from print photography. Ritchin says, "The production of content and its publication are now considered to be the right of anyone technologically enabled, bypassing conventional editorial and curatorial filters."[10] These celebrities have demonstrated how to control one's image (and build one's own media empire). Geoffrey Bachen suggests, "This really represents the shift of the photograph serving as a memorial function to a communication device."[11]

Perhaps rabid self-imaging is an appropriate response in an era of mass surveillance. We would rather define ourselves than submit our image to others' control. Our pictures are always being taken. To participate in society, we have to provide some form of photo ID. Whenever we pop into a convenience store, withdraw from an automated teller, cruise down the freeway, or reenter the country, our faces and actions are being recorded. Our phones know where we are and maybe even whom we're with. Facial recognition programs do the tagging for us. Our gymnasiums are lined with mirrors so we can admire our progress. We may turn the camera on ourselves to analyze our golf swing or basketball shooting touch. Our smartwatches record our daily steps. We track our heartbeat with precision once previously reserved solely for our babies in utero. We monitor our sleep. Self-surveillance starts early.[12]

Research into why we take selfies has only just begun. Five master's students at Brigham Young University gave frequent selfie takers a list of forty-eight statements that answer "why I take and share selfies."[13] The possibilities included "to socialize," "to express myself," and "to impress people."[14] They then ranked the responses, from statements they most agreed with—"to show people where I am" and "so I can record memories"—to reasons they rejected, such as "to accept the way I look" and "to be someone I'm not."[15] The eighteen- to forty-five-year-old participants selected two statements that were "most like they believe" and "least like they believe." After conducting interviews and analyzing the data, the researchers found three distinct groupings emerged. They labeled these archetypal groups as "the self-publicists," "the communicators," and "the autobiographers."[16] The self-publicists want to share and show events and places to other people, but primarily to set themselves apart. They focus upon themselves as a way to control their personal image. The communicators take and share selfies primarily for communication. They want to show and share information with others. Autobiographers take selfies to record memories and express themselves. They want to show the world who they are and simultaneously learn to accept who they are.

This chapter will consider these three sets of motivations residing behind our selfies today.

Self-Publicists: The Art of Southern California

> We'd all be remiss if we didn't take a moment and thank Narcissus. He doesn't get enough of a shout-out.
>
> —Michael Keaton[17]

Self-promotion is an art in Southern California. So many aspiring actors, models, directors, talk-show hosts, reality-TV stars, and YouTubers compete for the spotlight that self-promotion is the primary art of Southern California. The star-making machinery was established in the entertainment industry by the 1920s. Hollywood studios changed aspiring actors' names, looks, and social calendars in an effort to create a star. Archibald Leach became Cary Grant. Frances Gumm was remade as Judy Garland in *The Wizard of Oz*. A brunette named Norma Jean Mortensen was transformed into the platinum blonde Marilyn Monroe. Agents, publicists, photographers, costumers, and makeup artists dedicated themselves to burnishing these actors' new images. Nowadays, we're all invited to self-promote via social media.

Self-publicists seek to tell their story and show the world who they are. According to the Brigham Young researchers, self-publicists especially want to control their image and present themselves in a positive light. One self-publicist admitted, "I HATE candid pictures of me. I don't feel like I'm photogenic, and when others take pictures that I'm in, I almost always hate the way they turn out. I'm too concerned with how I look and how other people perceive me, so I like the idea of ME being able to take my picture and being in control of how it looks."[18] We may think of self-publicists as vain or egotistical, but their selfies may be rooted in self-doubt. They only want to share extraordinary images of themselves. This goal feels laden with potential performance anxiety and perfectionism (Instagram users, beware!). Self-imaging offers a strong form of self-empowerment and self-determination—controlling their own narrative. But they aren't interested in two-way communication. Their selfies are carefully curated, but they do not see selfies as introspective.[19]

With the publication of *Selfish*, a 448-page collection of Kim Kardashian selfies taken primarily between 2006 and 2014, Kardashian and the selfie phenomenon may have reached an apotheosis.[20] It begins with a photo taken in 1984, when Kim was just four, but focuses primarily on her years of rising fame and association with fellow celebutantes like Paris Hilton and eventual husband Kanye West. Reaction to the collection of photos ranged from enthusiasm to indifference. Laura Bennett of *Slate* expresses our collective conflict: "*Selfish* is an insane project, a document of mind-blowing vanity and deranged perseverance. It's also riveting. I can't recommend it enough."[21] Via shots taken in and around bathroom mirrors, *Selfish* reveals how much work it takes for her glam team to make Kim look so fabulous. Megan Garber of the *Atlantic* notes how the book allows us to "see the *work* that goes into making Kim Kardashian, the person, into Kim Kardashian, the icon. What *Selfish* depicts, more than anything else, is the labor that goes into beauty."[22]

Unfortunately, we tend to see only the self-publicists and Instafamous models' results rather than their process. We fall for the image rather than investigating the lived reality. Photographer Cindy Sherman's *Society Portraits* (2008) (like the one featured in the beginning of this chapter) reveals the gap between the imagined body image and the actual body image. She portrays aged celebrities and mavens trying to hold on to their glamour from a prior era. Keeping up the effortless facade takes even more work as we age. Sherman shows the great sadness that overcomes women who are past what society deems as their prime. Barbara Vinken suggests that Sherman's work "reflects the endeavor for perfection as a distortion to which the rich and the beautiful subject themselves in pursuit of perfection. This perfection can be achieved only at the price of objectification, mortification, death in life, becoming a foreign body to oneself."[23] At some point, the formerly famous become overwhelmed by the work involved in maintaining their image. Self-publicity is exhausting. But the physical and psychological toll is tough to convey to a celebrity while they're still on top (Kim Kardashian) or rising (Kendall Jenner).

What happens when celebrities' fame diminishes? Thankfully, Los Angeles has a celebrity doctor to assess the situation: Drew Pinsky (commonly known as Dr. Drew). He hosted six seasons of the reality television series *Celebrity Rehab with Dr. Drew* on VH1. Dr. Drew coauthored, along with S. Mark Young, *The Mirror Effect: How Celebrity Narcissism Is Seducing America* (2009). They trace how "a whole host of narcissistic traits—extreme self-importance, inflated sense of specialness, vanity, envy, and entitlement—come into play in diva shows like *Real Housewives of Orange County, Kimora: Life in the Fab Lane*, and *Keeping Up with the Kardashians.*"[24] Given his expertise in treating addiction, Dr. Drew reserves his harshest criticism for what he considers the most malicious reality-show format, the train-wreck series. He and Young cite the harsh labels applied to reality-TV stars like Tila Tequila, Paris Hilton, Nicole Ritchie, and Kim Kardashian. "They have been dubbed celebutantes (debutante-age girls famous only because of their wealth, lifestyle, and perceived glamour); celebuspawn (offspring of a celebrity or celebrity couple); and most cruelly, celebutards (stars known for ignorant behavior or opinions)."[25] Why do these young women subject themselves to such scrutiny?

Dr. Drew and Dr. Young distinguish between egotists and narcissists. For egotists, their "self-importance is unshakeable, so much so that it generally allows them to disregard reality." They are truly the center of their own universe (and media empire). They operate out of confidence. In contrast, narcissism "springs from an opposite relationship with the self: not self-improvement, but a *disconnection* with oneself. . . . True narcissists are not self-aware." The average viewer may not notice a difference in the two kinds of self-publicists. The authors cite seven traits classically associated with narcissism: authority, entitlement, exhibitionism, exploitativeness, self-sufficiency, superiority, and vanity. A healthy narcissist will reign in these tendencies to moderated levels. The pathological do not merely crave an audience (as do committed egotists like the Kardashians); they desperately need an audience to cover their fragile sense of self. Dr. Drew concludes, "For the narcissist, the whole world is a mirror; life is spent in constant pursuit of a gratifying reflection, a beautiful self-image to stave off feelings of internal emptiness."[26] Narcissists perform not to stroke a healthy ego but to compensate for the gaping hole inside their self-image.

Given over twenty years of experience dealing with celebrities and their addictions, Dr. Drew and Dr. Young conclude that "reality TV personalities are more narcissistic than any other segment of performers."[27] Narcissists will likely exhibit at least five of these nine behaviors:

1. A grandiose sense of self-importance
2. A preoccupation with fantasies of unlimited success, power, brilliance

3. A sense of specialness

4. A need for excessive admiration

5. A heightened sense of entitlement, leading to unreasonable expectations

6. A tendency to be interpersonally exploitative

7. A lack of empathy

8. An envy of other people or a belief that other people envy them

9. A tendency toward arrogant behavior or attitude[28]

These destructive blind spots that we all potentially share get heated up under the glare of television lights. The attention, gifts, and compliments doled out in an industry fueled by publicity only add to the delusions and expectations. Psychiatrist Robert B. Millman coined the term "acquired situational narcissism" to describe how this fawning behavior in the entertainment industry (and from adoring audiences) may heighten celebrities' narcissism.[29] We do not know what childhood trauma or inability to attach to parental love and affection might have drawn these personalities to Hollywood. Reality TV feeds their manias rather than healing them.

Self-publicity is fun while it works, but it is tough to sustain. Audiences' attention and affection are both limited. When hearty egotism turns toward self-destructive narcissism, the fall can be swift. We may tune in for one round of the talk-show circuit of confession, repentance, and restoration, but rarely two. Jesus challenges us to forgive one another seventy-seven times (Matt. 18:21–22), but most reality stars are renewed for only a season or two.

I can respect the self-publicists who turned their limited talent into social-media capital and a highly profitable enterprise. We might consider them sellouts, but they would likely argue they "sold in" on their own terms. Don't hate the players; hate the game. The astute Susan Sontag surmises, "A capitalist society requires a culture based on images. It needs to furnish vast amounts of entertainment in order to stimulate buying and anesthetize the injuries of class, race, and sex. . . . The camera's twin capacities, to subjectivize reality and to objectify it, ideally serves these needs and strengthens them—a spectacle for the masses and surveillance for the rulers."[30] Self-publicists have mastered the art of the social media spectacle. They have learned how to "break the internet" by fashioning themselves into NSFW (not suitable for work) objects. What will be their legacy? A generation of admirers wondering how much dignity must be sacrificed in order to be "liked" (or elected)? Christians' challenge will be to resist the temptation to treat self-publicists as objects. We must peer behind the lens to find the hurting narcissist that may reside within.

Jesus had nothing but love and patience for the train wrecks he encountered. Jesus repeatedly challenged his followers to have eyes to see and ears to hear things from God's perspective. Consider his patient perception in conversation with a Samaritan woman in John 4. While she draws water from a well, Jesus asks her for a drink. The focus soon shifts from physical thirst to the need for long-term spiritual sustenance, "living water" (v. 10). She recognizes that Jesus has overstepped social barriers between Samaritans and Jews to talk to her. Perhaps she also had things she was ashamed of and didn't want to surface or talk about. Jesus sees past her decisions that have resulted in multiple partners (five husbands) and gets to the core of her need. Where can we find a wellspring of love that will keep us from a gnawing spiritual hunger? The woman asks Jesus, "Where can you get this living water?" (v. 11). Jesus identifies himself as that source—"I am he" (v. 26)—even for the most self-destructive self-publicist.

Communicators: Collecting Experiences

> The most grandiose result of the photographic enterprise is to give us the sense that we can hold the whole world in our heads—as an anthology of images.
>
> —Susan Sontag[31]

We can almost hold the entire world in our hands via smartphones. We follow our friends' stories via Snapchat and Instagram. We can see what they're experiencing via Facebook Live. We can spot any corner of the globe via Google Earth. Best of all, we don't have to collect or store these images. Social media does it for us.

Communicators take selfies to share part of their life, to show people "where I am" and "what I'm doing." The research done by Brigham Young students determined that communicators want to tell their story, to be part of the ongoing conversation that is social media. They do not use selfies for self-analysis. A survey participant noted, "I don't feel like I need them [self-ies] for feeling important or to get noticed."[32] For communicators, social media is all about two-way exchange. It is an open invitation to connect. Posting a selfie is an easy way to let friends and family know we're thinking of them. Communicators want to share life even when they're apart. Selfies are a way of reaching out, including others, building community. Communicators come closest to posting selfies selflessly.

Parents may resent selfies as a waste of time. Teachers may consider them an unnecessary distraction. Adults would be wise to acknowledge their importance as a growing means of communication. Some write letters. Others make phone calls. The next generation prefers to text—visually. This can be a communal act, designed to include others (rather than merely draw attention to ourselves). Our affinity for this form of communication (as opposed to self-publicity) makes us susceptible to pride. It seems more noble. Communicators can point to Scripture verses like the opening line of Psalm 133—"How good and pleasant it is when God's people live together in unity!"—to justify our online activity. We are living out the charge of Dietrich Bonhoeffer to practice "life together": "Let him who is not in community beware of being alone."[33] Preserving a Snapchat streak is an inherently relational and communal act. It is a lo-fi test of our loyalty and attentiveness. The most valuable social-media platforms were created to enhance communication. We see our selfies as an open invitation to respond.

How many photographs are in your stream? Digital photography enabled us to shift from taking select images to obsessively documenting almost every moment of our lives. To what end? When we are taking photographs on vacation or curating images on Instagram, what are we collecting? We may express our aesthetic on Pinterest or Tumblr, but what kind of activity are we engaging in? Sontag suggests, "To collect photographs is to collect the world."[34] But why *so many* photographs? "Photographs really are experience captured," Sontag says, "and the camera is the ideal arm of consciousness in its acquisitive mood."[35] The desire for new things to photograph and post and celebrate can result in an endless pursuit of peak experiences. There is a legitimate high that comes from living life boldly and purposefully. Yes, you only live once—YOLO—but when our love for life crosses over to a love of the photograph of us loving life, we may have lost the meaning amid the experience. Sontag warns that "photograph collections can be used to make a substitute world, keyed to exalting or consoling or tantalizing images."[36] Do we love our photographs more than the gift of life itself?

The ease with which we can take photographs makes taking them so tempting. When we paid to develop each image, photographs were taken much more sparingly. Consider those old family photographs. Great-grandparents may have passed down a single photo of their children. Perhaps they couldn't afford more. Or perhaps they simply thought differently at that time about the purpose of a photograph. One printed photo of a parent or child may have sufficed when photographs were seen as a record of existence. In the digital era, the democratization of images makes photos more like the outsourcing of memory. The camera remembers so we don't have to. As Sontag writes, "Photographs are not so much an instrument of memory as an invention of it or a replacement."[37]

So why do I take so many pictures on vacation? What kinds of memories and experiences am I trying to store up? Sontag suggests that rather than relishing the moments when we're away, we may be dealing with our insecurities within a strange place or space. Consider how quickly we retreat to our phones when we're caught in an awkward spot. With my phone out, I don't have to engage with those around me. If I don't feel part of the scene, I can photograph it instead. In holding up the camera, I may actually draw others toward me. My social status may rise (at least momentarily) as people pay attention to my lens, my perspective on the world. Sontag says, "As photographs give people an imaginary possession of a past that is unreal, they also help people to take possession of space in which they are insecure" (like tourism!).[38] Is this how we deal with the *other* on our vacations? New places, new faces, and new experiences can be scary. We can mask our cultural incompetence or signal our lack of facility with language by carrying a camera. The smartphone can be our defense mechanism. The iPhone in pano mode cries out, "Don't judge me—I'm just a tourist!"

I have hiked up so many mountains in search of a perfect photo. I've dragged my family down trails they never wanted to traverse. Sometimes the visual payoffs are spectacular. Yet all too often I fail to enjoy the journey. Instead, I focus on the end goal—the photograph that reveals how intrepid, adventurous, and exotic I can be. Sontag's insights convict me: "A

Kayla Ferguson

Machu Pichu selfie

way of certifying experience, taking photographs is also a way of refusing it—by limiting experience to a search for the photogenic, by converting experience into an image, a souvenir. Travel becomes a strategy for accumulating photographs."[39] What does your search for a mountain vista look like? We may not enjoy the journey or even care about the destination. We photograph what is expected of us.

Having made a commitment of time and money to travel, perhaps I feel the need to justify my decision. Posting exotic photographs on Facebook or Instagram communicates wealth, power, and artistry. It also redeems the time spent away from work or family. We have to come back from vacation with something to show, don't we? Sontag suggests, "Using a camera appeases the anxiety which the work-driven feel about not working when they are on vacation and supposed to be having fun. They have something to do that is like a friendly imitation of work: they can take pictures."[40] Some of the most driven cultures on earth are also the most snap-happy. As the sun sets, I can be found on the shoreline, searching for the perfect image. No time for lounging in a beach chair. I want the reflection in the water, not in my personal life. There is a conquering impulse behind the relentless pursuit of the perfect shot.[41] I salute those who can find rest in a spectacular sunset. All too often, I approach it as yet another experience to be captured (and shared).

In the Psalms, God challenges us to "be still, and know that I am God" (Ps. 46:10). I am rarely still, *especially* on vacation. When the stated goal is rest and relaxation, I'm usually snapping as many images as possible. Taking photos can be an odd form of disengagement. It is a way to collect experiences while standing outside of them at the same time. When we post a selfie, we can comment on a situation rather than be invested in the moment we're in. I haven't experienced enough of what poet Gerard Manley Hopkins called "the selfless self of self, most strange, most still."[42] Self-reflection could be a form of retreat, an opportunity to assess our health, our well-being, the status of our soul. I relish experiences more than retreats. And I can justify it as a way of celebrating the God-given gift of life. Yet I spend so much time documenting the life I'm living that I wonder if I've missed God in the midst of it all. Be still. Know God. Constant connection with our phone may result in no God. Thankfully, "if we confess our sins, he is faithful and just and will forgive us our sins and purify us from all unrighteousness" (1 John 1:9). This is the fresh start we all long for.

What are the practices of healthy communicators? They do not drag friends and family out of their way just to capture an epic photo. They do not do it for the "gram."[43] They share their lowlights as well as their highlights online. They do not enhance their images to boost their reputation. They are not out to impress (honestly, isn't there more than a little self-promoter in us all?). They do not fear missing out on a photo-worthy moment. They can put their camera down. They can cherish the memory without preserving it. It may be an act of faith to take back our privacy, to not overshare.

Could we hold back a few photos as private moments that aren't meant to be shared? For our children's birthday parties, we attempted a social-media blackout. We ask guests not to post photos from the party. If there are friends who weren't invited, we don't want them to see photos and feel excluded or left out. Sensitivity to others' FOMO (fear of missing out) supersedes our own lust for YOLO. I want to make sure that our #blessed life and celebratory selfies do not end up pouring coals on our friends' heads. Our kids' accomplishments, a new job, our perfect vacation are lovely things to celebrate, but what's the downside? "Facebook envy" is a verified phenomenon.[44] The longer we stare at others' idealized lives on social media (without sharing our own updates), the more depressed we get. The conclusion: "Facebook is a lifestyle magazine featuring my friends, who are doing it better than me."[45] I don't want my #blessed photos to cause jealousy in others. Pride doesn't look good on any of us, even when masked as a humblebrag. A #gloatie is inherently dangerous. Gratitude can be a form of public praise, but can't it also be private? We don't have to communicate all our peak experiences to give God the glory. Perhaps we can recover a more robust relationship with God by allowing some of our most precious moments to be private rather than public. Even Kendall Jenner advises restraint. "You don't want to do too many posts. . . . You want to leave them wanting to come back." She summed up this secret in one word: "Mystery!"[46]

Autobiographers: Trying on New Selfies

> I don't want to write an autobiography because I would become public property with no privacy left.
>
> —Stephen Hawking[47]

We used to make photo albums. We would get our photos printed at a drugstore or camera shop and then sort through the images, usually twenty-four or thirty-six at a time. The best ones, the keepers, made it into a scrapbook. We had so many misfires and exposure and focus problems that it might take a year to fill up an entire album. For the most part, those images remained private, tucked away, inside our houses, for our eyes only.[48] They may have been passed down as family heirlooms. We would never have dreamed of subjecting our awkward selves to public comments. Digital media changed all that. Now we rarely print photos. It is cool to have all our pictures online. We can scroll through seasons of life to find the selfie we want to share in seconds. We let our photos do the talking. Yet the flow of images generated by those we follow is so voluminous that we may feel overwhelmed, drowning in our friends' current.

Autobiographers take selfies to record memories and express themselves. The Brigham Young University researchers found that they "are truly interested in authoring their story and in the process, hope to experience self-discovery."[49] Don't we want others to know who we are, what we think, and how we feel? It reassures autobiographers to know that "an honest portrait of themselves was seen." There is a bit of disconnect when it comes to their motives regarding self-image. Respondents may check boxes in the survey that indicate they aren't trying to show off their looks or get validation from others, but in one-on-one interviews they will admit, "I'm concerned with the perception of others."[50]

We are all engaged in self-discovery. Questions like "Who am I?" "How do I look?" and "Am I desirable?" dominate adolescence, but they never go away. We always seem to be in transition. When we view ourselves through the lens of social media, it creates a bit of space. Jill Walker Rettberg writes, "Putting a filter on our selfies, or framing them by placing them in a blog or an Instagram feed, gives them a distance that makes them new to us. We see ourselves and our surroundings as if we are outside of ourselves, through a retro filter or in the same poses and layouts as we see fashion models or homes in magazine spreads."[51] We cast ourselves to star in our own life story.

Selfies allow us to try on personas and perform for the camera. It can be frivolous and fun goofing around with our image. Snapchat is a safe place to not be taken too seriously. We can cut loose with the promise that our photos will disappear (or if they're downloaded, we can track the creepers who snatched them). The stakes rise with Instagram. We may not enjoy the night out with friends until we get the perfect shot to summarize it. We measure ourselves via metrics. How many likes? There's additional Instapressure on dating sites. Am I swiped left or right on Tinder? We know who stands out as the mini-celebrities in our social-media circles. They may have the Instafamous numbers to prove it. Social media raises the stakes on our selfies. We may get a dopamine rush when we receive notifications about new followers. This endless game of self-promotion and curating our social-media profiles can be exhausting. Managing our Twitter feed, keeping streaks alive on Snapchat, or talking to our followers on YouTube can drain our best energies away. Ever suffer from performance anxiety? This happens when we treat ourselves as clickbait. It is a short leap from objectifying others to objectifying ourselves. The provocation of some self-publicists can make it tough for an old-fashioned autobiographer-type to compete.

How might a simple effort to document our lives devolve into a daily referendum on our self-worth? In a Pew Research Center survey, 51 percent of eighteen- to twenty-five-year-olds said that becoming famous was their generation's either first or second most important life goal.[52] Fame is one way to seek a kind of eternity. Teens may develop an intense connection to a particular celebrity they admire or aspire to be like. Devotion may morph into a one-sided, voyeuristic, parasocial relationship. As we become enmeshed with the celebrity's life, we may comment about minute details of their behavior. These "nonrelationships are based on the illusions of interaction and intimacy."[53]

Dr. Drew and Young worry about the dangers of the "mirror effect": imitative behavior cued by how we see celebrities solve their problems.[54] The vast majority of people will not fall into these traps. But the subtle, pervasive influence that arises from consuming self-promoters' lives sinks into our collective psyche. Dr. Drew observes, "The average teenager's sense of the boundaries between everyday life and stardom often deteriorates until it's replaced with something like a delusion. The young person who admires a celebrity begins to believe she can *be* that person."[55] A steady diet of *Hannah Montana* might lead to a fixation on being discovered on *The Voice*.

When our dreams are frustrated, we may sink into depression ("I'm a loser") or a deep-seated aggression ("They're a loser"). Once-loyal fans may end up tearing down a celebrity via online chatter to make themselves feel better about their own blocked goals.[56] They can quickly unite around a shared sense of mission: "Let's all destroy that stupid idiot and take over her privileged life."[57] We may enter into social media thinking ourselves above the fray. "I'm not here to feel better about myself. I feel good about my self-image." But as the numbers rise for self-promoters, the autobiographers may wonder what's left for them. When measuring our average days against friends' idealized images, we may envy or even hate those closest to us.

Idealized images on Instagram can impact parents as well as teens. The pressures on parents, especially mothers, to construct a home life as picture-perfect as that of an Instamom like Amber Fillerup Clark can be enormous. Rob Fishman runs Niche, an ad network for online influencers who are paid to embed products in their social media posts, what's known as "native advertising." Fishman said, "We're seeing people following almost idealized versions of themselves. It's this attainable perfection."[58] What an insidious combination. Is "attainable perfection" possible for fallen humanity? No, it is an illusion, a ruse that does not conform to our experience of our selves or other people. Only God is perfect. We always have a shadow side. John makes it clear: "If we claim to be without sin, we deceive ourselves and the truth is not in us" (1 John 1:8). Pioneering mommy blogger Heather Armstrong has seen a shift from discussing the challenges and frustrations of parenting to "an air-brushed, Pinterest-ready version of parenthood, one that can leave readers feeling jealous, inadequate, or ashamed when they almost inevitably fall short."[59] There are so many financial incentives to convey a perfect image. Armstrong says, "Because the way to make money now is through sponsorships, we've lost the grit, truth, and messiness. . . . It's all staged. It's all fake. It's like, 'How many photos did you have to take to get that one photo?'"[60] Where does the imperfect parent find consolation?

Relief arises when we acknowledge that we are not perfect, when we cease striving for an absurd ideal. I admire the honesty communicated by my friend Aarti Sequeira of the Food Network. She has juggled the pressures of becoming a celebrity chef and a new mother with remarkable aplomb. Her selfies are comic and honest and glamorous and less-than-perfect. Her winsome Christian faith comes through in her smile and in her acknowledgment of the struggles she and husband, Brendan McNamara, have faced as parents and performers. We will never be Instaperfect. We may want to abandon that exhausting ideal now rather than later. Dr. Drew prescribes seven ways to regain a healthy sense of perspective:

1. Strive for increased self-insight and embrace the concept of something greater
2. Practice rigorous honesty
3. Keep things simple and live up to commitments
4. Spend time with a broad range of people
5. Share your feelings
6. Learn to appreciate the feelings of others
7. Be of service[61]

These are simple ways to recover some balance and rediscover the value of our own lives. Rooting our worth in God's image of us allows us to rise above comparisons. Retaining such groundedness will not be easy. The digital temptations to resort to an airbrushed self are pervasive.

The Instapressure builds as soon as we start scrolling. We get anxious when we're about to be photographed, because we fear the camera's disapproval. What if the all-seeing lens magnifies our blemishes or imperfections

Aarti Sequeira

Birthday selfie

for all the world to see? Even before the advent of social media, Sontag had concluded that "people want the idealized image: a photograph looking their best. They feel rebuked when the camera doesn't return an image of themselves as more attractive than they really are."[62]

Photographs have been retouched from their beginning. At the 1855 Exposition Universalle in Paris, a German photographer dazzled crowds with his technique for retouching a negative. Sontag says, "The news that the camera would lie made getting photographed much more popular."[63] Body modification and alterations were initially reserved for the rich. They could afford to hire the best portrait painters and fire those who failed to deliver a flattering image. Art history is laden with idealized images of kings and queens portrayed as they wished to appear. Photoshop made body modification available to all, as simple as shifting pixels.

Dove's "Campaign for True Beauty," which started with a survey of three thousand women in ten countries, revealed that only 2 percent considered themselves beautiful. Their 2006 "Evolution" video chronicled how easily a digital makeover transforms models into unattainable ideals.[64] In the three-minute "Real Beauty Sketches" video from 2013, women described their appearance to a forensic artist.[65] The ladies' self-criticism is quite detailed. Then someone else enters and describes the same women to the artist. The far more generous descriptions from strangers result in demonstrably different portraits. Confronted by the beauty of how other women see and describe them, the subjects shed healing tears. Dove's "Real Beauty Sketches" became the most watched ad on YouTube of all time. It was translated and uploaded in twenty-five different languages.[66] Dove's message: "You're more beautiful than you think," resounded around the globe.

In 2015 an Instafamous Australian model decided to reveal the painful truths behind the images she was posting. After amassing more than a million followers across Snapchat, YouTube, Tumblr, and Instagram, nineteen-year-old Essena O'Neill declared, "Social media is not real life. It's purely contrived images and edited clips ranked against each other. . . . And it consumed me."[67] She shut down all of her accounts except for Instagram. There, she altered the captions on her photos, revealing her true feelings at the time. On a close-up selfie of her face, O'Neill wrote, "I had acne here, this is a lot of makeup. I was smiling because I thought I looked good. Happiness based on aesthetics will suffocate your potential here on earth." On a photo taken along Australia's rugged Sunshine Coast, O'Neill admitted, "Only reason we went to the beach this morning was to shoot these bikinis because the company paid me and also I looked good to society's standards. I was born and won the genetic lottery." It is helpful to find an Instafamous model admitting she was paid to push products to her followers. Her candor regarding her appearance is also intriguing. It is a thin line between hubris and humilty. O'Neill urged her followers, "Read between the lines, or ask yourself, 'why does someone post a photo?'"[68] She started asking core questions that we all must consider about the relationship between perfectionism, capitalism, and our selves.

O'Neill's dramatic exit from social media sparked more criticism than praise. Former friends called it "100 percent self-promotion." Two months later, O'Neill responded with an email to her followers. She reiterated, "I was lost, with serious problems so beautifully hidden. . . . If anything my social media addiction, perfectionist personality and low self esteem made my career."[69] She longed to start a new life and backed that up with clear, dramatic actions. O'Neill was accused of making it all up, being a hypocrite, staging a hoax, and being a genius manipulator. By calling into question the entire capitalist enterprise of women selling themselves in order to sell products, O'Neill attacked core tenets of social media. We rarely stop to think about the companies who are actually selling us to advertisers every time we like an image. We have become so consumed by consumption that anyone who opts out of the system may be subject to abuse (O'Neill even received death threats). To her credit, O'Neill has honored her commitment to no social media.

Should autobiographers abandon social media? By no means. There must be sustainable ways to document our lives without losing ourselves in pursuit of likes. But if seeking online approval starts to spark psychic pain, be wary rather than weary. One may have to sacrifice selfies for long-term health, like O'Neill did. What about those who feel called to record their story via social media? How might we proceed in faith rather than fear?

The Orthodox Christian tradition encourages us to recognize the beauty and gifts already inherent within us. Nonna Verna Harrison assures us that "God is the one who makes us who we are. He makes each individual unique so that we are not all photocopies of one another. Each of us reveals God's creativity in a different way."[70] Apple tapped into this on the iPhone X with authentication via Face ID. Perhaps that is also why face swaps look so strange. Snapchat equips us to strip away our face and paste it onto another person (or thing). It looks inherently wrong, downright comic, in its absurdity. An app that entertains can also affirm: "Your face was made only for you." We should cherish God's gift. We are the face of God. So why don't we always feel that way and live with that confidence? Why do we fail to recognize God's beauty and goodness in others? Blame it on the fall, for how sin has distorted our self-image. Gregory of Nyssa compares the image of God in us to a mirror covered with dirt. The light of God may shine onto the mirror, but it cannot be reflected when the mirror is dirty. In his essay "On the Beatitudes," Gregory writes, "Evil, however, overlaying the Godlike pattern, has made the good useless to you, hidden under curtains of shame. If, by conscientious living, you wash away once more the filth that has accumulated on your heart, the Godlike beauty will again shine forth for you."[71] As the Spirit cleanses our hearts and purifies our minds, our vision becomes much clearer. Judgment and shame are washed away. The fullness of our beauty is revealed.

While I admire the chutzpah of the self-promoter who controls her own image, I wonder what is lost when we only view social media as a one-way form of communication. We lose the opportunity to be in active relationship with others and may end up cut off and alone (like Echo and Narcissus). As a communicator, I enjoy keeping up with friends and family via social media. When I am solely focused on communicating with others, I may miss the experience itself, cutting myself off from my surroundings for the sake of reaching an audience. The autobiographer who is in the moment, making memories and sharing with others, may come closest to approximating God's best for social media. The danger (and Instapressure) comes from defining our worth via others' responses to our selfies. We must proceed with the powerful understanding that only the individual-in-the-community is the image of God.[72]

Questions to Consider/Discuss

1. Analyze the last five selfies you posted. Which of the three types (self-publicists, communicators, autobiographers) seems to best characterize the impetus behind them? Is there a different category and motivation that the researchers might have missed?

2. Which kind of selfie taker most annoys you and why? How does God view them? What's one thing Jesus may be asking of you?

Selfie Challenge

Think about how you envision yourself and who you'd like to be. Create a photo of that aspirational self—the self(ie) you're becoming. Print it and put it up where you will see it every day. Consider keeping that powerful image private—for your eyes only.

Macaque selfie

Augmented and Transfigured

The Selfie Tomorrow

We don't think of our future normally as experiences. We think of
our future as anticipated memories.

—Daniel Kahneman, Nobel laureate in economics
and professor of psychology at Princeton University[1]

THOSE WHO DERIDE THE SELFIE as an empty form of self-promotion
that requires no skill whatsoever may be encouraged by the discovery
that even a macaque monkey in Indonesia photographed herself. Nature
photographer David Slater set up his camera in North Sulawesi hoping
that the local inhabitants would be intrigued enough to press the shutter
button. The macaques took plenty of blurry photos, failing to understand
that subjects are supposed to hold still to get the best results. The framing and presence in this shot by Naruto, a six-year-old macaque, was so
perfect that it became an online sensation, which meant the possibility
of hefty profits. One problem to sort out: who owned the image—the

photographer or the monkey? American courts ultimately ruled that an animal cannot own a copyright (and neither can the photographer who provided the camera).[2]

This unexpected court case illustrates the contentious issues that continue to swirl around self-imaging. Notions of power and property remain remarkably relevant. It has never been easier to take a self-portrait—even an untrained monkey can do it! When everyone can take a selfie, the value of individual images may be fading. Veteran press photographers trained on film are annoyed by digital photographers' obsession with the screen on the back of their cameras. They refer to the editing that occurs amid the action as "chimping" (a put-down derived from the actions of a chimpanzee).[3] They wonder what kind of photographer looks down at a screen, pressing buttons, during an event? The answer is, increasingly, the twenty-first-century kind. Digital photographers may fire back that they'd rather be an animal than an old-style "shooter" linked to the early days of photojournalism. Taking someone's photograph can be a kind of violence. We are still figuring out how to juggle care for ourselves and others and God's world with a camera almost constantly in our hands.

How shall we practice an authentic faith in a pixelated era? Rapid technological change is pushing us with reckless abandon into uncharted ethical areas. Some changes may be easy to embrace. We have expanded our reach. We can see more and reach further than ever before. For people of faith, called to go and make disciples of all nations (Matt. 28:18–20), the opportunity to reach the far corners of the globe via social media is quite enticing. Yet many have retrenched, apparently threatened by people who do not already look or think like us. The twenty-first century is global, polyglot, diverse. In all that variety, our reach will exceed our grasp. We have to be willing to surrender a certain amount of control. Consider our images. Once we have taken a photo and posted it for all the world to see, we have lost control of that image. It can be morphed, blended, and photoshopped into all kinds of strange and disconcerting memes. We can be co-opted into a surrealistic painting or melded into someone else's dream. Once our photo is on the internet, almost anyone can monkey with it. Ask former congressman Anthony Weiner, now a registered sex offender, how quickly a political career can unravel. The wrong photo in the wrong hands can undo our life in an instant.

Propriety and privacy are important concepts to master when our reach exceeds our wisdom.

We will also be challenged by the rate of change. It has never been easier to distribute our images instantaneously around the globe. Fred Ritchin notes, "In the digital environment the new photography is nearly eye-to-mind. Unlike the analog version, it does not require processing and is capable of being immediately transmitted worldwide."[4] There is no longer any lag time. All is available for immediate broadcast, no developing or reflection required. Yet faith requires patience, endurance, stillness. A fast-paced culture challenges our spiritual health. It is easy to feel overwhelmed by the speed with which new opportunities and applications arise. Teenagers fiddling with computer code have undermined long-established institutions almost overnight. Expedia replaced travel agents. Lyft and Uber threatened taxis. Google's driverless cars may send truckers to an early retirement. Napster's file-sharing app nearly leveled the music industry. Netflix and Amazon muscled into movies and television at a remarkable pace. Even our most vaunted institutions like democracy were seemingly unprepared for the rate of change. Fake news shared via Facebook assaulted the bulwark of democracy, "a well-informed citizenry," in the 2016 US presidential election. Creative destruction in the new economy doesn't ask if we're ready to make a change.

In the twentieth century we debated, "How are we different from monkeys?" The twenty-first-century question seems to be shaping up as, "How are we different from machines?" Is the singularity coming? How close are we to merging with robots or cloning ourselves? These will be key questions as the lines between augmented reality and the authentically human continue to blur. The ability to edit our images coincides with scientists' ability to isolate and potentially alter our DNA. We have reduced ourselves to code. With augmented reality, we apply an extra layer or "skin" atop the world we reside in. Snapchat used augmented reality to transform the selfie via lenses. Snap users embraced the opportunity to apply flower crowns, rosy cheeks, and cat ears to their faces.[5] Thousands of pets were subjected to face-swapping with their owners. The results were strange, disorienting, and hilarious. World lenses allow users to transform objects within view by, for example, having a cloud barf rainbows.[6] By constantly rotating and withdrawing the popular lenses, Snapchat keeps users engaged, checking back in for updates and surprises. The introduction of Spectacles made

Snap selfie

such augmentation even easier to implement.[7] A phone is no longer necessary to add emojis, captions, stickers, and filters to your snaps. Snapchat made it easier than ever for us to layer a new skin atop the world.

Filters built into our smartphones allow us to alter our appearance. Skin smoothing, face narrowing, and eye widening are available at the touch of a button. Caucasian beauty standards are baked into Samsung's appliance. The free Meitu app has been available in Asia since 2008. It offers users a virtual face-lift to smooth out blemishes, remove acne, or firm wrinkles. *Business Insider* says the app really shines in "'hand-drawn' mode that is like a Snapchat filter on steroids. It slims jawlines, enlarges eyes, and adds a bit of sparkle to the whole package. Basically, it makes you look like a cartoon."[8] Among the filters available are these: "youthful," "angelic," or the goth-like "baroness." The results can be hilarious. Images of Donald

Trump have been put through Meitu with frighteningly comical results. FaceApp allows users to envision themselves in old age or to try on a different gender.[9] In the digital age, our bodies are fully adjustable. One major problem with FaceApp: the "hot" filter actually lightened people's skin color.[10] Code can reflect and reinforce racial bias.

Our ability to manipulate images, including our face and body, places us in a precarious position. Initial photos are just the beginning of a process of manipulation that buffs, boosts, and polishes our digital selves. Students who grew up playing Nintendo's Wii have always been comfortable creating a portable Mii. We have dropped our avatars into everything from *Guitar Hero* to *Half-Life*. Surrogates now speak for us via Bitmojis, personal avatars that come in all kinds of shapes and sizes with built-in responses like "Amazing," "Love it," and "Yaaaaas."[11] Thanks to facial tracking, the Animojis (animated emojis) introduced with the iPhone X can transform our selfies into talking chickens or singing monkeys. Bitmojis are faster and more convenient than sending a selfie. If an earlier generation turned to Hallmark cards, a digital age can depend on these personalized electronic answers. Animojis and Bitmojis are a playful way to respond, but the more we rely on bits and bytes to stand in for our authentic selves, the more we reduce ourselves and others to objects. The initial joy of scrolling through our Snapchat feed can devolve into a daily chore to complete. We may eventually look back and consider selfies a quaint form of something approximating face-to-face communication, something we used to do in the good old days, when I took the time to send you my actual face. Consider how revolutionary it already seems to take the time to show up in person. Enjoying a cup of coffee, having a face-to-face conversation, and exchanging a physical hug are acts of resistance in an accelerated and augmented era.

The cultural debates swirling around questions of sexuality (like "Who can pee where?") will seem so quaint, so early twenty-first century, when we start to really debate, "How much augmentation is allowed and/or how much genetic purity is necessary to separate humans from machines?" I do not expect us to agree anytime soon on who has rights, when they start, or when they end. Whether we are talking about abortion or euthanasia or transgender issues, we are arguing about human beings and what they can do with their bodies and when. We are also simultaneously arguing about the rights of animals and debating whether it is our duty to protect them. Some march for the rights of the unborn, others protest on behalf of orcas. If we do not figure out how to protect the environment of polar bears, we all may be facing an apocalypse soon. I maintain that the core question amid it all remains, "What is a human?" What is our calling? What is our responsibility? The answers are found in the beginning of the Bible, in Genesis, where God sets us apart as image and likeness, as male and female in community, with responsibility to cultivate and care for creation.

This book has been an effort to broaden our understanding of the long, celebrated history of self-portraiture and to appreciate the thought and artistry that can often accompany our finest work. It is a blessing to be able to communicate our thoughts, to convey our words and images to friends (and strangers) far and wide. With this great power comes considerable responsibility. In reflecting on our self-imaging, we discover competing claims about humanity in Scripture. We are made in the image of God. We are crowned a little lower than the angels. But we are also capable of demonic acts that attack others and even murder God's image. So how do we engage in self-imaging with the best of intentions rather than depraved inclinations? How do we love ourselves and our neighbors via our digital devices?

I will conclude by exploring four shifts, grounded in Scripture and rooted in church history, that may help us respond to the future with faith rather than fear. These are shifts in emphasis, changes in communication strategies, not capitulations to our times. I am not implying that we abandon core tenets of faith practices, like the preaching of the Word or gathering for worship. I am suggesting that we reach back to earlier eras, when images were the primary means of communicating God's story, as a way to refine our public witness in a digital age. It may work just as well to adopt a countercultural stance to the selfie era. I truly admire those who dare to resist digital domination. Consider these conclusions aesthetics for ascetics.

From Words to Images to the Word

> The more photographs you take, the less time you'll spend looking at each one.
>
> —David Hockney[12]

Images used to be costly. Only the rich and powerful could afford to hire a painter or sculptor to preserve their visage. Photography was more affordable. It took twenty dollars to buy a roll of film and develop the images.

Each photo cost approximately one dollar to produce. Many were not worth keeping. Consequently, we thought carefully about each photo we took. Was it the right framing, the proper angle, the best lighting possible? Jill Walker Rettberg recalls, "The cost wasn't simply financial; we also had to consider how many shots were left on the roll of film, as we wouldn't want to run out of film before we had captured a range of interesting images. With digital photography, individual photos have no cost."[13] We are limited only by our storage capacities. Thanks to the cloud, we live in an image-saturated age.

This is a book about images. I've used words to sharpen our sense of sight. We have tended to think of words and images as distinct forms of communication. Hopefully, we've discovered that this is a false divide. We now engage in visual texting. Words have been supplanted, or rather combined, with visual replies in the form of photos. These pictures aren't always meant to convey a thousand words—maybe just ten or twelve. It requires a robust visual literacy to translate these images into meaning. What are we communicating via our Instagrams? How do we convey care and concern through an ephemeral medium like Snapchat?

While some may bemoan this shift to image-driven communication, we should be encouraged that God created humanity in his image and likeness; male and female he created them. We were meant to relate to each other, to be in community. It is not good for humans to be alone. Social media is a natural extension of our God-given calling to relate to our surroundings, our fellow animals, and our fellow humans. We've been told to think before we speak, but do we think before we tweet? Social media has empowered us to communicate more rapidly to more people than ever before. Yet we may not have reflected enough on this remarkable opportunity and responsibility (especially when it involves pictures rather than words).

In the wondrous 1998 Japanese film *After Life*, the recently deceased gather at a way station between heaven and earth.[14] They are given an assignment. They are to choose one moment of pure joy from their life. They have one week to write, cast, and re-create that scene for the camera. Director Hirokazu Koreeda intercuts the drama with interviews of real people, not actors, about the highs and lows of their lives. Some of those interviewed struggle to choose just a single moment from a lifetime of memories. Others aren't sure they've ever felt anything worth preserving. Eventually, the scenes are chosen, shot, and edited, ready to be premiered.

The deceased all gather in a screening room. They laugh and cry, reliving the beauty of the moments on-screen. As their scenes of pure joy unspool, the deceased disappear. They are transported, perhaps to live within that beautiful moment for eternity. *After Life* doesn't answer the question of what happens when we die, but it does prompt us to more thoughtfully reflect on the life we've been given. When it is time to write our story, what images or moments will endure?

Thankfully, Orthodox Christianity has great resources to help us reconcile the (false) dichotomy between word and image. Orthodox iconographers do not paint icons; they "write" them. Elizabeth Zelensky and Lela Gilbert have helped Protestants and Catholics understand this distinction in the Orthodox tradition. They write, "This emphasis on the word *writing* underscores icons' rootedness in the central 'text' of Christianity, that of the incarnation."[15] While Protestants emphasize Jesus as the Word of God, the Orthodox focus on the incarnation as a text to be read. Jesus dwelt among us as the icon of the invisible God. Images are good. Images are signs of the divine. We are a glorious reflection of our Creator. What a lofty (and humbling) calling. So why do we so easily debase ourselves with blatant self-promotional stunts or come-hither looks that reduce us to objects rather than embodied souls? We may be confused by conflicting biblical claims that we were created as a little lower than the angels and yet "all have sinned and fall short of the glory of God" (Rom. 3:23). Are we crowned with honor and glory, or are we more comparable to the grass or the flowers, which wither and fade (1 Pet. 1:24)? The answer is both.

We can find our aspirational selves on Instagram, where our carefully curated photos present an idealized and aestheticized version of us. We see our more ephemeral selves on Snapchat, where our photos don't last and where our absence is only noted when a Snapstreak ends. If Instagram is designed to make a lasting impression and to convey a striving for perfection, Snap reminds us how fleeting our time on earth amid the pleasures of everyday life can be. It is important to remember that our physical bodies may fail, but the impressions we've made on others will remain. Instagram is curated; Snap is simply lived.

This book looks at the history of self-portraits as a way into understanding these competing social media platforms. The classical art of ancient Greece and Rome idealized beauty in ways we're still trying to conform to today. The masterpieces of the Renaissance elevated humanity to center stage and suggested that art could elevate and secure our social standing. Photographic self-portraits arose from the timed release of the shutter. Early photographs captured us in time and place, often commemorating holy events like weddings and baptisms. Photography has always coincided with sacred moments, preserving important milestones and making those images available now and later.

Now, adolescents face much Instapressure to put forth an idealized image. We must define ourselves (or certainly our days) via a single image, not just in our profile picture, but also in our daily posts. As teens are still developing their sense of self, no wonder they try on multiple selves via photos in an effort to figure out which one fits and feels right. We may feel judged before we've even finalized who and whose we are. The selfie is a way of buying time, trying on versions of "Mii" before deciding which one to wear. We may tire of the pressure to respond with a quip or rejoinder to our friends' photos. Bitmoji offers a myriad of ready-made options, digitized versions of ourselves, to distribute far and wide.

In an image-saturated culture, we may have forgotten or ignored the promises of God gathered in Scripture. The Word of God remains a resonant anchor for defining ourselves apart from the crowd. Perhaps we can find comfort in turning from images back to the Word. The Orthodox tradition encourages us to contemplate the glory of the Word revealed in the iconic Jesus. Words and images both remind us that we are the crown of God's creation. We are royal sons and daughters, set apart by a King for a heavenly calling. We may feel like a failure, but Christ considers us worthy of sacrifice. No matter how lost we may be, Jesus steps away from the masses to seek us out, to find us and restore us and bring us into his fold. We may come as we are, even naked and ashamed. God the Father bore us. Jesus adores us. The Spirit of God restores us. How do we respond to such abundant amour?

From Idols to Icons to the Icon

Protestants are traditionally people grounded in the Word of God—read, studied, and proclaimed. So an era of ubiquitous cameras in our pockets and constant visual updates can feel daunting. This book is an effort to expand our visual literacy as a way to deepen our lived theology. Protestants have been comfortable communicating the perils of idolatry, particularly when it comes to graven images. We have ample biblical support for such suspicion. Lost in the desert, desperate for direction, the Hebrews rallied around a golden calf. Well before the arrival of the golden iPhone 5s or the $1000 iPhone X, we had reason to worry that our smartphones were securing a little too large a place in our hearts. Steve Jobs's products were becoming the apple of our eye.

There are so many examples of how cell phones have contributed to our self-centeredness. From the first moments that Facebook asked us "What's your status?" we have been prompted to think first and foremost about ourselves. Selfie culture is so pervasive that Kim Kardashian's cell phone photos can easily be compiled into a 448-page coffee-table book titled *Selfish*. It is far too easy to compare our social media use against others and conclude: "At least I don't talk about myself as much as they do." We are reminded, "Do not think of yourself more highly than you ought, but rather think of yourself with sober judgment, in accordance with the faith God has distributed to each of you" (Rom. 12:3). Taking a break from selfie-taking may be necessary for self-regulating.

While I am concerned about the idols residing in my heart, I also want to tap into the iconic power of images. For centuries, the Christian faith was communicated to a mostly illiterate people through nonliterary means. When early church father St. Anthony was relegated to the desert, he was asked how he could endure without books. St. Anthony replied, "My book, philosopher, is the nature of created things, and whenever I wish I can read it in the works of God."[16] Churches eventually invested in cutting-edge architecture, stained glass, and pipe organs to tell God's story. Changes in the church calendar were conveyed via colorful vestments, which announced when special seasons were arriving. Religious pilgrims were invited to meditate before and upon the face of Christ speaking from iconic sculptures and paintings. Catholic and Orthodox traditions rooted in the spiritual power of signs and symbols may have a competitive advantage in a highly visual era.

We all need to learn how to *sit with* and *see through* an icon to the invisible power behind or within it. As the icon (*eikōn*) of the invisible God celebrated in Colossians 1:15, Jesus endures as our living witness, our embodied Savior. Paintings of Jesus are an invitation to look further, to see the invisible God made manifest in Christ. We sit before an icon that may have been painted centuries before, and yet we are invited to experience a transcendent moment with God today. We must train our eyes to see the immaterial Reality that resides beyond the image. Yes, we can reflect upon and appreciate the work of Jesus accomplished two thousand years ago. But the icon offers us the opportunity to appropriate the historical sacrifice of Jesus into our spiritual lives even now. Sitting with an image of Jesus does more than remind us that "God is our refuge and strength"; it offers God as "an ever-present help in trouble" (Ps. 46:1).

Why does the gaze of Jesus in icons feel so piercing and personal? Iconographers go to great lengths to alter the normal focal points in a painting. When they write an icon, they are not adhering to the vanishing points that have dominated Western painting since the Renaissance. The icon is not designed to draw the viewer into Jesus's world inside the frame. The flatness of the portrait, the gold leaf in the background, encourages us to focus solely upon the face of Jesus. As we stare into his eyes, we realize that the focus of Jesus is upon us, the viewer. We are the vanishing point in the painting. Jesus is entering our world, eager to enter into our thoughts and concerns. When we make Jesus the subject of our attention, we discover that we are the object of his eye.

Perhaps we can redeem the selfie by learning from this iconic encounter. When we turn the camera on ourselves, we are definitely the subject. We treat the camera as an object. But we do not consider it as having a life beyond. Could we peer into the camera with something more akin to the communion we experience with an icon? Can we envision the camera lens as looking into someone's eyes? Can we see Jesus staring at us through the lens? How does he view us? What does he see? And how might that change how we pose? If we understand that we are being seen with eyes of love, of encouragement, of compassion and support, then we have no need to act up or act out or really even to act at all. We can relax. And be honest. Be fully ourselves in moments of triumph or trial. We begin to love the camera as if it is a person who appreciates us. We respond to the camera with eyes of love and gratitude, something much more sublime than a smile.

This kind of spiritual discipline will prove increasingly important in an image-saturated culture. We are exposed to so much visual information that we must develop keener perception. As we scroll through thousands of images, we are tempted to settle for only a surface reading. Idolatry

Saint Catherine's Monastery, Sinai

Christ Pantocrator

arises when our gaze fixates on an object and begins to venerate it. We may latch on to a celebrity, a prize, a title that feels like an elusive source of life. We may become attached to fame as the key to immortality. Such idolatry will end in frustration when our attachments prove unworthy of our attention. Yet this book is about learning to see God in the many-splendored selfies flooding our feeds.

Will we allow our hearts to ache with those crying out for attention and validation? We can celebrate with those who have been blessed with moments of breakthrough and mourn with those sharing their grief via social media. We can make the leap from Jesus as the image of the invisible God to ourselves as the image and likeness of God. This doesn't mean that we think of ourselves more highly than we ought. It means thinking of ourselves with sober judgment, keeping in mind the faith that God has given to each of us (Rom. 12:3). We must not be satisfied with merely seeing ourselves in that electronic mirror in our pocket; instead, we should reflect on where we are and whose we are.

This may mean putting down our phones long enough to recognize the blessings and opportunities that surround us. Maltbie Babcock was a pastor in upstate New York during the turn of the twentieth century. His walks around "the escarpment" near his church inspired the lyrics to the hymn "This Is My Father's World."[17] In the first verse, Babcock celebrates what he has heard: "to my listening ears, all nature sings, and round me rings the music of the spheres." He had trained his ears to connect nature to the music made by the planets themselves. Are these the "ears to hear" that Jesus wants in his disciples? What about developing eyes to see? Even surrounded by mountains and freshwater lakes, when it came to vision, Babcock spoke of dreaming: "I see his face, I open my eyes, and in glad surprise cry, 'The Lord is in this place.'" It may be easier to see God in wondrous settings. We may Instagram a sunset as an act of praise. But what about when we aren't in the most stunning surroundings? Can we develop God's heart for urban settings and city dwellers as well (Jonah 4:11)? Can we see God even in circumstances that might be dire? Babcock allowed himself to dream long enough to see the face of God, to open his eyes and exclaim, "The Lord is in this place."

This book aims to harness that kind of spiritual perception. We may be surrounded by a sea of selfies demanding our attention, overwhelmed by Snapchat Stories to keep up with and streaks to maintain. Yet in our Father's world, we must pause to dream long enough to see his face and recognize that "the Lord is in this place."

This is the kind of magical, spiritual seeing that informs the revolutionary theology of Jean-Luc Marion.[18] He pushes past Protestant, Catholic, and Orthodox divides to challenge us to see God as far greater than our theological categories. He recognizes how attractive idols remain. We can even make our existing image of God into an idol. When we fixate on our known understanding of the divine and limit God to our confines, we have hedged in the living God. We must be open to the correction and expansion offered by the Icon that endures across the centuries and reveals new challenges today. When our gaze is fixed upon the Invisible that cannot be bound, our empathy and love may be expanded beyond our previous limits. We bow before and receive God's revelation "as pure gift, indeed as excess," far more than we ever thought or imagined.[19]

This is the profound truth of why we must learn how to see more clearly. The apostle Paul writes about how "we all, who with unveiled faces contemplate the Lord's glory, are being transformed into his image with ever-increasing glory, which comes from the Lord, who is the Spirit" (2 Cor. 3:18). In fixing our gaze upon Christ and in contemplating the glory of God, we are transformed into visible manifestations of that elusive, eternal, and unbound Triune God. We become living witnesses radiating the love that we experienced in our worship of the "immortal, invisible God only wise, in light inaccessible hid from our eyes."[20] This is how we become conduits of patience and love en route to eternity. We do not claim the glory for ourselves, but instead suggest that we are only experiencing "a reflection as in a mirror"; we know that the invisible will be fully revealed, and "then we shall see face to face" (1 Cor. 13:12). Marion says the true icon "transforms us in its glory by allowing this glory to shine on our face as its mirror."[21] This is the high calling that resides within our cell phones. We can snap and post as mirrors of God's glory and carry ourselves with humility and power. We would never want to desecrate that glory or hoard it for ourselves. The same tension that resided in the Tower of Babel drives our social-media marketing today. The question remains, "Who or what is being elevated via our platforms?"

From Worship to Witness to Worship

One of the most problematic aspects of social media is that it is almost always public. And public piety is almost always dangerous. Jesus talks about the eternal rewards of private piety in the Sermon on the Mount. God hears those prayers we utter in private. He honors those aches and pains we air behind closed doors. What about public displays of religion? The reviews aren't good. In fact, Jesus offers a fairly stern warning: "And when you pray, do not be like the hypocrites, for they love to pray standing in the synagogues and on the street corners to be seen by others" (Matt. 6:5). Some may say that Jesus isn't talking about worship. In a theocracy like ancient Israel, public worship took the form of marches, as in the royal psalms sung in the streets at festive occasions. We can almost hear the Israelites rejoicing as the king comes marching in, described in Psalm 72: "Long may he live!" (v. 15). Christmas caroling is also a form of public proclamation. It is an effort to bless others with the gift of song, to celebrate Jesus's birthday with a chorus or two. We sing "O Come, O Come Emmanuel" because we anticipate the advent of "God with us." This form of evangelism is mostly welcomed and maybe even rewarded with a cookie or a cup of hot cider. Yet, according to Jesus, we aren't supposed to take our worship practices into the public square.

While the doors of our churches and synagogues are always open to guests, we aren't supposed to parade through town with worship songs in the hope of being noticed (especially if that attention is intended to make us feel holier than others). Worship is about putting ourselves in proper relation to God (as well as to each other). It is a collective act, a statement of solidarity, an opportunity to remember whose we are and who we are. It is comparable to a pep rally before a big game. But the game of serving others isn't played for acclamation and cheers. We perform for an audience of (three in) one. Public acts of piety that pump up our self-esteem are among the most blatantly condemned acts in the entire Bible. Devices that make our prayers public are laden with spiritual danger. While social media may be a great place to solicit prayer and support, it isn't necessarily the proper forum for celebrating God's blessings. Our answered prayers may not inspire others. Facebook envy is a real, verified phenomenon. So how do we live out our private faith in such a public forum? The particulars of digital discipleship are still being sorted out.[22]

Worshiping God and taking selfies do not go together. Worship keeps our egos in check. When we bow down before God, we regain our perspective regarding who is the center of the universe and the source of our sustenance. We cease striving in order to focus on gratitude. We stop cultivating long enough to give thanks. We remember that we have not made ourselves. We pause to focus on the One in whose image we are created and whose likeness we strive to reclaim. We confess our sins in worship as a way of renouncing the powers that seek to undo us. We kneel before the Lord our God and Maker as an act of contrition, a recognition that we are from dust, and to dust we shall return. We acknowledge the gift of life and remember those saints who've gone before us. We bring our prayers and needs before God and the community. We share from the abundance we've been given. We enjoy a meal together. We break bread passed down from Jesus to the disciples to us. We share a common cup. We embrace the other as family. We rehearse heavenly songs in anticipation of choruses to come. Worship is a beautiful private act (in community) that equips and empowers us to engage in public service (to others).

What kind of public witness can we practice via social media? Selfies are a time-honored but complex form of communication. We need to recover the roots of photography as capturing sacred moments. As we've seen, the camera was initially reserved for special occasions like baptisms and weddings. People wanted to commemorate rites of passage. Now, the ubiquity of smartphones collapses the gap between the sacred and the everyday. We always have a phone with us. So what kinds of moments are we seeking to capture, preserve, and promote? Thanks to smartphones and platforms like Instagram, we are learning to find the sacred amid the mundane. Beautiful moments abound, if we have eyes to see them (and a phone with which to capture them). We can approach the composition of a photograph as a form of prayer, pausing before a meal, admiring the beauty around us, offering praise to God in a very public (but still reverential) way. The challenge before us is to approach photography as a sacred craft and a potential form of prayer. We bring an attitude of gratitude and worship into our daily lives.

In church tradition, we break out special colors and liturgy for Advent, Lent, and Easter, but what about Ordinary Time? Finding blessings in everyday life is a spiritual discipline worth developing. It is an artistic *and* religious way of being: the place where our ascetic tendencies can revel in the aesthetic. In "Pied Beauty," poet Gerard Manley Hopkins writes, "Glory be to God for dappled things," from finches' wings to plotted landscapes.[23] Emily Dickinson prefers a Sabbath "with a Bobolink for a Chorister—and an Orchard for a Dome."[24] Wendell Berry spends Sundays on his farm in Kentucky composing Sabbath poems. He writes, "A heron hunched at stream mouth fishes quietly as he ought."[25] Ann Voskamp makes this ritual practical by challenging readers to list one thousand things to be grateful for.[26] We may make the mistake of thinking it is easier for someone like Berry or Voskamp to slow down while living on a farm, yet Voskamp finds "one thousand gifts" amid considerable pain and heartbreak, from the loss of a sister to the burial of her nephews. An attitude of gratitude can emerge amid any and all circumstances. This sense of *eucharisteo*, a joyful thanksgiving, can transform our hearts.

Imagine what one thousand days of grateful Instagrams might look like. These are not selfies of God (pantheism) or selfies for God (evangelism). These are selfies with God (panentheism). What a powerful potential testament to the presence of God in and around us. We all have the ability to capture tiny snapshots of goodness on our phones. We can pause before unspoiled pleasures and share them far and wide. The Instapost may cover today's dinner, tonight's sunset, or tomorrow's sunrise. The wizened author of Ecclesiastes reminds us to drink our wine with gladness, every wonderful, meaningless day (Eccles. 9:7–9). Our photos are a conduit for praise and worship. St. Leontius of Cyprus writes, "It is through me that the heavens declare the glory of God, through me that the moon worships God, through me that the stars glorify him, through me all the waters and showers of rain, the dews and all creation worship God and give him glory."[27] Instagram could become a new form of praying the hours—posting them as well as reciting them. What an intriguing challenge to transform our public witness into a hidden form of worship.

What about those struggling to survive, who have few flowers or fields to photograph? When we witness inequities and atrocities, those also must be recorded. Brazilian photographer Sebastião Salgado has focused upon the plight of "the other Americas" from those caught in famines and mass migrations to workers laboring in mines.[28] Poet Gwendolyn Brooks recounts driving through the wealthy suburbs of Beverly Hills, near Chicago, where "Even the leaves fall down in lovelier patterns here. / And the refuse, the refuse is a neat brilliancy." She writes, "We do not want them to have less. / But it is only natural that we should think we have not enough."[29] Can our selfies convey a longing for equality, for economic justice, for everyone's prosperity? In his poem, "Imagine the Angels of Bread," Martín Espada describes what the biblical notion of jubilee might look like in our lifetime. He declares, "This is the year that squatters evict landlords," and "shawled refugees deport judges," and "this is the year that darkskinned men / lynched a century ago / return to sip coffee quietly / with the apologizing descendants / of their executioners."[30] We must train our eyes to see the world with God's sense of justice. Perhaps we need to include more discomforting pictures in our stream. Worship includes an understanding of what it means to live out our prayer for "Thy kingdom come." Our photos can be a form of prophetic witness.

From Practice to Theory to Practice

We stockpile experiences in search of our best selfie. The ultimate high may come via crowdsurfing at Coachella or rotating above England in the London Eye. It could be in skydiving selfies. But we have compiled so many photos that we need multiple apps to contain them. When it comes to photos, we are all en route to being digital millionaires, possessing terabytes of digital information in the cloud. But those experiences often lack contemplation. The Latin word *contemplatio* involves the act of carefully looking at something. To truly contemplate, we must release our prejudices and assumptions and to-do lists. *Contemplatio* finds an equivalent in the Greek word *theoria*. We may consider theories as dry concepts stuck in textbooks and classrooms. But theories stem from seeing clearly. They are borne out of contemplation, taking time to figure out what things "mean." The danger in selfie culture is becoming all praxis—"I did this"—without any accompanying theory or reflection. What was happening in us when we took that photo of us?

This book is a call for us to move toward *contemplatio*, to recover *theoria*. Hopefully, we've learned how to see ourselves, our neighbors, and God with more clarity. In studying Narcissus's (lack of) reflection, painters' use of mirrors, writers' mining of memories, and photographers' keen eye, we've sharpened our own sense of selfies. We may still feel divided against ourselves, projecting multiple images across social media. I fully expect us all to stumble as we sort out the difference between self-study and self-promotion in our picture taking. Overcoming our self-seeking instincts isn't easy, especially when so many social-media prompts encourage us to think about me, rather than we, first. No one supports us with more patience and vigor than God. Yet following God involves sacrifices that we aren't always prepared to make.

In the Gospel of Luke, Jesus spelled out a costly way forward, "Whoever wants to be my disciple must deny themselves and take up their cross daily and follow me. For whoever wants to save their life will lose it, but whoever loses their life for me will save it. What good is it for someone to gain

Selfie in London Eye

the whole world, and yet lose or forfeit their very self?" (Luke 9:23–25). I invested seventeen years in building up my "very self." How dare Jesus call me to renounce all that I'd acquired in order to follow him! Yet I needed a clean break from my past, to distance myself from toxic relationships and my self-destructive tendencies. As a freshman in college, I had grown disgusted by my duplicity. I had assembled an impressive résumé and earned a valuable scholarship—in quite a calculating way. I was involved in a sexual relationship that served me well. But I had really given only my body, not my being, to my partner. My efforts to fill the hole in my soul felt empty and vain. Serving my self-interests was exhausting and unfulfilling. I decided to discard my awards and alter my career path for a restart. Craig 2.0. It was a costly commitment that I've never regretted. It was exhilarating to wipe my dirty slate clean. Knowledge of my limits led to a hunger for God. Introspection inspired me to seek transformation.

Some may consider Jesus's call too costly. The acquisitive self may seem more viable or rewarding than the inquisitive self. It is a vexing paradox—renouncing ourselves to save ourselves. Yet the most profound spiritual mystics leaned into this spiritual paradox. They understood that self-knowledge is a prerequisite to God-knowledge. Studying ourselves, staring at our selfies, is an essential part of a spiritual search. Eight days after Jesus issued this shocking call to self-renunciation, God responded with a transfiguration. In Luke 9:28–36, Jesus was lifted up, higher than ever before. Jesus and three of his disciples headed to a mountain to pray. Their spiritual trek resulted in transformative visions and divine pronouncements—they literally heard from the Father. The route to a mountaintop experience with God begins in the valley where we discover the truth about ourselves.

Luke recounts how Jesus "took Peter, John and James with him and went up onto a mountain to pray" (9:28). Peter, John, and James must have been exhausted by the journey. They are described as "very sleepy" (v. 32). Yet as Jesus was praying, "the appearance of his face changed, and his clothes became as bright as a flash of lightning. Two men, Moses and Elijah, appeared in glorious splendor, talking with Jesus" (vv. 29–30). This augmented reality definitely woke up Peter and his companions. Luke writes, "A cloud appeared and covered them, and they were afraid as they entered the cloud. A voice came from the cloud, saying, 'This is my Son, whom I have chosen; listen to him'" (vv. 34–35). This is the voice that Jesus challenges all of his disciples to hear. This is the heavenly vision that we are all invited to see. It is available for those who have eyes to see and ears to hear. Jesus is transfigured, with his clothes glowing, and with two long-departed spiritual exemplars beside him, and the disciples almost missed it.

The transfiguration is the major event, the big reveal, between Jesus's baptism and his crucifixion. God's voice of affirmation, first heard when Jesus rises from the water of baptism, returns (see Mark 1:11 and Matt. 3:17). The divinity of Christ is established both in the light emanating from his appearance and in the heavenly voice urging his disciples to listen to him. This is a sight and sound spectacular, an immersive spiritual experience, an epiphany. It is a heavenly vision, a divine lightning bolt that transforms Jesus, the disciples, and hopefully the reader. Did it really happen? Were Moses and Elijah literally raised from the dead to appear alongside Jesus? None of us were there, so we're left to interpret the vision reported by Luke. The presence of Moses and Elijah can be seen as symbolic of the Old Testament law and prophets. But their appearance also points toward the resurrection to come. New Testament scholar Dorothy Lee notes how "this rapturous experience serves as a hinge point in the Gospel of Luke and a turning point in history." She concludes, "The transfiguration bridges the gulf between Creator and creation, facing two directions at one and the same time: backwards to the vision of the incarnation and forwards to the hope of the resurrection and parousia," the return of Christ.[31] This is the kind of transformative vision that sears our soul and inspires us for an eternity.

When we seek to be augmented, we are longing to be transfigured. The restless search for beauty will not cease until we are overwhelmed by the radiance of Jesus. Our obsession with our appearance can be satisfied by a radical vision of glory divine.

Unfortunately, the next day, when Jesus descended the mountain, his disciples seemed to have forgotten all the lessons they had learned. They failed the immediate test—the opportunity to heal a demon-possessed boy. The disciples felt unequipped to deal with this freaky encounter. The power and glory revealed in the transfiguration was lost on them a day later. They had the experience but missed the meaning. Or at least they could not appropriate what they had (allegedly) learned. Jesus grows frustrated and scolds, "You unbelieving and perverse generation." He wonders, "How long shall I stay with you and put up with you?" (Luke 9:41). This is decidedly who we do not want to be: blessed by mountain-top experiences but unable to deal with the messiness of a child's screams and spasms. We want to experience the ultimate selfie, but we may want to avoid those awkward and uncomfortable moments that require faith beyond the realm of our self-confidence.

Selfie culture encourages us to seek mountaintop experiences (like the transfiguration and ascension) but to avoid or at least deny the dark nights of the soul (like Jesus's crucifixion and the disciples' subsequent suffering). The Spanish priest St. John of the Cross is renowned for how he navigated the dark nights of the soul. Selfies celebrate our moments of triumph, but what about those periods of depression or defeat? St. John of the Cross suggests, "It is great wisdom to know how to be silent and to look at neither the remarks, nor the deeds, nor the lives of others."[32] When we're judging our lowest moments against others' highlight reels, we are bound to feel overwhelmed. When we turn outward for affirmation, we are bound to be disappointed. St. John of the Cross counters, "Strive to preserve your heart in peace; let no event of this world disturb it."[33] When we slow down long enough to quiet our anxieties, we may begin to see or hear God. St. John of the Cross says, "It is best to learn to silence the faculties and to cause them to be still so that God may speak."[34] No one wants to suffer in silence, but St. John of the Cross promises that "the endurance of darkness is the preparation for great light."[35]

Activists must make space for contemplation. In Luke 10, Jesus affirms the activism of the Samaritan caring for a neighbor in need. Such radical hospitality is celebrated as compassion in action. This is followed by the hospitality of Martha making preparations to host Jesus. While Martha scurries about, her sister Mary sits at Jesus's feet, "listening to what he said" (Luke 10:39). Mary adopts the posture of a rabbinical student, choosing to listen and learn rather than engaging in domestic work. A frustrated Martha asked Jesus to sort Mary out: "Tell her to help me" (v. 40). Instead, Jesus chastises Martha for her distractedness, "You are worried and upset about many things, but few things are needed—or indeed only one" (vv. 41–42). Carolyn Custis James notes how "Jesus defied all expectations when, instead of sending Mary scurrying back to the kitchen, he defended her in the strongest possible terms."[36] Mary's reflection and repose set her apart as the first theologian in the New Testament. In this situation, Mary understood what mattered, but Martha clearly missed it amid her activities. What is the one thing? The parable of the good Samaritan and the encounter with Martha and Mary seem to provide contradictory answers. Are we to stop what we're doing and attend to the need at hand? Or is it better to sit with Jesus, put our distractions aside, and simply listen? Does Jesus prefer theory or practice? These stories suggest we need both action and contemplation.

What I Learned / What We Need

What is my takeaway from writing this book? As partakers of the divine nature, we may all have a masterpiece within us, waiting to be captured on camera (and posted with those beautiful Instagram filters). But we may also need the leveling reminders of rainbow barf pouring from our mouth to keep our egos in check (à la Snapchat). We are noble sons and daughters of the living God and ignoble ignoramuses capable of petty and envious self-promotion.

I did not expect to find so many resources for navigating our selfie culture concentrated in the ancient church. While debating about the nature of Jesus, these saints forged timeless and helpful insights into the nature of humanity. They saw the incarnation as the beginning of our divination. St. Athanasius, Bishop of Alexandria declared, "For the Son of God became man so we might become God."[37] That is a much loftier view of humanity than is usually heard. We honor and praise God when we reflect our status as the image and likeness of God. That calling is not singular: it is plural, male and female. It is communitarian, found in the Trinity.

Corrosive narcissism arises from a failure to attach our selves to a trustworthy object of our affection. Christians know that object as Jesus. We need more attachments to Jesus. My research reveals that, instead of bemoaning how narcissistic we are, we need to investigate our attachments. When we circle back to the desert fathers and Julian of Norwich and Catherine of Siena, we find role models who acknowledged their sin but who also recognized that their humanity leads to glory via redemption in Christ. By selling short the glory of our image in Christ, the Protestant and Catholic churches may have unleashed our endless pursuit of self-help that leads to self-doubt, self-deceit, and self-defeat. The rise of selfie culture reflects an identity crisis that can only be transfigured through a fresh encounter with the icon of the invisible God.

Here are a few key convictions that emerged from my own "selfie analysis":

1. We are not defined externally (by how many people like or follow us).
2. We are loved and valued by God independent of our performance.
3. God's unconditional love for us doesn't mean that our choices and actions don't matter. But they should flow out of a healthy relationship with God and our selves.
4. As we follow Jesus, we are being transformed by the Spirit into God's likeness.
5. This allows our actions to spring from a sustainable well of genuine (rather than coercive) love.
6. We are free to be ourselves, to express ourselves on social media with an eye toward the health and well-being of our (online) neighbors.

7. We can create and photograph and paint and write to bless others and extend justice rather than seeking to elevate our own reputations.

8. The resulting circle of generosity can lead to a reformation of community, grounded in healthy selves encouraging each other to thrive.

These are not sacrosanct. I focus my camera on a subject (especially myself). I've ended up taking and posting more selfies through this process. I hope I'm photographing myself from a healthy and sustainable place that honors God's creation and investment in me. Feel free to check out my progress on social media. I'd be honored to converse online or in person. Invite me to your campus or community to talk further about our selfies as the image of God.

Even with careful attention to the best practices of self-imaging, there are inherent problems and limits to what a selfie can convey. We may think we are being subtle, clever, or clear, while our intended audience fails to get the message. We can end up creating an online storm with a post that was merely intended to be playful. We must not place too much faith in our audiences' interpretive abilities.

May grace abound in our online interactions. Before we pounce on Princess Breanna for her ill-advised (or rather non-advised) post from Auschwitz, we should remember the limits of the medium. Jesus's wisdom endures, especially in social-media practices: "Do not judge, or you too will be judged. For in the same way you judge others, you will be judged, and with the measure you use, it will be measured to you" (Matt. 7:1–2). Or perhaps: "Why bash your brother's or sister's post without realizing you have a massive selfie stick poking you in the eye?" A more gracious social media starts with us. A selfie can only say so much, even with a raft of clever hashtags attached to it. We must learn how to *see through* the selfie and *read between* the captions.

We need to see through the image that others are projecting, to recognize the cry of the heart residing behind the Gram or the Snap. Thoughtful reflection on who God created us to be, as image and likeness, can lead us toward contentment and compassion rather than compulsion and confusion. Recognizing the image of the invisible God in Jesus can enable us to be content with who we are and confident in whose we are. We can learn to capture (and cherish) the sacred moments preserved on Instagram and try on new or aspirational aspects of ourselves in Snapchat filters.

A keen eye can inspire an attitude of gratitude that drives our online decision making. Our pictures, our posts, and our captions can all point to the glory of God and honor the humanity in and around us. May we rest and rejoice in the person God has made us today. May we strive to become the best selfie that God is calling us to: pursuing justice, loving mercy, and walking humbly.

On their journey out of Egypt, the Israelites witnessed the faithfulness of God. In Deuteronomy 29, Moses reminds the people of "those signs and great wonders" (v. 3), miracles like the parting of the Red Sea and the provision of manna. And yet Moses still sees a blind and recalcitrant people: "But to this day the LORD has not given you a mind that understands or eyes that see or ears that hear" (v. 4).

Jesus takes up the same theme in his parables, challenging his followers to develop eyes to see and ears to hear. After Jesus was crucified on a cross, his body was wrapped and placed in a tomb. The entrance was sealed with a stone. Mary Magdalene takes her grief to the grave and is shocked to see the stone had been rolled away. While she weeps in confusion, wondering where Jesus's body has been taken, the risen Jesus appears to her. He acknowledges her tears, asking, "Woman, why are you crying?" (John 20:13). Mary is so focused upon the missing body that she fails to recognize Jesus. Her trauma and pain are understandably blinding.[38] Jesus asks, "Who is it you are looking for?" (v. 15). Mary still fails to identify him. Only when Jesus calls her by name—"Mary"—(v. 16), does she turn and recognize the One she seeks. We all have reasons to weep. Have we heard Jesus call our name? Have we turned, like Mary, amid pain or confusion to recognize Christ is risen?

When we take photos of ourselves, I urge us to consider Jesus's question, "Who is it you are looking for?" Clarity of vision and keen auditory ability are a prerequisite for discipleship. Proverbs celebrates the blessings of sight and sound: "Ears that hear and eyes that see—the LORD has made them both" (Prov. 20:12). Jesus said, "The eye is the lamp of the body. If your eyes are healthy, your whole body will be full of light" (Matt. 6:22). I leave spiritual listening to another volume. For now, I hope this book equips us to raise our smartphones with a more prayerful attitude. We are often so enraptured with our screens that we fail to recognize the person next to us in class, on the bus, or across the border.[39] I hope we will take time to notice what's going on with the person next to us. It could be a parent, a sibling, a roommate, a stranger. Hopefully, in studying our self-ies, we start to see the beauty and wonder that reside within all of us. Technology is a wondrous gift loaded with possibilities and temptations. May the Spirit prompt us to think before we Snap or at least pray while we post, making it a godly discipline, a way to develop eyes to see. May we be transfigured, like Jesus, into our best selfies. May God make God's face to shine upon us and give us peace.[40]

Questions to Consider/Discuss

1. What is the craziest selfie you've taken of yourself via augmented reality? What do you like about it? What makes it especially funny or weird or interesting?

2. What's the longest you've ever stared at a photo or painting? Have you ever tried to look at an icon of Jesus or a saint? How does it feel? Gaze upon an icon of Jesus until you start to see yourself through his eyes.

Selfie Challenge

Take the challenge to view your smartphone in a new way. Imagine Jesus behind the lens pouring affirmation upon you. How does that transfigure your image? Look into the lens as if you're gazing into the loving eyes of Jesus. Now snap. The mere thought of the resulting image evokes tears of joy and gratitude.

Illustrations

Notes

Chapter 1 Introduction

1. Howard Thurman, *The Search for Common Ground: An Inquiry into the Basis of Man's Experience of Community* (Richmond, IN: Friends United Press, 1971), xiii.

2. Jessica Durando, "Auschwitz Selfie Girl Defends Actions," *USA Today*, July 23, 2014, https://www.usatoday.com/story/news/nation-now/2014/07/23/selfie-auschwitz-concentration-camp-germany/13038281/.

3. Craig Detweiler, "'Smiling for Auschwitz Selfies,' and Crying into the Digital Wilderness," *Belief Blog*, July 22, 2014, http://religion.blogs.cnn.com/2014/07/22/defending-the-auschwitz-selfie/.

4. Ariane Lange and Emily Orley, "Is Anne Frank's Role in *The Fault in Our Stars* Offensive?," BuzzFeed, June 5, 2014, https://www.buzzfeed.com/arianelange/anne-frank-the-fault-in-our-stars?utm_term=.ifeAqlbWV#.ftVavxW6p.

5. T. S. Eliot, "The Dry Salvages," in *The Complete Poems and Plays, 1909–1950* (New York: Harcourt Brace Jovanovich, 1971), 133.

6. Elie Wiesel, *Night* (New York: Bantam Books, 1982), xv.

7. Miroslav Volf, *The End of Memory: Remembering Rightly in a Violent World* (Grand Rapids: Eerdmans, 2006), 29.

8. Philip Oltermann, "'Yolocaust' Artist Provokes Debate over Commemorating Germany's Past," *Guardian*, January 19, 2017, https://www.theguardian.com/world/2017/jan/19/yolocaust-artist-shahak-shapira-provokes-debate-over-commemorating-germanys-past.

9. Renee Ghert-Zand, "Citing Success, Creator Takes Down YOLOCAUST Webpage," *Times of Israel*, January 26, 2017, http://www.timesofisrael.com/citing-success-creator-takes-down-yolocaust-webpage/.

10. Jason Farago, "The Scourge of the Selfie," BBC, January 21, 2015, http://www.bbc.com/culture/story/20150121-the-scourge-of-the-selfie.

11. Alison Herman, "Kara Walker Knew People Would Take Dumb Selfies with 'A Subtlety,' and That Shouldn't Surprise Us," Flavorwire, October 14, 2014, http://flavorwire.com/482585/kara-walker-knew-people-would-take-dumb-selfies-with-a-subtlety-and-that-shouldnt-surprise-us.

12. Caroline A. Miranda, "Kara Walker on the Bit of Sugar Sphinx She Saved, Video She's Making," *Los Angeles Times*, October 13, 2014, http://www.latimes.com/entertain

ment/arts/miranda/la-et-cam-kara-walker-on-her-sugar-sphinx-the-piece-she-saved-video
-shes-making-20141013-column.html.

13. Donna Freitas, *The Happiness Effect: How Social Media Is Driving a Generation to Appear Perfect at Any Cost* (New York: Oxford University Press, 2017), 85.

14. The Chainsmokers (Andrew Taggart and Alex Pall) 2014 viral video for "#Selfie" has been viewed over half a billion times on YouTube: https://www.youtube.com/watch?v=kdemFfbS5H0.

15. Jerry Saltz, "Art at Arm's Length: A History of the Selfie," *New York Magazine*, February 3, 2014, http://www.vulture.com/2014/01/history-of-the-selfie.html.

16. Bryn Lovitt, "Death by Selfie: Eleven Disturbing Stories of Social Media Pics Gone Wrong," *Rolling Stone*, July 14, 2016, http://www.rollingstone.com/culture/pictures/death-by-selfie-10-disturbing-stories-of-social-media-pics-gone-wrong-20160714.

17. Heather Saul, "Daredevil or Reckless? 'Russia's Spiderman' Kirill Oreshkin Takes Extreme Selfies from Moscow's Tallest Buildings, *The Independent*, March 25, 2104, http://www.independent.co.uk/news/world/europe/daredevil-or-reckless-russias-spiderman-kirill-oreshkin-takes-extreme-selfies-from-moscows-tallest-9214540.html.

18. Cover line referring to the article inside by Timothy Egan with Casey Egan, "Unplugging the Selfie Generation," *National Geographic* 230, no. 4 (2016).

19. M. Delatorre, "The Story behind the Selfie: Why Those Sorority Girls Seemed Selfie-Obsessed," KFOR, October 19, 2015, http://kfor.com/2015/10/19/the-story-behind-the-selfie-why-those-sorority-girls-seemed-selfie-obsessed/.

20. Erving Goffman, *The Presentation of Self in Everyday Life* (New York: Anchor Books, 1959), 208.

21. Kara Fox, "Instagram Worst Social Media App for Young People's Mental Health," CNN, May 19, 2017, http://www.cnn.com/2017/05/19/health/instagram-worst-social-network-app-young-people-mental-health/index.html.

22. Christopher Lasch, *The Culture of Narcissism: American Life in an Age of Diminishing Expectations* (New York: Norton, 1979).

23. Robert D. Putnam, *Bowling Alone: The Collapse and Revival of American Community* (New York: Simon & Schuster, 2000).

24. Pete Brook, "Fred Ritchin Redefines Digital Photography," *Wired*, September 2, 2011, https://www.wired.com/2011/09/fred-ritchin/.

25. Charles Taylor, *Sources of the Self: The Making of Modern Identity* (Cambridge, MA: Harvard University Press, 1989).

26. Thomas Aquinas, *Questiones Disputatiae de Potentia Dei* (On the Power of God), trans. by the English Dominican Fathers, The Newman Press, 1952, question 7, article 5, paragraph 14.

27. G. K. Chesterton, *Orthodoxy* (London: John Lane, 1908), 35.

28. Sherry Turkle, *Alone Together: Why We Expect More from Technology and Less from Each Other* (New York: Basic Books, 2011), 266.

29. Dorothy S. Hunt, ed., *Love: A Fruit Always in Season; Daily Meditations from the Words of Mother Teresa of Calcutta* (San Francisco: Ignatius Press, 1987), 112.

30. Elizabeth A. Johnson, *She Who Is: The Mystery of God in Feminist Theological Discourse* (New York: Crossroad, 1992), 54.

31. Sarah Coakley, *God, Sexuality, and the Self: An Essay 'On the Trinity'* (Cambridge: Cambridge University Press, 2013), 58.

32. John Milton, *Paradise Lost,* book 1, line 26, https://www.poetryfoundation.org/poems/45718/paradise-lost-book-1-1674-version.

33. For much more on this seminal truth, see Stanley J. Grenz, *The Social God and the Relational Self: A Trinitarian Theology of the Imago Dei* (Louisville: Westminster John Knox, 2001).

34. Blaise Pascal, *Pensées*, trans. A. J. Krailsheimer (New York: Penguin Books, 1966), 75.

35. Carol Lee Flinders, *Enduring Grace: Living Portraits of Seven Women Mystics* (New York: HarperCollins, 1993), 111.

36. Dan B. Allender, *The Wounded Heart* (Colorado Springs: NavPress, 1990), 44.

37. Coakley, *God, Sexuality, and the Self*, 58.

38. Freitas, *Happiness Effect*, 13, emphasis original.

39. Freitas, *Happiness Effect*, xvi.

40. Twenty One Pilots, "Stressed Out," posted by Fueled by Ramen, April 27, 2015, https://www.youtube.com/watch?v=pXRviuL6vMY.

41. Tyler Joseph, "Stressed Out," from Twenty One Pilots, *Blurryface*, produced by Mike Elizondo, released by Fueled by Ramen, 2016.

42. Craig Detweiler, *iGods: How Technology Shapes Our Spiritual and Social Lives* (Grand Rapids: Brazos, 2013).

43. Christian Smith and Melinda Lindquist Denton, *Soul Searching* (New York: Oxford University Press, 2005).

44. See especially Hans Urs von Balthasar, *The Glory of the Lord: A Theological Aesthetics*, trans. Andrew Louth, John Saward, Martin Simon, and Rowan Williams (San Francisco: Ignatius, 1986).

45. Balthasar, *Glory of the Lord*, 80.

46. Dwight N. Hopkins, *Being Human: Race, Culture, and Religion* (Minneapolis: Fortress, 2005), 34.

47. Eboni Marshall Turman, *Toward a Womanist Ethic of Incarnation: Black Bodies, the Black Church, and the Council of Chalcedon* (New York: Palgrave Macmillan, 2013), 158.

Chapter 2 Reflected Beauty

1. Ovid, *Metamorphoses*, trans. Frank Justus Miller (Cambridge, MA: Harvard University Press, 1921), 1:3.

2. *Portrait of a thin-faced, bearded man*, Metropolitan Museum of Art, http://www.metmuseum.org/art/collection/search/547856.

3. Euphrosyne Doxiadis connects the large spiritual eyes in Christian icons to the expressive eyes of these earlier Greco-Egyptian images: "The power of the gaze of the Fayum portraits was inherited by the icons. . . . The eyes, as 'windows of the soul,' convey their subjects' spirituality." Euphrosyne Doxiadis, *The Mysterious Fayum Portraits: Faces from Ancient Egypt* (New York: Harry N. Abrams, 1995), 92.

4. Sarah M. Coyne, "Pretty as a Princess: Longitudinal Effects of Engagement with Disney Princesses on Gender Stereotypes, Body Esteem, and Prosocial Behavior in Children," *Child Development* 87, no. 6 (2016): 1909–25.

5. Valentina Zarya, "Study: Disney Princesses Negative for Girls, Positive for Boys," *Fortune*, June 22, 2016, http://fortune.com/2016/06/22/disney-princesses/.

6. Blake Bakkila, "Ashley Graham Makes History as the First Size 16 Model to Cover *Sports Illustrated*: 'This is Going to Change My Life Forever,'" *People*, January 26, 2017, http://people.com/style/ashley-graham-makes-history-as-the-first-size-16-model-to-cover-sports-illustrated-this-is-going-to-change-my-life-forever/.

7. Anne E. Becker, "Television, Disordered Eating, and Young Women in Fiji: Negotiating Body Image and Identity during Rapid Social Change," *Culture, Medicine and*

Psychiatry 28, no. 4 (2004): 533–59, cited in Sarah Grogan, *Body Image: Understanding Body Dissatisfaction in Men, Women, and Children*, 2nd ed. (London: Routledge, 2008), 33.

8. Grogan, *Body Image*, 25.

9. Susan Bordo, *Unbearable Weight: Feminism, Western Culture, and the Body* (Berkeley: University of California Press, 2004).

10. Gerard Manley Hopkins, "To What Serves Mortal Beauty?," in *Poems of Gerard Manley Hopkins*, ed. Robert Bridges (London: Humphrey Milford, 1918), 43.

11. Christopher Lasch, *The Culture of Narcissism: American Life in an Age of Diminishing Expectations* (New York: Norton, 1979).

12. Tom Wolfe, "The 'Me' Decade and the Third Great Awakening," in *Mauve Gloves and Madmen, Clutter and Vine* (New York: Farrar, Straus & Giroux, 1976).

13. Joel Stein, "The Me, Me, Me Generation," *Time*, May 20, 2013, http://time.com /247/millennials-the-me-me-me-generation/.

14. Jean M. Twenge, *The Narcissism Epidemic* (blog), *Psychology Today*, https://www .psychologytoday.com/blog/the-narcissism-epidemic.

15. Case Western Reserve University, "Millennials Admit to Being Narcissists, But Don't You Dare Call Them That," *Science Daily*, March 24, 2016, https://www.sciencedaily.com /releases/2016/03/160324105059.htm.

16. Brook Lea Foster, "The Persistent Myth of the Narcissistic Millennial," *Atlantic*, November 19, 2014, http://www.theatlantic.com/health/archive/2014/11/the-persistent -myth-of-the-narcissistic-millennial/382565/.

17. Ovid, *Metamorphoses*, 1:151.

18. Mary H. K. Choi, "Like. Flirt. Ghost: A Journey Into the Social Media Lives of Teens," *Wired*, August 25, 2016, https://www.wired.com/2016/08/how-teens-use-social-media/.

19. Ovid, *Metamorphoses*, 1:155.

20. Louise Vinge, *The Narcissus Theme in Western European Literature up to the Early Nineteenth Century*, trans. Robert Dewsnap (Lund: Gleerups, 1967), 11.

21. Ovid, *Metamorphoses*, 1:157.

22. Vinge, *Narcissus Theme*, 12.

23. Julie Kristeva, *Tales of Love*, trans. Leon S. Roudiez (New York: Columbia University Press, 1987), 126.

24. See Eli Pariser, *The Filter Bubble: What the Internet Is Hiding from You* (New York: Penguin Books, 2011).

25. Ray S. Anderson, *On Being Human: Essays in Theological Anthropology* (Pasadena, CA: Fuller Seminary Press, 1982), 22.

26. Michel Foucault, "Technologies of the Self," in *The Essential Foucault: Selections from the Essential Works of Foucault 1954–1984*, ed. Paul Rabinow and Nikolas Rose (New York: New Press, 1994), 147.

27. Joanna Woods-Marsden, *Renaissance Self-Portraiture: The Visual Construction of Identity and the Social Status of the Artist* (New Haven: Yale University Press, 1998), 13.

28. Woods-Marsden, *Renaissance Self-Portraiture*, 13.

29. Hans Urs von Balthasar, *A Theological Anthropology* (New York: Sheed & Ward, 1967), 101.

30. Kristeva, *Tales of Love*, 376.

31. Kristeva, *Tales of Love*, 377, emphasis original.

32. Kristeva, *Tales of Love*, 122, emphasis original.

33. Kristeva, *Tales of Love*, 122.

34. Gerard Manley Hopkins, "The Leaden Echo and the Golden Echo," in *Poems of Gerard Manley Hopkins*, 36.

35. Kristeva, *Tales of Love*, 122.
36. M. Shawn Copeland, *Enfleshing Freedom: Body, Race, and Being* (Minneapolis: Fortress, 2010), 18.

Chapter 3 Mastering the Mirror

1. Nikos Kazantzakis, *Report to Greco* (London: Faber & Faber, 1961), 150.
2. Joanna Woods-Marsden, *Renaissance Self-Portraiture: The Visual Construction of Identity and the Social Status of the Artist* (New Haven: Yale University Press, 1998), 9.
3. Maria H. Loh, *Still Lives: Death, Desire, and the Portrait of the Old Master* (Princeton: Princeton University Press, 2015), ix.
4. Loh, *Still Lives*, ix–x.
5. Woods-Marsden, *Renaissance Self-Portraiture*, 31.
6. James Hall, *The Self-Portrait: A Cultural History* (London: Thames & Hudson, 2014), 43.
7. David Hockney and Martin Gayford, *A History of Pictures: From the Cave to the Computer Screen* (New York: Abrams, 2016), 122.
8. Hall, *Self-Portrait*, 40.
9. Woods-Marsden, *Renaissance Self-Portraiture*, 34.
10. Quoted in Hall, *Self-Portrait*, 46.
11. Hall, *Self-Portrait*, 81.
12. Woods-Marsden, *Renaissance Self-Portraiture*, 1.
13. Woods-Marsden, *Renaissance Self-Portraiture*, 35.
14. Loh, *Still Lives*, ix.
15. Loh, *Still Lives*, xviii.
16. Woods-Marsden, *Renaissance Self-Portraiture*, 241.
17. Pascal Bonafoux, *Portraits of the Artist: The Self-Portrait in Painting* (New York: Rizzoli, 1985), 62.
18. Hockney and Gayford, *History of Pictures*, 112.
19. On Velázquez's chest is a red cross, symbol of the honorary Order of Santiago, national patron of Spain. Interestingly, the honor was not bestowed upon Velázquez until 1659 (three years after he completed the painting). Legend suggests that King Philip IV painted the honor upon Velázquez's chest in the painting. Here we see how far the lowly profession of artist has risen. The finest painters are now knighted by kings with symbols of church blessing.
20. Bonafoux, *Portraits of the Artist*, 79.
21. Woods-Marsden, *Renaissance Self-Portraiture*, 193.
22. Emma Hope Allwood, "Why We Still Need John Berger's *Ways of Seeing*," *Dazed*, January 3, 2017, http://www.dazeddigital.com/artsandculture/article/34166/1/why-we-still -need-ways-of-seeing-john-berger.
23. Quoted in Allwood, "Berger's *Ways of Seeing*."
24. Woods-Marsden, *Renaissance Self-Portraiture*, 199.
25. Adapted from Lucy Whitaker, Martin Clayton, and Aislinn Loconte, *The Art of Italy in the Royal Collection: Renaissance and Baroque* (London: Royal Collection, 2007).
26. Allwood, "Berger's *Ways of Seeing*."
27. Natasha Walter, "Feel My Pain," *Guardian*, May 21, 2005, https://www.theguard ian.com/artanddesign/2005/may/21/art; and Antonio Rodríguez, "Una pintora extraor-dinaria," *Así*, March 17, 1945.
28. Andy Warhol, *Self-Portrait*, 1966, Museum of Modern Art, https://www.moma.org /learn/moma_learning/andy-warhol-self-portrait-1966.

29. Danielle Shang, "Yayoi Kusama, Narcissus Garden," Khan Academy, https://www
.khanacademy.org/humanities/ap-art-history/later-europe-and-americas/modernity-ap
/a/yayoi-kusama-narcissus-garden.

30. Jean-Michel Basquiat, *Self-Portrait*, 1982, http://www.everypainterpaintshimself
.com/article/basquiats_self-portrait.

31. Alex Taylor, "Ten Things You Might Not Know about Basquiat," *AnOther*, July
7, 2015, http://www.anothermag.com/art-photography/7569/ten-things-you-might-not
-know-about-basquiat.

32. Nathan Smith, "The Philosophy of Ai Weiwei (From Andy Warhol and Back Again),"
Los Angeles Review of Books, January 31, 2016, https://lareviewofbooks.org/article/the
-philosophy-of-ai-weiwei-from-andy-warhol-and-back-again/.

33. "The 20 Best Ai Weiwei Selfies," *HuffPost*, August 31, 2013, http://www.huffington
post.com/2013/08/31/ai-weiwei-selfies_n_3829361.html.

34. Smith, "Philosophy of Ai Weiwei."

35. "An Argument for Something Else: Dieter Roelstraete in Conversation with Kerry
James Marshall," in *Kerry James Marshall: Painting and Other Stuff*, ed. Nav Haq (An-
twerp: Ludion, 2014), 22.

36. "Argument for Something Else," 28.

37. Lanka Tattersall, "Black Lives, Matter," in *Kerry James Marshall: Mastry*, ed.
Helen Molesworth (New York: Skira Rizzoli, 2016), 69.

38. Hockney and Gayford, *History of Pictures*, 208.

39. Hall, *Self-Portrait*, 107.

40. Hall, *Self-Portrait*, 126.

41. Giovanni Pietro Bellori, "Life of Caravaggio," in *Vite de' pittori, scultori ed ar-
chitetti moderni* (Rome, 1672), http://arthistoryresources.net/baroque-art-theory-2013
/bellori-caravaggio.html.

42. Hall, *Self-Portrait*, 109.

43. Hall, *Self-Portrait*, 110.

44. Basil the Great's theological anthropology can be found in *On the Human Condition*, trans. Nonna Verna Harrison (Yonkers, NY: St. Vladimir's Seminary Press, 2005).

45. Nonna Verna Harrison, *God's Many-Splendored Image: Theological Anthropology
for Christian Formation* (Grand Rapids: Baker Academic, 2010), 14.

46. Harrison, *God's Many-Splendored Image*, 70.

47. Gregory of Nyssa, "On Perfection," from his *Ascetical Works* in *The Fathers of
the Early Church*, trans. Virginia Woods Callahan (Washington, DC: Catholic University
of America Press, 1967), 110.

48. Harrison, *God's Many-Splendored Image*, 71.

Chapter 4 Reframing Memories

1. Marilynne Robinson, *Gilead* (New York: Farrar, Straus & Giroux, 2004), 106–7.

2. In order, quotations are from Charles Dickens, *David Copperfield* (London: Penguin
Classics, 2005); Maya Angelou, *I Know Why the Caged Bird Sings* (New York: Virago,
2015); Ralph Ellison, *Invisible Man* (New York: Ishi Press, 2015); and Herman Melville,
Moby Dick: Or, The Whale (London: Penguin Classics, 2010).

3. Charles Dickens, *David Copperfield* (New York: Sheldon and Company, 1863), 42.

4. Herman Melville, *Moby Dick: Or, The White Whale* (Boston: The St. Botolph Society, 1892), 7.

5. Ralph Ellison, *Invisible Man*, 1.

6. Maya Angelou, *I Know Why the Caged Bird Sings*, 1.

7. "Nadine Gordimer: A Life in Quotes," *Guardian*, July 14, 2014, https://www.the guardian.com/books/2014/jul/14/nadine-gordimer-a-life-in-quotes.

8. Julie Phillips, "Out of Bounds: The Unruly Imagination of Ursula K. Le Guin," *New Yorker*, October 17, 2016, 38.

9. F. Scott Fitzgerald, *The Great Gatsby* (New York: Scribner, 2004), 1.

10. Octavio Paz, *The Labyrinth of Solitude* (New York: Grove, 1961), 195.

11. Jill Walker Rettberg, *Seeing Ourselves through Technology: How We Use Selfies, Blogs, and Wearable Devices to See and Shape Ourselves* (London: Palgrave Macmillan, 2014), 29.

12. Alice Walker, *The Color Purple* (Boston: Mariner Books, 1982), 196.

13. Walker, *Color Purple*, 1.

14. Walker, *Color Purple*, 177.

15. Walker, *Color Purple*, 195.

16. Walker, *Color Purple*, 40.

17. Walker, *Color Purple*, 285.

18. Walker, *Color Purple*, preface.

19. Alice Walker, *In Search of Our Mother's Gardens: Womanist Prose* (New York: Harcourt Brace Jovanovich, 1983).

20. Sarah Sentilles, "The Photograph as Mystery: Theological Language and Ethical Looking in Roland Barthes's *Camera Lucida*," *Journal of Religion* 90, no. 4 (October 2010): 525–26, http://www.jstor.org/stable/10.1086/654822.

21. Sarah Pulliam Bailey, "Bono: David Sang the Blues and Jesus Did Some Punk Rock," *Washington Post*, June 24, 2013, https://www.washingtonpost.com/national/on-faith/bono -david-sang-the-blues-and-jesus-did-some-punk-rock/2013/06/24/f7398bde-dcfd-11e2-a4 84-7b7f79cd66a1_story.html?utm_term=.93bb0f5df45c.

22. She can be found on Instagram, Twitter, and YouTube under the moniker "beckiej brown." Her YouTube channel is https://www.youtube.com/user/beckie0.

23. Beckie Jane Brown, "She Takes a Photo: 6.5 Years / BeckieJBrown," YouTube, June 8, 2014, https://www.youtube.com/watch?v=eRvk5UQY1Js.

24. Beckie Jane Brown, "Trichotillomania / BeckieJBrown," YouTube, May 25, 2009, https://www.youtube.com/watch?v=CiBIXMBEqgE.

25. Rettberg, *Seeing Ourselves through Technology*, 39.

26. Brown, "She Takes a Photo."

27. Rettberg, *Seeing Ourselves through Technology*, 4.

28. Saint Augustine, *Confessions*, trans. R. S. Pine-Coffin (London: Penguin Books, 1961), 21.

29. Rettberg, *Seeing Ourselves through Technology*, 4.

30. Rodger M. Payne, *The Self and the Sacred: Conversion and Autobiography in Early American Protestantism* (Knoxville: University of Tennessee Press, 1998), 37–38.

31. Rettberg, *Seeing Ourselves through Technology*, 4.

32. Rettberg, *Seeing Ourselves through Technology*, 5.

33. Rettberg, *Seeing Ourselves through Technology*, 6.

34. John Fuller, "To the Reader," in the preface to John Beadle, *The Journal or Diary of a Thankful Christian* (London, 1656), quoted in Payne, *Self and the Sacred*, 20. You can see the original journal at https://archive.org/details/journalor00bead.

35. Payne, *Self and the Sacred*, 20.

36. Beadle, *The Journal or Diary of a Thankful Christian*, quoted in Payne, *Self and the Sacred*, 20.

37. Payne, *Self and the Sacred*, 20.

38. Payne, *Self and the Sacred*, 22.

39. Ann Voskamp, *One Thousand Gifts: A Dare to Live Fully Right Where You Are* (Grand Rapids: Zondervan, 2011).

40. Voskamp, *One Thousand Gifts*, 108–9.

41. Christine Valters Paintner, *Eyes of the Heart: Photography as a Contemplative Practice* (Notre Dame, IN: Sorin Books, 2013), 3.

Chapter 5 Seizing the Light

1. Iris Murdoch, "Metaphysics and Ethics," in *Existentialists and Mystics: Writings on Philosophy and Literature*, ed. Peter J. Conradi (London: Chatto & Windus, 1997), 75.

2. Nicholas Mirzoeff, *How to See the World* (New York: Pelican Books, 2015), 4–5.

3. Mirzoeff, *How to See*, 5.

4. I have been encouraged and inspired by colleagues and their collective wisdom gathered in places like the Brehm Center at Fuller Theological Seminary. Great starting points include William A. Dyrness, *Visual Faith* (Grand Rapids: Baker Academic, 2001), Daniel A. Siedell, *God in the Gallery* (Grand Rapids: Baker Academic, 2008), and Makoto Fujimura, *Culture Care* (Downers Grove, IL: InterVarsity, 2017).

5. Roland Barthes, *Camera Lucida: Reflections on Photography*, trans. Richard Howard (1980; repr., New York: Hill & Wang, 2010), 31.

6. Sean O'Hagen, "Capturing the Light by Roger Watson and Helen Rappaport," *Guardian*, April 21, 2013, https://www.theguardian.com/books/2013/apr/21/capturing -light-watson-rappaport-review.

7. "Robert Cornelius' Self-Portrait: The First Ever 'Selfie' (1839)," *Public Domain Review*, http://publicdomainreview.org/collections/robert-cornelius-self-portrait-the-first -ever-selfie-1839/.

8. Jillian Lerner, "The Drowned Inventor: Bayard, Daguerre, and the Curious Attractions of Early Photography," *History of Photography* 38, no. 3 (2014): 218–32.

9. Edward Weston, *The Daybooks of Edward Weston* (1973), quoted in Susan Sontag, *On Photography* (New York: Farrar, Straus & Giroux, 1977), 186.

10. Sontag, *On Photography*, 86.

11. Barthes, *Camera Lucida*, 30.

12. Charles Baudelaire, *The Mirror of Art*, ed. and trans. Jonathan Mayne (London: Phaidon, 1955), excerpt available at http://www.csus.edu/indiv/o/obriene/art109/readings /11%20baudelaire%20photography.htm.

13. Baudelaire, *Mirror of Art*.

14. Charles Baudelaire's original review was published in the *Révue Française, Paris, June 10–July 20, 1859*, and is quoted in Steven Z. Levine, *Monet, Narcissus, and Self-Reflection: The Modernist Myth of the Self* (Chicago: University of Chicago Press, 1994), 1.

15. Mary Warner Marien, *Photography: A Cultural History* (New York: Harry N. Abrams, 2002), 169.

16. Sontag, *On Photography*, 7.

17. Barthes, *Camera Lucida*, 79.

18. Barthes, *Camera Lucida*, 87.

19. Barthes, *Camera Lucida*, 105.

20. Jill Walker Rettberg, *Seeing Ourselves through Technology: How We Use Selfies, Blogs, and Wearable Devices to See and Shape Ourselves* (London: Palgrave Macmillan, 2014), 54.

21. Barthes, *Camera Lucida*, 85.

22. Barthes, *Camera Lucida*, 92.

23. Rettberg, *Seeing Ourselves through Technology*, 54.

24. Christopher Isherwood, from the first page of his "Berlin Diary" in *Goodbye to Berlin* (London: Hogarth Press, 1939).

25. Marien, *Photography*, 23.

26. Sontag, *On Photography*, 156.

27. Sontag, *On Photography*, 5.

28. Marien, *Photography*, 162.

29. Charles Milton Bell, *Otoe Delegation*, 1881, http://www.metmuseum.org/art/col lection/search/285710.

30. Arthur Schopenhauer, "Physiognomy" (1850), in *Religion: A Dialogue and Other Essays*, trans. T. Bailey Saunders (London: George Allen and Unwin, c. 1890), 75, found in Robert A. Sobieszek and Deborah Irmas, *The Camera I: Photographic Self-Portraits from the Audrey and Sydney Irmas Collection, Los Angeles County Museum of Art* (New York: Harry N. Abrams, 1994), 20.

31. James W. Redfield, *Comparative Physiognomy, or Resemblances between Men and Animals* (New York: J. S. Redfield, Clinton Hall, 1852), 11. The absurdity of blatant stereotyping by Redfield is only mildly relieved in seeing "Frenchmen compared to Frogs and Irishmen to Dogs." Our ability to judge the other can spring from even more than race or gender.

32. Marien, *Photography*, 143.

33. *National Geographic*, "About," http://www.nationalgeographic.com/about/.

34. Lewis Hine, quoted in Marien, *Photography*, 234.

35. Sontag, *On Photography*, 4.

36. Sontag, *On Photography*, 87.

37. Dorothea Lange, quoted in Milton Meltzer, *Dorothea Lange: A Photographer's Life* (Syracuse, NY: Syracuse University Press, 1978), vii.

38. Arthur Rothstein, *African-American Family from Gee's Bend, Alabama*, 1937, http://www.metmuseum.org/art/collection/search/284663.

39. Marien, *Photography*, 285.

40. Marien, *Photography*, 282.

41. Marien, *Photography*, 312.

42. Sontag, *On Photography*, 32.

43. Sontag, *On Photography*, 192.

44. Marien, *Photography*, 314.

45. Rettberg, *Seeing Ourselves through Technology*, 53.

46. Marien, *Photography*, 445.

47. A film has been made about Vivian Maier titled *Finding Vivian Maier*, codirected by John Maloof and Charlie Siskel (Ravine Pictures, 2013).

48. Marien, *Photography*, 239.

49. Kurt Schwitters, quoted in Marien, *Photography*, 242.

50. Näkki Goranin, "The History of the Photobooth," *Telegraph*, March 7, 2008, http://www.telegraph.co.uk/culture/donotmigrate/3671736/The-history-of-the-photobooth.html.

51. Rettberg, *Seeing Ourselves through Technology*, 42.

52. Rettberg, *Seeing Ourselves through Technology*, 43.

53. Marien, *Photography*, 257.

54. These words from Henri Cartier-Bresson are taken from *Images a la Savette* published in France in 1952 and quoted in Marien, *Photography*, 262.

55. Rettberg, *Seeing Ourselves through Technology*, 43.

56. Barthes, *Camera Lucida*, 32.

57. Barthes, *Camera Lucida*, 13.

58. Sobieszek and Irmas, *Camera I*, 30.

59. Richard Avedon, *Borrowed Dogs* (New York: The Richard Avedon Foundation, 2002), quoted in Sobieszek and Irmas, *Camera I*, 23.

60. Cindy Sherman, *The Complete Untitled Film Stills* (New York: The Museum of Modern Art, 2003), quoted in James Hall, *The Self-Portrait: A Cultural History* (London: Thames & Hudson, 2014), 271.

61. Hall, *Self-Portrait*, 271.

62. Gabriel Schor, "Cindy Sherman: Force of Circumstance, Ambiguity, Horror, Aging," in *Cindy Sherman*, ed. Ingvild Goetz and Karsten Löckemann for the Sammlung Goetz Museum (Ostfildern, Germany: Hatje Cantz Verlag, 2015), 53.

63. Rosemary Radford Ruether, *Sexism and God-Talk: Toward a Feminist Theology* (Boston: Beacon, 1983), 19.

64. Errol Morris, *Believing Is Seeing: Observations on the Mysteries of Photography* (New York: Penguin, 2011), 270.

65. Barthes, *Camera Lucida*, 80–81.

66. Sarah Sentilles, "The Photograph as Mystery: Theological Language and Ethical Looking in Roland Barthes's *Camera Lucida*," *Journal of Religion* 90, no. 4 (2010): 516, http://www.jstor.org/stable/10.1086/654822.

67. Barthes, *Camera Lucida*, 80–81.

68. Sentilles, "Photograph as Mystery," 516.

69. Barthes, *Camera Lucida*, 82.

70. Sentilles, "Photograph as Mystery," 517.

71. Teresa of Avila, *The Life of St. Teresa of Jesus, of the Order of Our Lady of Carmel*, trans. David Lewis (New York: Benziger, 1904), 256.

72. Sentilles, "Photograph as Mystery," 517.

73. Sentilles, "Photograph as Mystery," 509.

74. Sentilles, "Photograph as Mystery," 518.

75. Sentilles, "Photograph as Mystery," 519.

Chapter 6 Behind the Mask

1. Paul Laurence Dunbar, "We Wear the Mask," in *Majors and Minors* (Toledo: Hadley & Hadley, 1896), http://nationalhumanitiescenter.org/pds/maai2/identity/text3/dunbar.pdf.

2. Gustav Janouch, *Conversations with Kafka*, trans. Goronmy Rees (Frankfurt-am-Main: S. Fischer, 1971), quoted in Susan Sontag, *On Photography* (New York: Farrar, Straus & Giroux, 1977).

3. William James, *The Principles of Psychology* (New York: Henry Holt, 1890), 1:294.

4. Donna Freitas, *The Happiness Effect: How Social Media Is Driving a Generation to Appear Perfect at Any Cost* (New York: Oxford University Press, 2017), xv.

5. Christian Smith, foreword to Freitas, *Happiness Effect*, iv.

6. Freitas, *Happiness Effect*, xvii.

7. Roland Barthes, *Camera Lucida: Reflections on Photography*, trans. Richard Howard (1980; repr., New York: Hill & Wang, 2010), 118.

8. See the pointed letter to the editor of the *New York Times* by Allen Frances, chairman of the task force that wrote the DSM-IV, urging readers to resist the urge to diagnose Donald Trump: "An Eminent Psychiatrist Demurs on Trump's Mental State," *New York Times*, February 14, 2017, https://www.nytimes.com/2017/02/14/opinion/an-eminent-psychiatrist-demurs-on-trumps-mental-state.html.

9. Karl Barth, *The Word of God and the Word of Man* (London: Peter Smith, 1958).

10. Sigmund Freud, *On Narcissism*, in *The Standard Edition of the Complete Psychological Works of Sigmund Freud*, trans. James Strachey (London: Hogarth, 1948), 14:73–102.

11. Martin Buber, *I and Thou*, trans. Walter Kaufmann (1923; repr., New York: Touchstone, 1971).

12. Julie Kristeva, *Tales of Love*, trans. Leon S. Roudiez (New York: Columbia University Press, 1987), 86.

13. Kristeva, *Tales of Love*, 94.

14. C. Fred Alford, *Narcissism: Socrates, the Frankfurt School, and Psychoanalytic Theory* (New Haven: Yale University Press, 1988), 3.

15. Rebecca Webber notes, "True pathological narcissism has always been rare and remains so. It affects an estimated 1 percent of the population, and that prevalence hasn't changed demonstrably since clinicians started measuring it" ("The Real Narcissists," *Psychology Today*, September/October 2016, 54).

16. David Riesman's *The Lonely Crowd* (New Haven: Yale University Press, 1950) and William H. Whyte's *The Organization Man* (New York: Simon and Schuster, 1956) noted how people subsumed their desires for the good of the company (or the crowd).

17. Christopher Lasch, *The Culture of Narcissism: American Life in an Age of Diminishing Expectations* (New York: Warner Books, 1979), 29.

18. Lasch, *Culture of Narcissism*, 31.

19. Lasch, *Culture of Narcissism*, 33.

20. From Karl Menninger's *Whatever Became of Sin?* (New York: Hawthorn Books, 1978) to Alasdair MacIntyre's *After Virtue* (Notre Dame, IN: University of Notre Dame Press, 1981) through Keith Miller's *Sin: Overcoming the Ultimate Deadly Addiction* (San Francisco: Harper & Row, 1987), the diagnosis has been clear and our prospects for self-improvement bleak.

21. Cornelius Plantinga Jr., *Not the Way It's Supposed to Be: A Breviary of Sin* (Grand Rapids: Eerdmans, 1995), 83.

22. Plantinga, *Not the Way*, 83.

23. Elizabeth Lunbeck, *The Americanization of Narcissism* (Cambridge, MA: Harvard University Press, 2014), 2.

24. Jean M. Twenge, *Generation Me: Why Today's Young Americans Are More Confident, Assertive, Entitled and Miserable Than Ever Before* (New York: Atria Books, 2014).

25. Charles Zanor, "A Fate That Narcissists Will Hate: Being Ignored," *New York Times*, November 29, 2010, http://www.nytimes.com/2010/11/30/health/views/30mind.html.

26. Blogger Matt Walsh blames all the self-worshiping Satanists: "Christians, Our True Battle Is Spiritual, Not Political," TheBlaze, March 29, 2017, http://www.theblaze.com/contributions/matt-walsh-christians-our-true-battle-is-spiritual-not-political/.

27. Alford, *Narcissism*, 2.

28. Rod Dreher, *The Benedict Option: A Strategy for Christians in a Post-Christian Nation* (New York: Sentinel, 2017).

29. Elizabeth Lunbeck, *The Americanization of Narcissism* (Cambridge, MA: Harvard University Press, 2014), 4.

30. Lunbeck, *Americanization of Narcissism*, 3.

31. Lunbeck, *Americanization of Narcissism*, 4.

32. Lunbeck, *Americanization of Narcissism*, 253. See Jean M. Twenge and W. Keith Campbell, *The Narcissism Epidemic: Living in the Age of Entitlement* (New York: Free Press, 2009).

33. Lunbeck, *Americanization of Narcissism*, 261.

34. Rebecca Webber, "The Real Narcissists," *Psychology Today*, September/October 2016, 58.

35. Lunbeck, *Americanization of Narcissism*, 263.

36. Read it and weep in 2 Chron. 26:15–16; 32:23–26.

37. Jessica Tracy, *Take Pride: Why the Deadliest Sin Holds the Secret to Human Success* (Boston: Houghton Mifflin, 2016), 35.

38. *The Twelve Books of John Cassian on the Institutes of the Coenobia, and the Remedies for the Eight Principal Faults*, in *A Select Library of Nicene and Post-Nicene Fathers of the Christian Church*, second series, book 11, chapter 3 (New York, 1894), http://www.osb.org/lectio/cassian/inst/inst11.html#11.1.

39. Cassian, *Institutes*, book 11, chapter 3.

40. Cassian, *Institutes*, book 11, chapter 6.

41. Tracy, *Take Pride*, 35.

42. Tracy, *Take Pride*, 43.

43. Tracy, *Take Pride*, 51.

44. Tracy, *Take Pride*, 174.

45. Tracy, *Take Pride*, 175.

46. Tracy, *Take Pride*, 196.

47. Paul Laurence Dunbar, *Majors and Minors* (Toledo: Hadley & Hadley, 1896), http://nationalhumanitiescenter.org/pds/maai2/identity/text3/dunbar.pdf.

48. Soong-Chan Rah's commentary on the biblical book of Lamentations is titled *Prophetic Lament: A Call for Justice in Troubled Times* (Downers Grove, IL: InterVarsity, 2015), 24.

49. William James, *The Principles of Psychology* (New York: Dover Publications, 1950), 294, quoted in Erving Goffman, *The Presentation of Self in Everyday Life* (New York: Anchor Books, 1959), 49.

50. Goffman, *Presentation of Self*, 244.

51. Goffman, *Presentation of Self*, 252.

52. Goffman, *Presentation of Self*, 253.

53. The research of MIT psychologist Sherry Turkle gathered in *Alone Together: Why We Expect More from Technology and Less from Each Other* (New York: Basic Books, 2011) is quite sobering.

54. Goffman, *Presentation of Self*, 2.

55. Goffman, *Presentation of Self*, 19.

56. Hans Urs von Balthasar, *Theo-Drama: Theological Dramatic Theory*, vol. 2, *Dramatis Personae: Man in God*, trans. Graham Harrison (San Francisco: Ignatius, 1990), 91.

57. Balthasar, *Theo-Drama*, 19.

58. Balthasar, *Theo-Drama*, 20.

59. Claudio Tolomei to Sebastiano del Piombo, *De le lettere di m. Clavdio Tolomei* (In Vinegia: Appresso Gabriel Giolito de Ferrari, 1547), https://archive.org/details/delelet teredimcl00tolo, quoted in Harry Berger Jr., *Fictions of the Pose: Rembrandt against the Italian Renaissance* (Stanford, CA: Stanford University Press, 2000), 161.

60. Eugene H. Peterson, *A Long Obedience in the Same Direction: Discipleship in an Instant Society* (Downers Grove, IL: InterVarsity, 2000).

61. Charles H. Cooley, *Human Nature and the Social Order* (New York: C. Scribner's Sons, 1922), 352–53, quoted in Goffman, *Presentation of Self*, 35.

62. Goffman, *Presentation of Self*, 36.

63. C. S. Lewis, *Mere Christianity* (San Francisco: HarperOne, 2015), 128.

64. Alford, *Narcissism*, 2.

65. Theodore Maynard, *Saints for Our Times* (Garden City, NY: Image Books, 1955), 77.

66. Raymond of Capua, *The Life of Catherine of Siena*, trans. Conleth Kearns, OP (Dublin: Dominican Publications, 1980), 1.10.92.

67. Catherine of Siena, *The Dialogue*, trans. Suzanne Noffke, OP, in *The Classics of Western Spirituality* (New York: Paulist Press, 1980), dialogue 4, 29.

68. Catherine of Siena, "Letter T226," quoted in Thomas McDermott, OP, *Catherine of Siena: Spiritual Development in Her Life and Teaching* (Mahwah, NJ: Paulist Press, 2008), 124.

69. Catherine of Siena, "Letter T226," 124.

70. Maynard, *Saints for Our Times*, 77.

Chapter 7 Instapressure

1. Julia Naughton and Peter Born, "Kendall Jenner on Caitlyn, Social Media, and Scents," *Women's Wear Daily*, September 20, 2015, http://wwd.com/beauty-industry-news /beauty-features/kendall-jenner-sisters-kardashian-estee-lauder-10232780/.

2. Justin Worland, "This is the Most-Liked Instagram Photo Ever," *Time*, June 28, 2015, http://time.com/3939231/kendall-jenner-instagram-photo/.

3. Kimberley Dadds, "Here's the Top Ten Most Liked Instagram Posts of 2015," BuzzFeed, December 2, 2015, https://www.buzzfeed.com/kimberleydadds/people-love -the-heart-hair?utm_term=.blBqAQBzVn#.atGDpnwveY.

4. Robert Sullivan, "How Kendall Jenner Stays Grounded with 68 Million Followers and Counting," *Vogue*, March 23, 2016, http://www.vogue.com/article/kendall-jenner-insta gram-brand-growth?mbid=KJ.

5. Sullivan, "Jenner Stays Grounded."

6. Rachel Torgerson, "This Justin Bieber Photo Dethroned Kendall Jenner's Heart-Shaped Hair Pic as Most-Liked on Instagram," *Us Magazine*, May 5, 2016, http://www .usmagazine.com/celebrity-beauty/news/justin-bieber-beats-kendall-jenner-for-most -liked-instagram-pic-w205341.

7. "Beyoncé's Pregnancy Picture Is Now the Most Liked Instagram of All Time," *Marie Claire*, February 2, 2017, http://www.marieclaire.co.uk/news/celebrity-news/most-liked -instagram-photo-29093.

8. This line is from *History of King Henry the Fourth, Part 2*, act 3, scene 1.

9. Fred Ritchin, *After Photography* (New York: Norton, 2009), 10.

10. Ritchin, *After Photography*, 12.

11. David Colman, "Me, Myself and iPhone," *New York Times*, June 30, 2010, http:// www.nytimes.com/2010/07/01/fashion/01ONLINE.html.

12. Even forty years ago Susan Sontag noted how new inventions like video cameras were being directed at ourselves with image feedback in her book *On Photography* (New York: Farrar, Straus & Giroux, 1977), 177.

13. Steven Holiday, Matthew J. Lewis, Rachel Nielsen, Harper D. Anderson, and Maureen Elinzano, "The Selfie Study: Archetypes and Motivations in Modern Self-Photography," *Visual Communication Quarterly* 23, no. 3 (July–September 2016): 175–87.

14. Holiday et al., "Selfie Study," 179.

15. Holiday et al., "Selfie Study," 181.

16. Holiday et al., "Selfie Study," 182.

17. Keaton made these comments at the Independent Spirit Awards in 2016 while accepting the best actor prize for his role as a self-obsessed actor in *Birdman*.

18. Holiday et al., "Selfie Study," 183.

19. Holiday et al., "Selfie Study," 184.

20. Kim Kardashian, *Selfish* (New York: Rizzoli, 2015).

21. Laura Bennett, "Self-Publishing," *Slate*, May 6, 2015, http://www.slate.com/articles/arts/books/2015/05/selfish_kim_kardashian_west_s_book_of_selfies_reviewed.html.

22. Megan Garber, "You Win, Kim Kardashian," *Atlantic*, May 13, 2015, http://www.theatlantic.com/entertainment/archive/2015/05/kim-kardashian-selfish/393113/.

23. Barbara Vinken, "Cindy Sherman, Woman as Image: The Artist Is Present?" in *Cindy Sherman*, ed. Ingvild Goetz and Karsten Löckemann (Germany: Hatje Cantz Verlag, 2015), 134.

24. Drew Pinsky and S. Mark Young, *The Mirror Effect: How Celebrity Narcissism Is Seducing America* (New York: HarperCollins, 2009), 65.

25. Pinsky and Young, *Mirror Effect*, 82.

26. Pinsky and Young, *Mirror Effect*, 88.

27. Pinsky and Young, *Mirror Effect*, 127.

28. Pinsky and Young, *Mirror Effect*, 98.

29. Pinsky and Young, *Mirror Effect*, 131.

30. Sontag, *On Photography*, 178.

31. Sontag, *On Photography*, 3.

32. Holiday et al., "Selfie Study," 182.

33. Dietrich Bonhoeffer, *Life Together*, trans. John W. Doberstein (San Francisco: Harper & Row, 1978), 77.

34. Sontag, *On Photography*, 3.

35. Sontag, *On Photography*, 3.

36. Sontag, *On Photography*, 162.

37. Sontag, *On Photography*, 164.

38. Sontag, *On Photography*, 9.

39. Sontag, *On Photography*, 9.

40. Sontag, *On Photography*, 10.

41. Sontag, *On Photography*, 42.

42. Gerard Manley Hopkins, "On the Portrait of Two Beautiful Young People," *Poems* (London: Humphrey Milford, 1918), http://www.bartleby.com/122/54.html.

43. This abbreviation of "Instagram" became so ubiquitous in youth culture that it was incorporated into rap hits by Meek Mill and Kendrick Lamar, http://www.urbandictionary.com/define.php?term=do%20it%20for%20the%20gram.

44. Peter Walker, "Facebook Makes You Unhappy and Makes Jealous People Particularly Sad, Study Finds," *Independent*, December 22, 2016, http://www.independent.co.uk/life-style/gadgets-and-tech/facebook-social-media-make-unhappy-jealous-people-particularly-sad-copenhagen-university-study-a7490816.html.

45. Cara Reedy, "Too Much Facebook Leads to Envy and Depression," CNN, March 2, 2015, http://money.cnn.com/2015/03/02/technology/facebook-envy/.

46. Sullivan, "Jenner Stays Grounded."

47. Roger Highfield, "Interview with Stephen Hawking," *Telegraph*, October 18, 2001, http://www.telegraph.co.uk/news/science/science-news/4766816/Interview-with-Stephen-Hawking.html.

48. Donna Freitas inspired me to reflect on my old, weathered photo albums, thanks to her important book, *The Happiness Effect: How Social Media Is Driving a Generation to Appear Perfect at Any Cost* (New York: Oxford University Press, 2017).

49. Holiday et al., "Selfie Study," 183.

50. Holiday et al., "Selfie Study," 184.

51. Jill Walker Rettberg, *Seeing Ourselves through Technology: How We Use Selfies, Blogs, and Wearable Devices to See and Shape Ourselves* (London: Palgrave Macmillan, 2014), 27.

52. Pew Research Center, "A Portrait of 'Generation Next': How Young People View Their Lives, Futures, and Politics," January 9, 2007, cited in Pinsky and Young, *Mirror Effect*, 148.

53. Pinsky and Young, *Mirror Effect*, 183.

54. Pinsky and Young, *Mirror Effect*, 154.

55. Pinsky and Young, *Mirror Effect*, 184.

56. Pinsky and Young, *Mirror Effect*, 159.

57. Pinsky and Young, *Mirror Effect*, 185.

58. Bianca Bosker, "Instamom," *Atlantic*, March 2017, 16–18, https://www.theatlantic.com/magazine/archive/2017/03/instamom/513827/.

59. Bosker, "Instamom," 17.

60. Bosker, "Instamom," 18.

61. Pinsky and Young, *Mirror Effect*, 240.

62. Sontag, *On Photography*, 85.

63. Sontag, *On Photography*, 86.

64. "The Evolution Video: How Images of Beauty Are Manipulated by the Media," Dove Self-Esteem Project, 2006, https://www.youtube.com/watch?v=iYhCn0jf46U.

65. "Dove Real Beauty Sketches: You're More Beautiful Than You Think," Dove, https://www.youtube.com/watch?v=XpaOjMXyJGk.

66. Samantha Murphy, "Viral Dove Campaign Becomes Most Watched Ad Ever," *Mashable*, May 20, 2013, http://mashable.com/2013/05/20/dove-ad-most-watche/#SLjO_79hfEqR.

67. Madison Malone Kircher, "Where Are You, Essena O'Neill?," *New York*, November 4, 2016, http://nymag.com/selectall/2016/11/esenna-oneill-one-year-after-quitting-social-media.html.

68. While Essena O'Neill no longer has an Instagram account, remnants of her revised posts (and the discussion surrounding them) can be found across the internet. These quotations are from my own survey taken in March 2017.

69. Megan McCluskey, "Instagram Star Essena O'Neill Breaks Her Silence on Quitting Social Media," *Time*, January 5, 2016, http://time.com/4167856/essena-oneill-breaks-silence-on-quitting-social-media/.

70. Nonna Verna Harrison, *God's Many-Splendored Image: Theological Anthropology for Christian Formation* (Grand Rapids: Baker Academic, 2010), 29.

71. Gregory of Nyssa's *Homilies on the Beatitudes*, quoted in Harrison, *God's Many-Splendored Image*, 32.

72. David Cairns, *The Image of God in Man* (London: SCM, 1953), 44, in Stanley J. Grenz, *The Social God and the Relational Self: A Trinitarian Theology of the Imago Dei* (Louisville: Westminster John Knox, 2001), 305.

Chapter 8 Augmented and Transfigured

1. Daniel Kahneman, "The Riddle of Experience vs. Memory," TED talk, February 2010, https://www.ted.com/talks/daniel_kahneman_the_riddle_of_experience_vs_memory#t-583613.

2. David Kravets, "Judge Says Monkey Cannot Own Copyright to Famous Selfies," *Ars Technica*, January 6, 2016, https://arstechnica.com/tech-policy/2016/01/judge-says-monkey-cannot-own-copyright-to-famous-selfies/.

3. Fred Ritchin, *After Photography* (New York: Norton, 2009), 145.

4. Ritchin, *After Photography*, 73.

5. Kerry Flynn, "Snapchat's 10 Most Popular Lenses of 2016," Mashable, December 31, 2016, http://mashable.com/2016/12/31/snapchat-lenses-2016/#zXkDefu5fqqE.

6. Raymond Wong, "Snapchat Will Soon Make Real Clouds Vomit Rainbows," Mashable, February 1, 2017, http://mashable.com/2017/02/01/snapchat-world-lenses-augmented-reality/#zXkDefu5fqqE.

7. Rob Marvin, "Snapchat Spectacles," *PCMag*, February 21, 2017, http://www.pcmag.com/review/350153/snapchat-spectacles.

8. Kif Leswing, "A Chinese Photo App Worth $4.5 Billion Is Trending in the US—Here's What It Does," *Business Insider*, January 19, 2017, http://www.businessinsider.com/what-is-meitu-selfie-app-photos-2017-1.

9. Miz Cracker, "The Magnetic and Emotionally Complex Power of FaceApp's Gender Filter," *Slate*, May 5, 2017, http://www.slate.com/blogs/outward/2017/05/05/faceapp_s_gender_filter_offers_possibility_for_trans_and_gender_curious.html.

10. Abby Ohlheiser, "Everything That's Wrong with FaceApp, the Latest Creepy Photo App for Your Face," *Washington Post*, April 26, 2017, https://www.washingtonpost.com/news/the-intersect/wp/2017/04/26/everything-thats-wrong-with-faceapp-the-latest-creepy-photo-app-for-your-face/.

11. The Bitmoji app can be found at https://www.bitmoji.com/.

12. David Hockney and Martin Gayford, *A History of Pictures: From the Cave to the Computer Screen* (New York: Abrams, 2016), 340.

13. Jill Walker Rettberg, *Seeing Ourselves through Technology: How We Use Selfies, Blogs, and Wearable Devices to See and Shape Ourselves* (London: Palgrave Macmillan, 2014), 53.

14. *After Life*, directed by Hirokazu Koreeda (Japan, 1998).

15. Elizabeth Zelensky and Lela Gilbert, *Windows to Heaven: Introducing Icons to Protestants and Catholics* (Grand Rapids: Brazos, 2005), 24.

16. Zelensky and Gilbert, *Windows to Heaven*, 25.

17. After Maltbie Davenport Babcock's death at age 42, his widow Catherine published a collection of his poems, including "This Is My Father's World," in *Thoughts for Every-Day Living* (New York: Charles Scribner's Sons, 1901), https://archive.org/details/thoughtsforever00babc.

18. Jean-Luc Marion, *God without Being*, trans. Thomas A. Carlson (Chicago: University of Chicago Press, 1991).

19. David Tracy, introduction to Marion, *God without Being*, xii.

20. Walter C. Smith, "Immortal, Invisible, God Only Wise," found in *Hymns of Christ and the Christian Life*, 1867.

21. Marion, *God without Being*, 22.

22. Colleagues contributing to this discussion include Kara Powell, Art Bramford, and Brad M. Griffin, *Right-Click: Parenting Your Teenager in a Digital Media World* (Pasadena, CA: Fuller Youth Institute, 2015); and Andy Crouch, *The Tech-Wise Family: Everyday Steps for Putting Technology In Its Proper Place* (Grand Rapids: Baker Books, 2017).

23. Gerard Manley Hopkins, "Pied Beauty," *Poems* (London: Humphrey Milford, 1918), http://www.bartleby.com/122/13.html.

24. Emily Dickinson, "Some Keep the Sabbath Going to the Church," in *The Poems of Emily Dickenson*, ed. R. W. Franklin (Cambridge, MA: Harvard University Press, 1999), https://www.poetryfoundation.org/poems/52138/some-keep-the-sabbath-going-to-church-236.

25. Wendell Berry, "Sabbaths 2011," in *This Day: Sabbath Poems Collected and New 1979–2013* (Berkeley: Counterpoint, 2013), http://www.terrain.org/2013/poetry/four-poems-by-wendell-berry/.

26. Ann Voskamp, *One Thousand Gifts: A Dare to Live Fully Right Where You Are* (Grand Rapids: Zondervan, 2011).

27. Zelensky and Gilbert, *Windows to Heaven*, 26.

28. Sebastião Salgado's work as a social photographer was chronicled by director Wim Wenders in the documentary *Salt of the Earth*, Sony Pictures Classics, 2014.

29. Gwendolyn Brooks, *Selected Poems* (New York: Harper Perennial Modern Classics, 2006).

30. Martín Espada, *Imagine the Angels of Bread: Poems* (New York: W.W. Norton, 1997).

31. Dorothy Lee, "On the Holy Mountain: The Transfiguration in Scripture and Theology," *Colloquium* 36, no. 2 (2004): 158.

32. St. John of the Cross, *Maxims and Counsels*, in *The Collected Works of St. John of the Cross*, trans. Kieran Kavanaugh, OCD, and Otilio Rodriguez, OCD (Washington, DC: Institute of Carmelite Studies, 1991), 30, http://www.jesus-passion.com/Minor_Works _StJohn.htm.

33. St. John of the Cross, *The Sayings of Light and Love*, in *Collected Works*, 154.

34. St. John of the Cross, *The Ascent of Mount Carmel*, in *Collected Works*, Book 3, Chapter 3.

35. St. John of the Cross, *The Dark Night of the Soul*, 1584–85.

36. Carolyn Custis James, "The First Great New Testament Theologian was a Woman, Mission Alliance," October 3, 2017, http://www.missioalliance.org/first-great-new-testament-theologian-woman/.

37. St. Athanasius, *De Incarnatione Verbi Dei* (*On the Incarnation*), 54, 3: PG 25, 192B, downloadable at http://www.copticchurch.net/topics/theology/incarnation_st_athanasius .pdf.

38. For a beautiful meditation on this scene, read Shelly Rambo, *Spirit and Trauma: A Theology of Remaining* (Louisville: Westminster John Knox, 2010), 83–91.

39. To learn how to incorporate more reflection into our daily lives, I recommend C. Christopher Smith and John Pattison, *Slow Church: Cultivating Community in the Patient Way of Jesus* (Downers Grove, IL: InterVarsity, 2014).

40. Thank you to Miroslav Volf, who offered this adaptation of Num. 6:24–26 as a benediction to us at Pepperdine University, March 29, 2017.

Index